THE JOURNEY

May God continue
to bless and keep
you! We love you!
Phillip, Anjie,
Josh & Sydney
2020

THE JOURNEY

GOD WITH US

SCOTT HOWARD

Illuminate Ministries

I want to thank the people who have stood by me and believed in me through the years. My loving wife Susan and my family in particular. You are amazing. To those who really stepped up (too many to mention without leaving someone out) and partnered with me and help get this project completed, I am so grateful. Thank you and God bless you abundantly. You are the best.

It is my desire to help people everywhere come into a deeper and more meaningful relationship with God. I pray that through the power of the Holy Spirit the words on the pages of this book come alive taking you into deeper intimacy with the Father.

Sin consciousness ruled after Adam and Eve fell in the garden, but God sent Jesus to bring us back. Jesus didn't die so we could have religion, He died so we could have a deep, intimate, personal relationship with God. You are created to be in relationship, first with your Heavenly Father and also each other.

You are not just a statistic or a meaningless wanderer journeying through life without purpose. Jeremiah 1:4-5 says, "Then the word of the Lord came to me, saying: Before I formed you in the womb, I knew you. Before you were born, I sanctified you; I ordained you."

God is saying, "You and I hung out in my heart before you ever got here. I knew you before you knew yourself. You are not your mothers' mistake, you are not an outcast, you are not an orphan, you are not Fatherless or forsaken. You are loved. You are wonderfully made for a personal relationship with me. You are created and fashioned to journey with me." Let Him lead you on "The Journey."

SCOTT HOWARD

DAY 1

I'm very much a person of empathy, and I try to write as someone who understands what it's like to experience life. I try not to sugarcoat real emotions that life can cause to rise to the surface. Believing in God doesn't make our emotions automatically disappear. Through Him, we learn how to walk through it all.

You may be walking through some very difficult times. I want to remind us all that the process of life, when fully surrendered to HIS purpose, can, at times, be painful and require greater degrees of trust, but He will always bring us into a more fruitful place. Sometimes instead of directly answering our questions, God will instead simply respond by reminding us who He is. He wants us to know His character, to put our hope in what He is capable of, and to decide that when we don't have all the answers, He is enough. Sometimes, what looks like a disappointment is simply God getting us into a position to see His greatness. Declare that His greatness will be on display this year.

Walking into the unknown in simple obedience to the Lord will always feel uneasy, but it keeps us dependent, and dependence on Him releases the miraculous! Mary was unknown until God chose her to be the mother of Jesus. Others will say, "Surely, this is God's doing." Abraham wasn't childless forever. Joseph wasn't in prison forever. Daniel wasn't in the lion's den forever. You won't be in your current situation forever; your God will make a way.

"But when the fullness of time had come, God sent forth his Son, born of woman, born under the law, to redeem those who were under the law, so that we might receive adoption as sons. And because you are sons, God has sent the Spirit of his Son into our hearts, crying, "Abba! Father!" So you are no longer a slave, but a son, and if a son, then an heir through God."

Galatians 4:4-7 ESV

DAY 2

No matter where you may be starting from, or starting over from, don't let disappointment make your decisions. The greatest power we possess is the power to choose, to choose one thought over another, to choose what we yield to and submit to. We have to think better of ourselves before we can do better for ourselves. Knowing what God says about us and who we are and who we can be will change our view on life and our future.

Everyone who got where they are started from where they were. Transitions can be scary and uncertain, but we must not allow fear and uncertainty to rule our decisions. Sometimes our plans don't work out because God has better ones. Sometimes it's in the winds of change we find our greatest satisfaction and true direction in life. These can be the times where God is enlarging us and our territory, where we choose to break free from small thinking and choose to stay open to God's possibilities!

Join me today in choosing God's promise. "I choose to set my heart on God and let this promise rise up in me like never before. My God always provides a way out of whatever I'm in; or a way INto wherever I've been left out. Every daily need I have will be met with a daily wave of God's grace. His all-sufficient grace is never lacking, abundant, and full for every challenge. God's favor is on my life and is being released on my behalf. It's a new day, and my Heavenly Father is the author of new beginnings! By faith, my heart is awakened to the possibilities that can enter my world as I imagine with faith what my God can do in me and for me. I choose to live today with expectation and anticipation of the goodness of God. I am made in God's image and graced to succeed. From this day forward, I live in the confidence that freedom from bondage is in my God-given DNA. I will overcome anything and everything that is trying to keep me bound. Thank you, Jesus."

DAY 3

Let's allow God to open our eyes today so that we can dream, envision, see, and imagine. He wants us to go far past where we are to a new level in Him, in our personal lives, families, jobs, business, and relationships. You are never too old to get a new attitude. So never stop learning, growing, reaching, and increasing! You are not too old to begin again and to get a fresh start. May we never lose our sense of wonder and amazement as we anticipate what God will do and what He has already done for us in Christ. Our God is continually drawing us forward and inviting us to experience abundant life with Him even in the midst of challenges. Our destiny involves REACHING out for the future and by faith bringing it into the present in your heart. May we dream big and believe big always, because we have a big God!

"Heavenly Father, we stand together in agreement today for everyone facing opposition and attacks. We ask now for the intervention of the Holy Spirit on our behalf—minister to us at every point of need we have and raise us up above our circumstances so that we might fulfill our divine destiny and purpose in life—to be blessed and be a blessing. Thank you for supernatural wisdom and guidance for every decision. May we rise up inside through your supernatural strength and fight the good fight of faith. Thank you that we are surrounded by your love and angels that are ministering to us and for us as well. May we draw power and assurance from your love, which never fails. May we experience supernatural faith, peace, strength, and trust. Bring Godly increase to every part of our lives. Amen!"

"I pray that the light of God will illuminate the eyes of your imagination, flooding you with light, until you experience the full revelation of the hope of his calling—that is, the wealth of God's glorious inheritances that he finds in us, his holy ones!"
Ephesians 1:18 TPT

DAY 4

Live long enough and you'll experience wounds. Some may be intentionally inflicted while others are simply the result of life events, relationships, rejection, misunderstandings, or tragedies. There is an old saying, "Time heals all wounds." But there are some wounds time alone won't heal. If all we're relying on is time, it can make us bitter and not better. Even when time heals, old wounds can be so easily reopened.

Rather than time heals all wounds, it is really, "Love heals all wounds." There are places in our lives that only the love of God can heal and fill. There is a perspective to the places of pain we go through that can only be processed when the ongoing flow of God's love is our guide. His love brings a grace to us that's greater than our natural understanding.

Jesus' sacrifice for us was deep and brutal because hurts can be deep and brutal. He was beaten, bruised, and wounded. His substitutional death on the cross secured a love for us that goes beyond anything time alone can heal. It is eternal in its provision for us, not just for heaven, but for here and now. He took our rejection, our grief, our failures, our pain, our sin, our sorrows, and made them His very own. It was and is personal. He was wounded, so we could heal.

I pray that each one of us allows His love to be the ointment that heals the wounds. I pray that each of us will personally be awakened to the overflowing, eternal, unconditional, deep, and precious healing love of God. I pray that each of us has an encounter like the apostle Paul spoke about in Romans 8 when he declared, "I am persuaded that nothing in the here and now or anything to come, no one on earth or any spirit being, nothing high or low, nothing ever, anytime, anywhere can ever separate me from the love of God."

DAY 5

No matter what you may be walking through right now, don't give up. Don't surrender your hopes and dreams to your fears. Transformation starts by believing in someone and something bigger than you. Today is a great day to remember, your future is as bright as the promises of God. By the grace of God, we are empowered. By the grace of God, we are illuminated, and we move forward. You are walking in grace, empowerment, and redemption today.

As you fulfill your responsibilities, it is birthing your rewards. He is shining on you, in you, and through you. Your today and your tomorrow are blessed. Something out of the routine and ordinary is coming your way; new levels favor, and awareness of God's presence is released and coming to you. No more just going through religious motions. It is time for powerful God encounters and interventions.

"I pray you will put your trust in God and in the great future He has already put in motion for you! That you will have an assurance that things are happening behind the scenes that you can't always see! I pray that you will keep dreaming, keep believing, and keep celebrating each step of victory, knowing that God is faithful! I pray that as you look toward your future, you are filled with hope and expectation because you know the plans God has for you, and you rest in that promise! I pray you are filled with great thoughts for your future, that your heart beats with deep feelings of hope and great anticipation of what God is doing and will do! I pray you won't let your vision die just because time has passed, that God's presence will keep it alive and fresh!"

"The Lord bless you and keep you; The Lord make His face shine upon you, And be gracious to you; The Lord lift up His countenance upon you, And give you peace."
Numbers 6:24-26 NKJV

DAY 6

Does it feel like you've been in a long time of waiting, uncertainty, and transition? I have such a deep sense in my heart that for many, we are being positioned for divine acceleration. Divine acceleration is the supernatural ability of God to bring His plans to pass at a much faster rate than in the past and is humanly possible. God has already started releasing new ideas, visions, and the right connections to take us to a level we never thought possible. He is breathing new life into dry bones. The Lord is bringing us into a greater manifestation of who we already are-victorious- and into what is already ours- victory!

Where the giants have been screaming the loudest, He is fighting for you. There is an awakening and a birthing of victory taking place right now. What has been delayed will not be denied to you. God is restoring the broken places and redeeming what has felt like lost time for you. God will restore you. He will turn it around. He is going to vindicate you as you trust Him!

You may have been through a storm, but He will bring you out better than you were before. He is decreeing victory over you now and it is going to be loud! Your testimony is going to be profound! Expect uncommon favor in every area of your life from this moment forward! Pay no attention to the words of those injecting their own doubt and skepticism into God's promises. There is no doubt. A new season, a new chapter, a new era is on the horizon for us. We are about to see an even greater manifestation of the power that is in the name of Jesus in our circumstances and life! I pray for divine acceleration to every held up and delayed promise of God! Let barriers, prolonged problems, demonic cycles, and setbacks be overturned in the name of Jesus!

"Great favor is upon you, for you have believed every word spoken to
you from the Lord."
Luke 1:45 TPT

DAY 7

Going forth with hope and expectation is often confronted by its enemy, weariness, and fatigue. I'm not talking about just physical fatigue, although that can be part of it. I'm talking about mental, emotional, and soul fatigue that threatens our future.

There are times in your walk when it seems like nothing is happening, or things didn't turn out like you thought it would, and disappointment tries to set in. Maybe you feel like that, like God isn't saying anything or there isn't anything visible taking place to encourage you to press forward and keep going.

When things don't go the way you think they should or happen as fast as you think they should trust that God is working behind the scenes on your behalf. Just because you don't think God is speaking to you doesn't mean He isn't speaking to someone else about you. God is taking care of you, even when it seems like you're all alone. God is working hard behind the scenes of your life. We have to know and believe that deep in our hearts. So, for every person who feels like your season of opportunity has passed you by, opportunities can still come your way. God is the God who restores lost opportunities!

Say it today, "It's not too late for me to live the life God intended for me to live. He is restoring lost years and opportunities. He is turning things around for my good today. Things are happening because my God is working even when my natural eyes can't see it. My future is filled with divine possibilities, awesome God moments, life-changing turn-arounds, overcoming obstacles, and supernatural favor coming my way. He is faithful and I will trust Him to bring it to pass. In Jesus' Name!"

And He said, "My Presence will go with you, and I will give you rest."
Exodus 33:14 NKJV

DAY 8

What do we do when we feel trapped by life? Times when we run out of money before we run out of month. Times when we don't know if we're going to make it or not, and we want to scream for someone to listen, but we feel like there is no one there to listen or anyone that cares enough to listen. Times when we can't enjoy today because we worry about tomorrow. Times when we feel like we are the only one that has problems this big.

We can be in a situation for so long, it becomes our identity. We need to make the word of God our identity. We are not what's been done to us. We are what Jesus has done for us.

When you feel like there is nowhere to turn, there is someone to turn to. Always. Jesus came to heal the brokenhearted, bring freedom to the captives, and set at liberty those who are experiencing oppression.

We may not have all the answers, but let's keep holding the hand of the One who does. Because no matter what problems are in your "boat," they are no match for the person in it.

God has not gone anywhere. He has not forgotten you. Even in the midst of darkness, He is surrounding you. God knows what's headed your way. He has a plan. You can trust Him and have supernatural peace because He loves you perfectly and unconditionally.

Wherever you are today, I'm praying for adversity to turn into victory. God did it for Joseph. He can do it for you. (Genesis 39) His favor can cause problems to become possibilities, obstacles to become opportunities, and troubles to become triumphs. Declare this, "I will overcome every obstacle, defeat every enemy, and become everything God has created me to be!"

DAY 9

The God that we serve is a God of might and miracles, hope and healing, life, and liberty. He has a way of showing up in the middle of trouble. Where others see failure, He sees a future. He found Gideon hiding out in a hole. He found Joseph in prison. He found Daniel in a lion's den. So, if you ever find yourself in the pit instead of on the pedestal, take heart, that's when He does His finest work! He knows where you are today, and He is not having a crisis wondering how He's going to help you!

Because God is your strength, you'll stand through storms, win battles, and get the victory where people said you were defeated. Just in case you didn't know this already, what man says to try to disqualify you, God will use to qualify you! Whatever obstacles you are facing, whatever struggle you have with not fitting in, whether you feel you aren't pretty enough, strong enough, big enough, fast enough, or smart enough, know that you are not an accident or a mistake. You are fearfully and wonderfully made. God never stops working toward something good in your life. He can turn every minus into a plus!

"Now the Angel of the Lord came and sat under the terebinth tree which was in Ophrah, which belonged to Joash the Abiezrite, while his son Gideon threshed wheat in the winepress, in order to hide it from the Midianites. And the Angel of the Lord appeared to him, and said to him, "The Lord is with you, you mighty man of valor! "Gideon said to Him, "O my lord, if the Lord is with us, why then has all this happened to us? And where are all His miracles which our fathers told us about, saying, 'Did not the Lord bring us up from Egypt?' But now the Lord has forsaken us and delivered us into the hands of the Midianites. "Then the Lord turned to him and said, "Go in this might of yours, and you shall save Israel from the hand of the Midianites. Have I not sent you?"
Judges 6:11-24 NKJV

DAY 10

"Father, we come boldly before your throne today to obtain grace to help in time of need. We have confidence in your ability to do what we can't. Thank you for the blessed assurance that all is well, and we will overcome!

Thank you for a supernatural impartation of strength for those who are tired and feel like they are continually fighting an uphill battle. God is causing faith and hope and expectation to arise in you!

I pray every chain restricting you, every bondage, every weight containing you is lifted, removed, and destroyed in Jesus' name! I break every spirit of weariness over you in the name of Jesus and pray for supernatural joy and strength! There is new energy released in your life! I declare the enemy will gain no advantage over you, no trap will prevail, and no bondage will hold! In the name of Jesus, let them break! The blood of Jesus secures you, your family, and your future.

Father, I ask you to restore every lost opportunity, stolen blessing, and good thing that belongs to your children! I pray an increase over you in favor, harvest, and success. I declare the blessing of the Lord to overtake you. You are blessed coming in and blessed going out. All that you put your hand to will prosper. I pray for divine revelation, clarity, and vision for you. I pray favor over you, a divine favor that will stick to you like honey and take you from your present season to your future destination!

I pray you say yes to the greatness that is calling you to stretch beyond the comfort of your familiar. You have circled this mountain long enough. It's time to take new territory! I pray for God to empower you for enlargement, expansion, increase, and advancement of your assignment and purpose in Christ. New strength for new things!"

DAY 11

People don't always see or understand what you're going through. They mean well, but many times, they are dealing with their own issues in life. But you always have somewhere to go. A place to run to- always. A safe place. That "place" is someone- your good, good Father.

The story we call the "prodigal son" gives us a beautiful portrait of our loving Father looking for the son in the distance. Reaching out, running toward him, embracing him, and welcoming him into his loving embrace!

Step by step, the good, good Father begins the process of restoration, clothing the son in garments of beauty and dignity. Bringing hope and security to his life again, taking him to that safe place of love and renewal.

That same good, good Father is running toward us today. Not distant and aloof but caring and safe. God loves you and will not forsake you. God did not create us and walk away. He created us, sent His son to die for us, and left the Holy Spirit to guide us!

His love is a mystery that meets us where we are but doesn't leave us where it found us. What He intends for us goes far beyond anything we can imagine. Never lose hope and hang on to God's hand. Take some time today and enjoy the hug of a good, good Father. He is there for you. You're always safe in His embrace.

"And he arose and came to his father. But while he was still a long way off, his father saw him and felt compassion, and ran and embraced him and kissed him."
Luke 15:20 ESV

DAY 12

May our Father bless you with life-changing breakthroughs from this day forward. I'm praying that every wall that's been holding you back is going to come tumbling down! I'm praying for you to get an unprecedented endorsement from God! I'm believing for God to do something fresh and inventive in your life! Every natural and spiritual hindrance to your fruitfulness is destroyed in the mighty name of Jesus! No matter how many people have written you off, I am declaring your life will become a fruitful field!

This week as the love of God grows in your heart; I see you soaring above frustrations on eagles wings! I pray you will experience deeper dimensions of God than you ever have before! More love, more grace, more power, more assurance, and more in the places where you've been stretched and challenged. No matter what past weeks have been like, this week you are strong and whole in Jesus' name. No more mental, physical, or spiritual exhaustion and fatigue. You are being refreshed by His presence! Hope is rising up in you that is grounded in your faith in Father God! I'm praying that the time has come to bring that promise God gave you to birth!

Declare it! "I affirm that I will never walk in darkness; for the path of the just is as the shining light, that shines more and more unto the perfect day. The Lord has perfected all that concerns me, and I am confident of a greater tomorrow, and day-to-day life of ever-increasing glory because the Lord is the one taking me by the hand and leading me to fulfill His perfect will for me. Christ is made unto me wisdom, righteousness, sanctification, and redemption; therefore, it doesn't matter what trouble I get into, one thing is certain, I am coming out of it. It doesn't matter what proclamation is made against me; it is to no effect because Jesus is my redeemer. He plucks my feet out of the miry clay. No weapon formed against me shall prosper, and every tongue which rises against me in judgment is condemned. There's no shame in my path! I go out with joy and I am led forth with peace."

DAY 13

To persevere in life usually involves some type of mental, emotional or physical hardship or discomfort. Though it sometimes feels like things would get better if God could just see us or understand our pain. The truth is, He already does!

Knowing God and trusting in His character and His ways is the secret to incredible faith. We do not need God to discover us or learn to understand us, He already does. We only need to trust Him enough to let Him develop us through it all.

Remember that every season is not a harvest season. There are seasons of watering, planting, pruning, cultivating, and fertilizing. A waiting season is not a wasted season. We can endure it and overcome it because we have a great God behind us. We have the powerful presence of the Holy Spirit to fill us.

Stay faith and future focused. Each day a new frontier of possibilities stretches out ahead of you. You haven't gone through all the hell, obstacles, and trials to just quietly lay down or hide in the corner! Don't let who you were yesterday prevent you from being all that you can be today!

You have a lot to live and believe for and every reason to keep moving forward. In Jesus' name, you are moving forward at an accelerated speed into the destiny God has for your life as you live yielded and surrendered to His Spirit. He's going to leave you in holy awe and wonder!

"Keep protecting and cherishing your chosen ones; in you they will never fall. Like a shepherd going before us, keep leading us forward, forever carrying us in your arms!"
Psalms 28:9 TPT

DAY 14

As we enter a fresh new day today, may we speak more to our hopes than our hurts and find the courage to love others as deeply as we long to be loved. Today, let's all "buy-in" to His plans for us instead of trying to get Him to "buy-in" to our plans. His ways are so much better than ours! Thank you, Lord for your will and design for us! You're a good, good Father!

Wherever you are right now in this journey called life, remember this is just one page or one chapter, but it isn't the end of the book! God sees your weariness today. He sees what others don't and what no one around you can even imagine you are going through. You don't always feel Him, but He is always present! Rely on the Holy Spirit, in every situation you are in. He is perfect at making a way where mankind can find none. Let His peace be greater than what your life feels like and stronger than what your mind thinks. Don't believe your situation is hopeless just because your human mind can't see a way out. There is someone greater, wiser, and more powerful than the ways of man. God works all things together for your good, even when what you're seeing isn't good!

Today, I pray against every discouraging and unfruitful spirit in your life! Your God is still on the throne. You are a person of destiny hand-picked by the Creator. You have not seen your best days! God has ingredients coming your way that will thrust you to a new level. His plan will not be stopped by disappointment, attack, setbacks, or people! Your God has the final say! May we always remember that God is able to bring us through the unknown, unseen, and unexpected as we trust Him with everything. This is our year! We will be unstoppable!

"For I know the plans I have for you," declares the Lord, "plans to prosper you and not to harm you, plans to give you hope and a future"
Jeremiah 29:11 NIV

DAY 15

You have an assignment from God. You're not here on this earth just to take up space. You're here to occupy space and be influential. When Jesus died for your sin, He gave you the power to thrive and live life in the victory that was won on the cross.

The joy of the Lord will give you the momentum you need to keep on keeping on. You won't back down, sit down, or quiet down because you've come too far towards your destiny to stop now. You will see and enjoy the goodness of the Lord *(Psalm 27:13)*.

So, when the road gets long- keep walking.

If your hill is steep- keep climbing.

If you are rowing upstream- keep rowing.

If there is a wall- march around it, 7 times if you must.

If there's a fiery furnace- look for the 4th man.

If there's a mountain- speak to it.

If you get knocked down- get up and go again.

May God favor you with unfair advantages and opportunities that others don't see and don't have the capacity to seize. May you always find yourself on the cutting edge, ahead of the curve, and head and shoulders above the attacks of the enemy. I decree you shall: Succeed! Progress! Prosper! Increase! Prevail! And you are about to get launched into the "much" season of your life! Declare it. "Yes, Lord! It's my time!"

"God himself will fill you with more. Blessings upon blessings will be heaped upon you and upon your children from the maker of heaven and earth, the very God who made you!"
Psalms 115:14-15 TPT

DAY 16

"I stand on the promises of God this day and declare over my life and my dreams that just like Esther, I am chosen and placed for such a time as this. My life matters and I am making a difference. I dare to believe in God-given dreams and visions for my future. I will be bold, believe God, increase the boundary mark of my faith, and dare to ask for bigger! Father by your grace, by your love, I will stand, and I will not give up or quit! I am chosen, I am on the way, I am needed, I am loved, I will make it. My dream will touch me and others and change our lives for the better! I am a finisher! God is for me!

Heavenly Father, because of your great love for me, by faith, I am filled with great thoughts for my future. My heart beats with deep feelings of hope and great anticipation of what You are doing and will do! Thank you, Lord! You make all things new. Father, it's a new day, with new mercies, new hope, new grace. Thank you for always being there for me. You are my faithful Redeemer! I know I can depend on You, for you have been faithful and will always be faithful. Thank you, Lord, for the gift of life. Thank you for getting me through every hard moment, every difficult season, and every dark place of my life. Even when I have failed, You have not. Thank you that You always stand by Your word! I command fear to go and doubt to flee. By faith my day and future will be filled with hope, love, peace, joy, and expectation! I choose to live in the land of your possibilities- God possibilities! I will walk in my God-given purpose and passion. I will see the provision of the Lord! I am chosen, I am on the way, I am needed, I am loved, I will make it, and I am yours!"

"The very moment I call to you for a father's help the tide of battle turns and my enemies flee. This one thing I know: God is on my side!"
Psalms 56:9 TPT

DAY 17

The scriptures remind us, "In Him, we live and move and have our being." God is the origin of our lives. We would have no existence without Him. Our God does nothing without purpose, so each of our lives has a purpose. We are not a random biological consequence or an accident. From our very first moment, we have mattered to God. And He is not looking for reasons to short-circuit our destiny. God is looking for ways to fulfill our destiny!

Our reality needs to be, I am a child of God! When I am hiding in the shadows and corners of life, it does not serve the kingdom and the world well. I was born to make manifest the glory of God within me.

So today, I pray an end to every spirit of Pharaoh that has taxed you, harassed you, and kept you in a place that you don't belong in Jesus' name! Don't be distracted by things that won't matter to your destiny! Difference makers and missionaries are not just in foreign countries; they are in business meetings, school rooms, athletic fields, hospitals, they are first responders, mothers and fathers in every walk of life.

I pray you have a renewed passion for your purpose this week and everything draining you is overcome through His strength.

God calls us, just like He called Caleb, to take our land, whatever that would be marriage, job, parenting, or health with strength and courage. While everyone is telling you why you can't do it, do it anyway and go for all that God has said!

"Then Caleb quieted the people before Moses, and said, "Let us go up at once and take possession, for we are well able to overcome it."
Numbers 13:30 NKJV

DAY 18

We've all have times in our lives where it looks like we are down for the count. Living a life of fullness and abundance does not exclude us from having to navigate challenging circumstances. Life is going to happen, but God is going to happen too.

It's so easy to get impressed by our problems. When we do, we stop worshipping, praising, thanking, and believing. Our vision for our future diminishes and our attitude limits our potential. Today, let's be more impressed with our God than we are our problems. All it takes is one moment of divine intervention and the walls can come down!

Always keep your attitude of conquest alive. With God what is broken can be fixed, what is closed can be opened, and what is lost can be recovered. No matter what comes up in my life, I know that 'this too will pass.' The favor of God means even when it is bad, God can turn it around for good. Yes, He is that good! Shake off that stress, put down that worry, and rise up. In one decision, you can change your attitude and in that one decision, you can change your entire future and life.

Declare out loud, "I will not be dominated by disappointment today. My hope is in God. My future is in God. The tables are turning in my favor today. My prayers are being answered. There is favor for my life. I will not despair or give up today because I will see the goodness of God show up in my life.

"Now may God, the inspiration and fountain of hope, fill you to overflowing with uncontainable joy and perfect peace as you trust in him. And may the power of the Holy Spirit continually surround your life with his super-abundance until you radiate with hope!"
Romans 15:13 TPT

DAY 19

I know that God has put some promises in your heart today. Never let the "experts" talk you out of the things God has spoken to you. If some of the things God has put in your heart seem overwhelming and impossible outside of God's divine intervention, take heart today. Our God is a God of divine intervention and He has demonstrated that He can and will overcome the "odds" to accomplish His promises and purposes in our lives. God can restore years of loss, things that should have been yours, and birth a future in you filled with endless possibilities with one moment of favor.

He can quiet the storms, part the sea, heal the sick, restore the broken, put money in a fish's mouth, bring promotion from prison, rain manna from the heavens, bring water from a rock, and bring life from death! With the Lord, nothing is ever hopeless! Your current battle isn't too big for God. Don't underestimate Jesus' ability to multiply what we put in his hands. 5 fish + 2 loaves x Jesus = the feeding of 5,000. When we are willing to release, Jesus is able to increase! In the young man's hand, it was lunch. In Jesus' hands, it was a feast with 12 full baskets leftover!

So today, when it feels like hope is gone, when it seems like there is no way, when all of the road signs say, "dead end," God can still make a way! Your prayers have no time, spacial, or geographic limit. Laws, ordinances, and even nature has to adjust to accommodate the power of prayer. So, trust in His timing. Rely on His promises. Wait for His answers. Believe His words. Rejoice in His goodness. Worship in His Presence. He is faithful!

"I will answer them before they even call to me. While they are still talking about their needs, I will go ahead and answer their prayers!"
Isaiah 65:24 ESV

DAY 20

The commanded blessing of God can find you no matter where you are or what is happening. It found Abram in Egypt, Joseph in prison, Daniel in the lion's den, and Moses on the backside of the desert. It will find you, even in the midst of the fire, in the storm, in the financial problem, in the betrayal, in the physical attacks, and in the setbacks. You are on God's radar. His eyes are on you.

You have seeds of greatness on the inside. Today can be your new beginning. Today could be the start of something amazing. Don't be afraid of life and don't be afraid of praying big prayers. Jesus came so that we may have life and have it to the full! So today, refuse to tiptoe through life in fear because God has made a covenant with you through the blood of Jesus. God didn't withhold His son; therefore, He will not withhold any good thing from you. Expect His best today in Jesus' name!

"Father, thank you for lifting up every precious person reading this to today. Keep them from being discouraged by causing the eyes of their faith to see what's possible through You. In Jesus' name, their territory is being enlarged; they will accomplish more than they thought was possible. I pray today for acceleration, new levels, divine favor, increase, abundance, and breakthroughs in their life."

"For I know your power and presence shines on all your lovers. Your glory always hovers over all who bow low before you. Your mercy and your truth have married each other. Your righteousness and peace have kissed.
Flowers of your faithfulness are blooming on the earth. Righteousness shines down from the sky. Yes, the Lord keeps raining down blessing after blessing, and prosperity will drench the land with a bountiful harvest. For deliverance and peace are his forerunners, preparing a path for his steps."
Psalms 85:9-13 TPT

DAY 21

Affirmations are important in our lives. The view and opinions we adopt for ourselves profoundly affect our lives. We need daily affirmations and perspective from God's word, just like we need daily nourishment and vitamins.

As we open our eyes and awaken today in the natural, I pray that we will also be inspired to rise up in the spiritual and like Moses did arise from isolation, exile, and doubt. As Abraham did, believe. As Sarah did, we will conceive (the dream is not dead) and as Lazarus did, begin to live again. Let's get our fire back!

Confess with me: "I affirm that my faith is alive and working. With my faith, I've connected into God's unending supply, taking full advantage of His inexhaustible grace, wealth, and wisdom. The Lord has set me on high; Glory and honor are in his presence; strength and gladness are in His dwelling! Yea, though I walk through the valley of the shadow of death, I fear no evil, for He's my shield and eternal protection. I am thoroughly nourished and furnished for the victorious life by the Word, through fellowship and meditation. I am making progress by the Spirit and the realities of the Kingdom are unveiled to me. The Holy Spirit is working through me to reveal the glory to glory realities of the Kingdom to every place in my world and beyond. Glory to God! My spirit is unbreakable. My vision is unobstructed. I am improving every day. My progress is unstoppable. My victory is inevitable. I am chosen, not forsaken. I am the lender and not the borrower. Through Jesus, I am undefeatable. I am who You say I am. My God is unbeatable. Therefore, nothing is impossible! Keep saying it, don't stop!"

"Jesus responded, "What appears humanly impossible is more than possible with God. For God can do what man cannot."
Luke 18:27 TPT

DAY 22

Plant good seeds today and every day from now on. Words are like seeds. They have creative power. Proverbs says, "We will eat the fruit of our words."

So, break every wrong word spoken over you in the past that is not in alignment with the word of God! Lock eyes with your naturally impossible circumstance and remind it, "You're finished. It is over. Jesus has already made a way where there seems to be none!" Remind every seemingly lifeless dream, "God is about to breathe new life into you! He is redeeming the lost time!"

I declare you will not spend another day lost in your past, blinded by disappointments. You will rise and thrive! You will go forward and overcome, climb mountains, and cross valleys. Rise up. Believe. Thrive. See with eyes of faith. God will prove Himself faithful! He will restore all the enemy has stolen from you!

"Tell the righteous it will be well with them, for they will enjoy the fruit of their deeds."
Isaiah 3:10-11 NIV

"This is what the Lord says— he who made a way through the sea, a path through the mighty waters, who drew out the chariots and horses, the army and reinforcements together, and they lay there, never to rise again, extinguished, snuffed out like a wick: Forget the former things; do not dwell on the past. See, I am doing a new thing! Now it springs up; do you not perceive it? I am making a way in the wilderness and streams in the wasteland."
Isaiah 43:16-19 NIV

DAY 23

Never allow yourself to be defined by someone else's opinion. When the opinions of others form bars in your mind, you can be held captive in "People Prison." Don't let anyone ruin your life and future. Keep your God dreams and future alive!

The moment you step away from the crowd to walk on water is the moment the crowd starts hoping you drown. The only people who have a problem with you being at your best are those who benefit from you being at your worst. When you understand who you are, you do not have to be jealous of who "they" are. Fulfill the destiny God gave you!

So, when people praise you, don't let it go to your head. When they criticize you, don't let it get to your heart! Do the thing you were born to do.

Your destiny is found as you move forward. Your purpose is found as you move forward. Your passion is found as you move forward. You are not an accident. You are not a mistake. You are loved and God has a purpose for you!

Let's go forward in faith, believing today. As we seek and walk with God, He will take us places we have never dreamed of!

"They will fight against you, but they shall not prevail against you, for I am with you, declares the LORD, to deliver you."
Jeremiah 1:19 ESV

DAY 24

Jesus once asked Peter, "Who do you say I am?" Let's answer it for ourselves today.

Dear God,

You are:

My anchor in the raging storm.

My comfort in times of pain and heartache.

My strength when I am weak.

My peace in the midst of chaos and confusion.

My hope when things go wrong.

My future when all seems lost.

My light in the darkness.

My grace in times of failure.

My relief for every sorrow and

My confidence for every tomorrow.

My passion when days get long and always my song.

My deliverer when I am bound

My healer when I am sick

My redeemer when I am held captive

My provider in need

You are faithful.

You are true

You are eternal

You are worthy

You are Kind of Kings

You are Lord of Lords

You are with me

You are steadfast, never failing, on time

You are all knowing

Now add your own personal list to this

DAY 25

Someone is praying and believing for a reversal, a divine intervention, a turnaround, a time of seeing the mighty hand of God in their circumstances. Let's cover our day with a word of prayer! "Father, it's a new day with new possibilities that we are determined to grab hold of with enthusiasm. Our day is going to be full of fresh ideas about the purpose You have created us to fulfill. Thank you today that You are the great God of the turnaround! You can take every dark situation in our lives and cause it to abound with blessing. You can cause every trial to become a testimony, every setback to become a come-back, every bad break to break forth with possibilities, and every place of lack and limitation to abound in fruitfulness! You have promised to give us beauty for ashes, the oil of joy for mourning, the garment of praise for the spirit of heaviness. Today we let go of the ashes and receive your beauty!

You have called us "trees of righteousness" planted by the rivers of water, bringing forth our fruit in season! You have declared that our leaf shall not fade or wither, and the things we put our hands to will prosper. You have spoken over us, "The righteous shall flourish like a palm tree, that we shall grow strong like a cedar in Lebanon." We receive it, Father God, therefore strength, security, steadfastness, and divine shifts are ours today. We leave our failures, fears, foes, and future in Your hands! We say, "Yes, Lord!" Our today and our week are abounding with awesome God possibilities! Thank You, Lord!

"Jesus looked at them and replied, "With people it is impossible, but
not with God—God makes all things possible!"
Mark 10:27 TPT

DAY 26

Our problems have voices. They say this problem will never end, but God says I'm bringing you out! They say you might as well give up the fight, but God says the battle is already won! They say it's over for you, but God says it has just started! They say you can't have it, but God says it's yours! They say you will never be enough, but God says I'm raising you up for my glory! They say there is no way, but God says I will make a way!

No matter what problems say, you have precious promises from God. Remember, we've all come through challenges and difficulties that should have stopped us. That wasn't luck or just a good break. It was the hand of God pushing back the forces of darkness and bringing favor to our lives. Lord, let every spirit of fatigue, stress, anxiety, and heaviness be removed in the name of Jesus. Let them be destroyed.

I hear the sound of "suddenly" in my spirit. Get ready for an instant outpouring and overflow of His goodness over every mountain in your life. You are valuable. You are worthy. You are loved. God says, "it is a new day and new mercies." Pharaoh is no longer your master. Egypt is no longer your home. You are not making bricks anymore. You are redeemed and restored, and your story will bring God glory!

"May God give you every desire of your heart and carry out your every plan as you go to battle. When you succeed, we will celebrate and shout for joy. Flags will fly when victory is yours! Yes, God will answer your prayers and we will praise him! I know God gives me all that I ask for and brings victory to his anointed king. My deliverance cry will be heard in his holy heaven. By his mighty hand miracles will manifest through his saving strength."
Psalms 20:4-6 TPT

DAY 27

I want to challenge all of us to believe this year!

What you believe about God and yourself is so important. It really matters! So, as a son or daughter of God, what do I believe?

Believe with all your heart that God is writing a story for your life and He's not finished! Believe that you are not an accident. You are not a mistake. Believe that you weren't born and then given an assignment. You were born because you have an assignment! Believe that you are loved, and God has a purpose for you! Believe that every lie of the enemy has no power over you! Believe that God is working and there are still things for you to do and accomplish!

Believe that He will make a way where there seems to be no way! Believe that you are His and He loves you, accepts you, and will take care of you! Believe that no matter what happened last year, yesterday, today or even five minutes ago- He still loves you! His love never fails you!

Declare, "I believe this year will be filled with the goodness of God. God is on the throne. Jesus is interceding for me. The Holy Spirit is filling me with power, gifts, and fruit. My name is written in the Lamb's Book of Life. I will keep my heart open to the work of the Holy Spirit and I will live the adventure I will walk in my God-given purpose and passion and I will see the provision of the Lord! I believe!"

"Jesus looked at her and said, "Didn't I tell you that if you will believe in me, you will see God unveil his power?"
John 11:40 TPT

DAY 28

Being strong doesn't mean you'll never get hurt. It means that even when you do get hurt, you will never let it defeat or control you. People disgusted with their own lives often envy and hurt others. Persistent critics tend to be miserable with themselves.

But if you're waiting for someone to apologize before you forgive them, it might never happen. Forgive them, even if they are not sorry.

Forgiveness is a choice, not a feeling. You know you've made that choice when your heart no longer wishes to inflict the same pain, they inflicted on you. Life in abundance comes only through love and forgiveness. Without love and forgiveness, your world is a tomb. Bitterness defiles everything. Perspectives are skewed by it. It kills personal growth. When you have bitterness in your heart, you stop reaching to grow and start grasping to "prove."

Forgiveness means I take control of my life from anyone who has hurt me. The past is over, and the future is mine. Father help us to let it go. Let us learn from the past but not live in it. I intentionally remind myself today that God has chosen me. I am His and He is mine.

"So now I live with the confidence that there is nothing in the universe with the power to separate us from God's love. I'm convinced that his love will triumph over death, life's troubles, fallen angels, or dark rulers in the heavens. There is nothing in our present or future circumstances that can weaken his love. There is no power above us or beneath us—no power that could ever be found in the universe that can distance us from God's passionate love, which is lavished upon us through our Lord Jesus, the Anointed One!"
Romans 8:38-39 TPT

DAY 29

God wants you to know He is still going to give you what He has promised you. The waiting may be hard and there are times you might not like where you are, but I want to encourage you that God is right there with you and He is preparing you for what He has prepared for you! Every struggle in your past has shaped you into the person you are today. Take God's hand and step into your future without fear. Refuse to allow the pain and hurt of yesterday to stop your overflowing blessed today! Live large! Believe big! Never forget who you are and whose you are!

When Israel had lived as slaves in Egypt so long, many of them had gotten comfortable in their bondage. They had forgotten that they were not citizens of Egypt. They had forgotten, "I may be here right now, but I'm a citizen of another place." They started asking to become better citizens of a place they didn't belong! We have been bought at a great expense and our lives are not ours to squander. God wants us to become all He created us to be!

Do not allow your current circumstances or surroundings to become your identity.

It's time to stop praying to become a better citizen of a place where you don't belong! God is calling you forward! May you have a wonderful new day launched into great God possibilities! Launched into a higher level of living!

"Let me be clear, the Anointed One has set us free—not partially, but completely and wonderfully free! We must always cherish this truth and stubbornly refuse to go back into the bondage of our past."
Galatians 5:1 TPT

DAY 30

Your life, your today, and your future is filled with potential, with Kingdom possibilities. Keep the growing going. Never apologize for your growth. Don't shrink and become "less than" for the comfort of others. Some people can only handle your level of favor as long as it does not exceed theirs. Keep believing to prosper. The only people who have a problem with you being at your best are the ones benefiting from you being at your worst.

You matter and your existence makes a difference in the hearts and lives of those around you. Your growth and blessings can give hope to others that they too can rise from the ashes of their past failures and live an abundant life. True prosperity is not just about making a living; it is about making a life.

So, stand firm and steady and face every decision with unshakable confidence in the goodness of God. As you step out in faith, may God cause you to excel in everything you do and may all you put your hands to produce fruit that will last. May you live with absolute certainty that God's hand is on your life and efforts. I speak strength to your heart, clarity to your mind, courage to your soul, and direction to your spirit. I'm declaring over you that God will provide every resource necessary for you to keep going forward with Him. Being blessed is not just about self-fulfillment, but also making the world and people around us better. Go get it!

"Yes, all things work for your enrichment so that more of God's marvelous grace will spread to more and more people, resulting in an even greater increase of praise to God, bringing him even more glory!"
2 Corinthians 4:15 TPT

DAY 31

No matter what we are up against right now, we are not alone in the dark. We can count on Jesus to be our light and our salvation. By His Spirit, He can illuminate even the darkest places in our lives. All He wants is for us to agree with Him, tie a knot around the Word of God, and hold on against every lying thing seen and unseen. Let's refuse the spirit of intimidation today and determine to move past previous limitations in our lives and see ourselves fulfilling the great dreams of God. I believe that the Lord would remind us today, "Never forget that my Spirit is with you. Ready to strengthen, sustain, love, and guide you. Even though you have been through heartache and pain and had disappointments and unfairness in your life, the pain of your past is nothing compared to the joy of your future! You have new opportunities in front of you."

"Father, thank you for the grace to live today without worry and anxiety for tomorrow or crippling guilt about yesterday. Thank you that You are working behind the scenes on our behalf, that things are happening right now in the unseen world to bring great blessings to our lives and families. Thank you, Father, that You will never stop being good! Your mercies are new every morning and your grace is more powerful than any failure of the past. Thank you for your great love today. And thank you for the light of eternal life that lives in our hearts."

"The glory of your splendor is our strength, and your marvelous favor makes us even stronger, lifting us even higher! You are our King, the holiest one of all; your wrap-around presence is our protection."
Psalms 89:17-18 TPT

DAY 32

There are times in life when you feel completely hidden, seemingly out of view, and obscure. But, destinies aren't born in the spotlight; they are birthed in the secret places. In order for a seed to achieve its destiny, it must go through a transformation process. It must spend some time out of the spotlight. It is pushed into the darkness and it's there that its destiny is born. It moves from being sown to being grown. Weariness tends to creep into our lives, not in the sowing season or reaping season but in the T-I-M-E season, the waiting season, the messy middle season. The Bible speaks of seed TIME and harvest. The waiting can be difficult and painful but something powerful is taking place. If you're in the hallway between the pain and the promise, keep walking through the process because the promise is on the other side of your pain. God is taking you where your own "smart" can't even figure it out. He sharpens us like arrows to be aimed with pinpoint accuracy at His target for our lives.

Don't let your mind dwell in the land of your pain and hurt. Don't let your choices be birthed out of your past failures. When you do, you end up getting stuck in the place you came out of because you keep speaking about your past as if it's in your present and future. Don't let your mind stay stuck in a season God already brought your spirit out of! Always appreciate what you have where you are, trust that even your challenges are part of a bigger plan, and believe the best is yet to come. There is a harvest in your future. So, when you are going through something that seems harder than you thought it would be and lasts longer than you thought it would last, I agree with you, it's going to turn out greater than you thought it could be!

"And He has made My mouth like a sharp sword; In the shadow of His hand He has hidden Me, And made Me a polished shaft; In His quiver He has hidden Me."
Isaiah 49:2 NKJV

DAY 33

Not everyone around you is always going to be for you but don't let the haters and doubters in life make you quit or turn you into one of them. Haters are usually people that are so insecure, they think the only way to build themselves up is to take you down.

Seek out relationships in life that are complementary, not competitive. God's pathway to promotion is through humility, not pride.

Always remember, don't hate, celebrate! Rejoice with those who are blessed and genuinely be glad for them. God doesn't have to deprive you to bless somebody else! You can never make your life better by 'hating' on someone else's life or success! In reality, they keep enjoying their success and you return to the same old life you had the day before. Start celebrating others' victories and start reaching for your own. God isn't poor, broke, barely getting by, or about to run out of mercy, grace, love, or anything else. He is the God of more than enough! The lights in heaven don't dim if you pray big and believe big. He's a great God! Proclaim it today, "I am not a victim, I am a victor! No one can keep me down! Because it's God who raises me up!"

"He raised us up with Christ the exalted One, and we ascended with him into the glorious perfection and authority of the heavenly realm, for we are now co-seated as one with Christ! Throughout the coming ages we will be the visible display of the infinite, limitless riches of his grace and kindness, which was showered upon us in Jesus Christ."
Ephesians 2:6-7 TPT

DAY 34

You were conceived by God before you were ever born to your parents. You were known in heaven before you were ever known on earth. He was thinking about you before you ever thought about Him. God chose you before you ever chose Him. He loved you before you ever loved Him. He provided for you before you ever had a need. Rest assured that He is pursuing and passionate when it comes to you. Never indifferent, never distant, never cold, and never callous. Always reaching, always caring, and always welcoming. May our lives be a reflection of the invitation we have been given. "I'm running toward you. My embrace awaits you. Come and join me at my table. I have a ring and a robe; I've prepared a feast and killed the fatted calf. A celebration is underway. All for you."

May we never forget or take for granted the glorious privilege of being sons and daughters of our great God, invited to sit at His table and break bread with Him. May our hearts beat with that same passion with which He invites us in. Let's RSVP today, "I'm here Father. Thank you for inviting me in, welcoming me such deep love and devotion. Thank you for including me and for preparing the best for me. My good good Father. I love you and I love being in Your presence."

"So the young son set off for home. From a long distance away, his father saw him coming, dressed as a beggar, and great compassion swelled up in his heart for his son who was returning home. So the father raced out to meet him. He swept him up in his arms, hugged him dearly, and kissed him over and over with tender love." "Turning to his servants, the father said, 'Quick, bring me the best robe, my very own robe, and I will place it on his shoulders. Bring the ring, the seal of sonship, and I will put it on his finger. And bring out the best shoes you can find for my son. Let's prepare a great feast and celebrate."
Luke 15:20; 22-23 TPT

DAY 35

We all have had setbacks and unfair things happen in our past. But God is working to turn it around! God is making things happen for you even if you don't see it, can't feel it, or if it is not evident! He's answering prayers now that you prayed last year!

So, get up! Get out! Get stirred up! And get going! Your life story is still being written and God's hand is guiding you! While you're believing for your miracle, take advantage of your opportunities! Long distances are covered one step at a time and big miracles sometimes take place one small miracle at a time! Remember, your God is amazing, you are amazing, and your future is going to be amazing. Isaiah 60 says this, "Arise, shine; For your light has come! And the glory of the LORD is risen upon you. For behold, the darkness shall cover the earth, and deep darkness the people; But the LORD will arise over you, And His glory will be seen upon you. The Gentiles shall come to your light, And kings to the brightness of your rising."

Remember, the Bible doesn't end with darkness, it ends with a bride and a bridegroom, with the Light defeating the powers of darkness! Radiance is in your future!

Instead of your shame you will receive a double portion, and instead of disgrace you will rejoice in your inheritance. And so you will inherit a double portion in your land, and everlasting joy will be yours.
Isaiah 61:7 NIV

DAY 36

There is no such thing as an insignificant Christian. Jesus knows your name; He endured your pain. He sees the depths of your heart and loves every fiber of your being. The Lord is involved with what concerns you every day. You are important to Father God. You are the apple of His eye. He wants to be good to you and He has made provision for you because you matter!

Remember, no matter what you are going through today, God has not given up on you, so don't give up on yourself. Stay encouraged by deciding to see beyond the present moment. God has a wonderful plan and place for you. And your future holds great promise!

I declare you will not spend the rest of your life poor, hurting, frustrated, defeated, or miserable. Any generational curse is broken! I declare you are salt and light and a city set on a hill for the glory of God! That you are raised up for such a time as this. That you are being empowered to be everything God has called you to be!

I declare doors are opening for you that no one can close, and God's favor surrounds you like a shield, in Jesus' Name! It's a new season, it's a new day, it's a season of power and blessing! Your greatest victories are still in front of you. You are loved!!!

"You can buy two sparrows for only a copper coin, yet not even one sparrow falls from its nest without the knowledge of your Father. Aren't you worth much more to God than many sparrows? So don't worry. For your Father cares deeply about even the smallest detail of your life."
Matthew 10:29-31 TPT

DAY 37

For those of you who are tired and feel like you are continually fighting an uphill battle, I'm here to stir you up to believe again today. The enemy tries to paint a hopeless, dark picture of your life, so you become discouraged, lonely, and depressed. You may be in a place like that right now, but God is causing hope to arise in you. Don't faint. God didn't bring you this far to leave you.

May God the Father touch your heart on this new day in a way that only He can. Don't start your day with the broken pieces of yesterday. Every morning we wake up is the first day of the future God has planned for us. Lord, let every spirit of fatigue, stress, anxiety, and heaviness be removed in the name of Jesus! Let them be destroyed! I declare peace and victory, provision for the vision. I speak hope and strength over your life and dreams! We serve the God of resurrection. Today is a new day. I pray for a new favor, new divine appointments, new hope, a wonderful new day, and season marked by the leading and blessings of the Lord. I am praying that this year, God will rewrite your story! Your secret tears shall be turned to public testimonies!

Don't worry about how things will work out; just know by putting your trust and faith in God that they will. The truth is that Jesus has destroyed the works of the devil! Rest in Him. Let go of the disappointments and setbacks and hang on to the promises of God for your future, and never forget that God loves you; He's with you, and He's on your side! When you believe that everything's going to be alright! Boldly proclaim, "God's grace is sufficient for me today. His power is perfected in my weakness today. I am strong in Him today in Jesus' Name! I am getting up, growing up, and going up today."

"Rise up in splendor and be radiant, for your light has dawned, and
Yahweh's glory now streams from you!"
Isaiah 60:1 TPT

DAY 38

Today is a priceless gift from God, so let's use it joyfully and encourage ourselves to remember, "All things are possible through Christ."

Today is a don't give up day! Yokes are being destroyed, burdens are being lifted, hearts are being healed, minds are being renewed, and joy is being restored!

Today is a day of going from poverty to plenty, emptiness to divinely accelerated overflow, and rejection to acceptance! A day to freely receive all God has given to us in Christ! He has blessed us with all things that pertain to life and godliness.

Today is a day to receive His great love freely. God doesn't just love us, He likes us! He doesn't just like us, He enjoys us! His love is always on, it is constant. It is not there only when we feel it, think about it, or have a "really spiritual" moment, it's eternal! Say it, "Today I welcome in the unconditional, no limits love God has for me!"

Today is a day to remember, love never fails. A day to look in the mirror and say, "I'm incomplete, but He loves me completely. I'm not perfect, but He loves me perfectly. When I fail, His love never does. I'm not there yet, but His love already is. Look who God loves!"

Today is a day to tell someone else you love them too because it's often the simplest and timeliest words that allow healing to enter a hurting person's heart and make their day.

"May mercy, peace, and love be multiplied to you."
Jude 1:2 ESV

DAY 39

The enemy constantly tries to remind you of your past failures, in-adequacies, shortcomings, and imperfections to try to sabotage your future success. Don't buy it! Don't allow your life to turn into a prison where you end up behind bars that are made of the failures, mistakes, wounds, hurts, and opinions of others. If it wasn't too late for Sarah and Abraham, Peter or Paul, it's not too late for you. Believe in the God of redemption. When the enemy brings up the past, remind yourself and others, yes, I have a past, but I'm not a prisoner of it. Don't judge me by my past. I've changed addresses and don't live there anymore.

God wants us to see the future with His eyes, seeing and believing that what has not yet entered our world will enter it as we imagine with faith what God can do. You were never created to live defeated, de-pressed, guilty, condemned, ashamed, or unworthy. You were created to live victoriously. We have been given the ability to dream, to imagine. We have the Holy Spirit who is the same Spirit who raised Christ from the dead. He imparts fresh faith and He is lifting your spirit to move past your past and jump into a great future! You have the opportunity and open doors.

God is for you and He prepared something even greater than you could dream up for yourself. This is a time when a divine reversal begins, when all that has been stolen from the generations is given back, and the set time of God's favor is released. I am believing for you and your entire family to walk in a new measure of freedom and breakthrough!

"I know you are about to arise and show your tender love to Zion.
Now is the time, Lord, for your compassion and mercy to be poured out—
the appointed time has come for your prophetic promises to be fulfilled!"
Psalms 102:13

DAY 40

"I stand on the promises of God this day and declare over my life and my dreams that just like Esther, I am chosen and placed for such a time as this. Just like Ruth, I am favored of the Lord. Just like David, I am called and set apart. My life matters and I am making a difference. I dare to believe in God given dreams and visions for my future. I will be bold, believe God, increase the boundaries of my faith, and dare to ask and believe bigger! I believe for divine connections that accelerate my move into the realm where the possibilities are endless in Christ, that my faith vision discovers unseen possibilities and opportunities as God opens doors I didn't even know were there!

I believe I will experience His goodness and favor in the name of Jesus! A flood of favor is coming my way, every yoke is broken, and every burden is lifted in Jesus name!

I declare peace to any raging storms in my life. I declare divine favor and uninhibited access to people and places that are connected to the fullness of the will of God for my life! I pray success and blessing over everything I put my hands to. I am chosen to succeed! God has prepared something even greater than I could dream of for myself. This is a time when a divine reversal begins, when all that has been stolen from the generations is given back and increase marks every step I take in obedience. I am believing for you and your entire family to walk free from every chain of bondage and lack.

"I continue to pray for your love to grow and increase beyond measure,
bringing you into the rich revelation of spiritual insight in all things.
And you will be filled completely with the fruits of righteousness that are
found in Jesus, the Anointed One—bringing great praise and glory to
God!"
Philippians 1:9, 11 TPT

DAY 41

Power points for abundant living:

- Sometimes breakthrough comes piece by piece instead of all at once.
- Be authentic but use wisdom. Everybody can't handle the raw and uncut version of who you were and even who you presently are. God's not finished with you yet.
- The brain does what the mind tells it to do. Having the mind of Christ can change the structure of our brain and our life!
- You don't just automatically outgrow bad belief systems; you confront them with the truth.
- The presence of trials doesn't destroy the potential for triumph.
- The places where we love the deepest are the places God uses to do His deepest work in our lives.
- When you think you don't have enough to give, start giving anyway. Give your time, give your energy, give your love, but show your faith in giving.
- Don't stay dysfunctional situations or places just to fit in.
- Attitude is a choice. Happiness is a choice. Optimism is a choice. Kindness is a choice. Giving is a choice. Respect is a choice. Whatever choice you make, makes you. Choose wisely.

"At each and every sunrise we will be thanking you for your kindness and your love. As the sun sets and all through the night, we will keep proclaiming, "You are so faithful!"
Psalms 92:2 TPT

DAY 42

It's common for people to be put down, criticized, maligned, and intimidated. Most people get far more jeers than cheers, more pokes than strokes, more cursing than blessings, and more put-downs than high fives. I refuse to give in to that spirit! Let's change it!

People never forget how someone makes them feel. Words can kill and words can bring life. It is amazing how far a few words of encouragement can go to give someone the extra push they needed to make it through a tough time. Be an encourager today! Speak words of blessing and encouragement, to others and to yourself!

Love ends when you stop caring. Life stops when you stop dreaming. Hope ends when you stop believing. Friendship ends when you stop sharing. Keep dreaming, keep believing, keep caring, and keep sharing. May God's love surround you and the sweet fragrance of His presence keep you loving, dreaming, believing, caring, and sharing.

By faith, I decree today, "In this season of your life you are now entering, you will not have to look back with disappointment and regret, your best days are here. You have so much to look forward to. You are coming into a new season of divine favor, peace, progress, increase, inheritance, and joy! YES, LORD!"

"Anxious fear brings depression, but a life-giving word of encouragement can do wonders to restore joy to the heart."
Proverbs 12:25 TPT

DAY 43

Sometimes we are reluctant to bring our lives to the feet of Jesus, almost as if we're waiting until we think we have everything in perfect order. I'm so glad Jesus is there for people who don't have it all together. Coming to the feet of Jesus isn't about discovering how great our strength is, it's about finding His strength for our weakness. No matter how long we've walked with Him and deeply spiritual we are, we never graduate from trusting and needing Him.

We all have "issues" in our lives like the woman in Luke 8 who had suffered from "issues" for 12 years. But something powerful happened when she pressed through the crowd and touched the hem of His garment. There are breakthroughs on the other side when we press through. It's been said, "faith is spelled R-I-S-K." Jesus said, "Daughter, you took a risk trusting me, and now you're healed and whole. Live well, live blessed." (Luke 8:48 The Message)

Jesus doesn't just respond to those whose lives are neat and orderly. He is looking for those who find themselves with nothing else to offer but to fall at His feet, those who've spent it all and are none the better. Those with "bloody issues" that can be uncomfortable to discuss in public. We can bring our messes to the Master, to the feet of Jesus today. His Word to us for our willingness to courageously press through the crowd, lay it all down, and take a risk is, "You're healed and whole, live well, and live blessed!"

"When the woman realized that she couldn't remain hidden, she knelt trembling before him. In front of all the people, she blurted out her story—why she touched him and how at that same moment she was healed. Jesus said, "Daughter, you took a risk trusting me, and now you're healed and whole. Live well, live blessed!"
Luke 8:47-48 MSG

DAY 44

We continually live in the grace and goodness of God. The awareness of it alone should lead us to deep places of praise, worship, and thanks that overwhelm us. God's grace, favor, and goodness are truly amazing. Grace has already won so many battles. For the woman at the well living empty and looking for one more drink, grace wins. For the woman thrown at Jesus feet caught in the very act of adultery, grace wins. For the one condemned to die on a cross next to our Savior who cried out "Remember Me," grace wins. "Today you'll be with me in paradise." For the Apostle Peter who cursed and denied he knew Him when the battle was so intense, grace wins. Jesus prepares breakfast for this broken man after His resurrection. For the prodigal son who spent it all and ended up eating what others throw out to survive, grace wins. Bring the best robe and kill the fatted calf.

For the things in us that are part of our lives that aren't yet fully what they need to be, the struggles, failures, and shortcomings, the guilt and shame of not always measuring up, the things in our past we wish we could change, grace wins. Grace empowers, grace overcomes, and grace takes us forward. God's grace is calling your name today. It's reaching out to empower and energize. Receive it.

"For the Lord is always good and ready to receive you. He's so loving that it will amaze you— so kind that it will astound you! And he is famous for his faithfulness toward all. Everyone knows our God can be trusted, for he keeps his promises to every generation!"
Psalms 100:5 TPT

DAY 45

When you feel overwhelmed and feel like you're going down, remember to focus on God and His promises. He is faithful and will keep you from drowning in your circumstances.

"My God is greater! Greater than my fears, greater than my insecurities, greater than my worries, greater than any problem I'm facing. I declare that no weapon formed against me will prosper. It's not too late for things to improve in my life. God is restoring lost years and opportunities. He is turning things around for my good today. God is writing a new chapter in my life and it's time to turn the page. I declare, "That it is well with my family and myself, no matter what it looks like to my natural eyes. There is victory in the battle, hope in every circumstance, and possibility in every trial. I will not have just enough, because El Shaddai gives me more than enough. I will prosper and be in health as my soul prospers. I will not lack prosperity, but whatever I do will prosper because I delight in the law of the Lord. I am a person of destiny. God is writing a story for my life and He's not finished. He has written every page of my life in His book and it's a book of victory! God is working and there are still things for me to do and accomplish in my future. The drought is over, and the curse is broken by the blood of Jesus. The pit I've been dealing with comes to an end and was only putting me in position for the palace. Divine grace and favor flood my life every day in every way and my mighty God turns every famine into a feast! Yes, Lord! The Lord will preserve my going out and my coming in from this time forth, and even forevermore and cause all my desert places to blossom as the rose!"

"That's where he restores and revives my life. He opens before me pathways to God's pleasure and leads me along in his footsteps of righteousness so that I can bring honor to his name."
Psalms 23:3 TPT

DAY 46

God has created us to be continually growing. But growth is not automatic; it's optional. Growing is a process. You have to feed it good thoughts and surround it with a good environment. Value and nurture it.

There is nothing we can do to stop change. It is inevitable. While we live our lives from day to day, we are surrounded by changes going on all around us. There is a certain mentality and cooperation level we must have in order to grow from our experiences. If we harden our hearts and close our minds, we will not be able to learn and grow, and we will waste the opportunity we've been given. May God give us grace and understanding in our hearts and minds so we don't waste opportunities, having to relearn lessons we could have learned the first time. As we allow God to shape us, mold us, and remove things in us that don't belong, we able to grow and overcome. Father, help us to be teachable and humble so we can grow in Your loving ways and use our free will to choose to be a continual learner and grower.

Remember Psalms 68 says, "Let God arise and His enemies be scattered." May that not only be our prayer for those things around us but also anything in us that hinders His best for us.

"God, the searcher of the heart, knows fully our longings, yet he also understands the desires of the Spirit, because the Holy Spirit passionately pleads before God for us, his holy ones, in perfect harmony with God's plan and our destiny. So we are convinced that every detail of our lives is continually woven together to fit into God's perfect plan of bringing good into our lives, for we are his lovers who have been called to fulfill his designed purpose."
Romans 8:27-28 TPT

DAY 47

One of the titles given to the enemy is the accuser of the brethren. He knows guilt and shame will keep you in fear and intimidation and chain you to your past and failure but, when you realize Jesus doesn't condemn you, the power to change comes.

One of the most powerful stories in the Bible is in John chapter 8. A woman caught in a sinful act was brought and put at the feet of Jesus by the religious leaders hoping to condemn and shame her. But they made a mistake trying to achieve their purpose by bringing her to Jesus! He writes in the dirt, rises to His feet, and asks, "Where are those who condemn you?" To her amazement, there were none left, and Jesus said so beautifully, "Neither do I condemn you. Go and sin no more." Bringing her to the feet of Jesus liberated her and set her free! When you begin to embrace grace, it empowers you to move on and break out of condemnation.

My question to you today is- Where are your accusers? Whatever they are, memories, mistakes, lies, or shame take them to the feet of Jesus. When Jesus speaks voices of accusation have to leave!

So, stop allowing your past limitations to set the boundaries in your life. God is the God of limitless possibilities. He wants to do great things for you and through you starting today! Let your expectations and hopes be God-filled and God birthed! Today you are crowned and encircled with God's goodness!

"For if, because of one man's trespass, death reigned through that one man, much more will those who receive the abundance of grace and the free gift of righteousness reign in life through the one man Jesus Christ."
Romans 5:17 ESV

DAY 48

Just because life hasn't unfolded with the timeline you laid down doesn't mean it's over. Don't let your frustrations push your faith off the cliff, things will get better. Even when time has passed, God can still redeem it.

Fear lies to you so much about the future- so much! Things can get tough in life. Notice how in every scenario, fear never presents God in the situation, but He will be there! If you're walking through the fire, God is going to cause the right people to see the smoke. He can and will cause any fire, any heartache, any season of brokenness, or hurt to turn around for your good and His glory. David said, "In my distress, God enlarged me."

It's time to bloom and blossom in your career, your health, your finances, your relationships, and in every place.

Remember, there is no pain, no season of weariness that God has not woven His faithfullness into. The fight is real, but so is the victory! When we remember God's trustworthiness in our past and cling to His promises about the future, it helps us to live with faith in our present! God is so good that He can take anything that the devil meant for our harm and use it for good! Don't fear! Don't panic! God has called you and He will faithfully lead you through!

Declare in faith today, "The Prince of Peace lives in me. Therefore, I will live stress-free. His presence in me is greater than the problems around me. God is my avenger! He will right every wrong. He will turn things around for my good! My Redeemer lives!"

"Then they remembered that God was their rock, And the Most High God their Redeemer."
Psalms 78:35 NLT

DAY 49

God doesn't get His opinion of you from others! He has already decided that you are His, you belong, He loves you, and He wants you! Even the things others have done to you, God can turn around to use for you! In one moment, God can turn around years of pain and disappointment! He will restore to you the years that have been wasted, damaged, or lost. This is your year to get back the lost years!!!

God sees the battles, the pain, the tears, and the scars on your soul. Others may treat you as though you had it easy, but He knows your story! He carries you when you don't have the strength to go on.

So, remember today, It's not over. Don't drown in the hopelessness of not seeing a change or shift yet. You can live with hope because you serve a God of restoration! God is working even when you can't see it with your eyes and leading you into victory!

With your God, what is broken can be fixed, what is closed can be opened, and what is lost can be recovered!

So today, thank Him by faith. The tables are turning in your favor. Your journey is not in vain. Your answer is on the way!

"Every seed buried in sorrow. You will call forth in its time. You are Lord, Lord of the harvest. Calling our hope now to arise!"

"But as for you, you meant evil against me; but God meant it for good..."
Genesis 50:20 NKJV

DAY 50

Don't give up on the things God has placed in your heart. Whatever you're worried about, God has a plan. He is bigger than your fears. He is stronger than your obstacles. Have faith. Keep going. I pray for supernatural joy and strength for you to keep on keeping on this year. I pray that God enlarges your territory and shows you great favor! I pray for a breakthrough in every area of your life and for you to walk in everything Jesus paid for you to have and that you rule and reign with Him in life! In Jesus name you will never again submit to the rule and reign of the enemy! Your chains are broken, and you are free!!! Spirit, soul, and body!!!

I pray God's peace over your mind and emotions. That He would heal your pain and comfort you with His presence in the name of Jesus. That His healing and health would fill every part of your physical body. Let the healing oil of God flow from the top of your head to the sole of your feet. Be made whole! I pray every chain restricting you, every bondage, every weight containing you is lifted, removed, and destroyed in Jesus' name! I break every spirit of fatigue, discouragement, and depression over you in the name of Jesus and pray for supernatural joy and strength! There is a new energy released in your life! I pray any soul-tie from your past is broken in the name of Jesus! The Blood of Jesus secures you, your family, your peace, and your future! I pray for divine revelation, clarity, and vision to you. I pray favor over you. Favor that brings provision that will carry you from your present season to your future destination! I pray that great things are coming your way and God is working to fulfill and give you the desires of your heart, for you and your family! I pray your life will be God-filled with many good things. That God opens up new doors for you that were not anticipated. That you will be blessed with new opportunities in the name of Jesus and because you have been faithful over a few things, the Lord will make you ruler over much!!!

DAY 51

This is a time and season when God is stirring a desire for you to do something bigger than yourself. A time when God's direction and purpose are awakening. We are here on this planet to live a life that causes our heart to come alive. But too many of us are not living our dreams because we are living our fears. So today, believe with all of your heart that you will do what you were made to do; that you will live a life of purpose.

Even though there are places and areas of our lives where we feel "less than" or "not enough," know that God will complete your incompletion! Remember it is not about just waiting for the "big things." A great life isn't just about big things; it is about the small things that make a big difference. Sometimes the smallest things have the biggest meaning. It takes a big person to do things that seem small and unnoticed. You are never taller than when you kneel down to help someone else.

Get ready, God is preparing you for something really small that will be connected to something really big. Never despise the day of small things. Who knows where it will lead! Be confident in God's power in your life today. There is nothing in the world that can come close to matching Him. No problem is too great. No dream is too big. When you are touched by God's favor, you can and will do amazing things!

"I tell you this timeless truth: The person who follows me in faith, believing in me, will do the same mighty miracles that I do—even greater miracles than these because I go to be with my Father! For I will do whatever you ask me to do when you ask me in my name. And that is how the Son will show what the Father is really like and bring glory to him. Ask me anything in my name, and I will do it for you!"
John 14:12-14 TPT

DAY 52

I don't care how hopeless you feel. God says you're coming out! God's love for you is so immense. It sweeps away fears. It is so deep it heals pain, mends broken hearts, and elevates expectations! It's never on and off. It is always on! His love moves you into victory. Nothing you are facing or ever will face is greater than His love! Jesus was willing to face the Father's rejection so that we could have the peace of knowing, as His children, He will never again reject us. God never mocks you when you fail, He never looks at you with disgust but greets you with love, forgiveness, and the gift of new beginnings. God knows your deepest flaws, yet still loves you outrageously! If we don't believe we are who God says we are, we'll never walk in our full identity as God's children. When you know who you are, see what God sees, you make no excuses for being fearless. Your boldness comes from His love in you. You are not rejected. You're not the things that steal your sleep. You are not every whispered lie. You are priceless, sacred, and loved. Relax in His love for you today! He loves you, even when you don't feel it! He leads you, even when you don't see it! His great love for you is unconditional, unchanging, eternal, and filled with grace and mercy. It's not based on your behavior but His faithfulness! I'm so grateful for this awesome God and this amazing love.

"So now I live with the confidence that there is nothing in the universe with the power to separate us from God's love. I'm convinced that his love will triumph over death, life's troubles, fallen angels, or dark rulers in the heavens. There is nothing in our present or future circumstances that can weaken his love. There is no power above us or beneath us—no power that could ever be found in the universe that can distance us from God's passionate love, which is lavished upon us through our Lord Jesus, the Anointed One!"
Romans 8:38-39 TPT

DAY 53

God is calling us to go deeper. Let's move past some of the old boundaries and limits of our lives and allow God to take us to a place of increased vision. Even when life hurts and it's hard. Even on the days your mind doesn't understand all that's going on around you. Even on those days, God is working!

The easy way isn't always the right way. The comfortable way isn't always the will of God. Sometimes when hardship comes, we tend to retreat and take the path of least resistance but many times in scripture, the right path wasn't the easy one. The right path was one of stretching and reaching beyond old boundaries and comfort zones, allowing God to bring great blessing and increase!

God is a good God, a God of abundance, a God of miracles, a big God, a living God, a great God, an all things are possible God, a God that doesn't get discouraged or give up, a God that is up to something so big, so powerful, and so amazing our minds can't contain it all! What we see God doing is never as big as what we don't see behind the scenes!

Let's live in expectation! Expect every one of your weaknesses to be swallowed up by the presence of Jesus, strengthened by His grace, and healed by His love! There is a grace (blessing) that God gives you; it is over your life! Your leaf will not wither! Remember, being blessed is not a condition; it is a position! It's not what surrounds me that determines my success; it is what's inside me! May we never lose our courage and inspiration to keep going forward and may we never lose our fight in hard times! If there was ever a time to follow our passion, that time is now! You were made to reflect God's glory! Arise, Shine!

"The Lord thy God in the midst of thee is mighty!"
Zephaniah 3:17 KJV

DAY 54

Some days are deeper than others. Days when the things that we depend on aren't enough. Days when those we love so much can't be there. Days when the questions aren't easy or simple and aren't answered with clichés or catchy slogans. Those deeper days call to a deeper truth within us. Those days demand more.

But those days can also be special days that take us back to the place of the greatest certainty in our lives. Jesus, you mean everything to me. Jesus, you have seen me through every hard place in my life, every time. Jesus, You have always been there for me. Nothing and no one can meet the deepest needs of my life like you can, like you have, or like you always will. Jesus, you have picked me up when I've been at my lowest. You have loved me when I didn't feel worthy to be loved. You've held me close when no one else even knew I needed it. Jesus, you see in me what others can't, what I can't see in myself sometimes, and you always keep believing in me through it all.

There will be days when IT isn't enough, whatever IT is. But there will never be a day Jesus is lacking. Thank you for days that remind us, Jesus, you are our source, our hope, our present, and our future. The deepest days and deepest places in our hearts can only be satisfied in Jesus. Thank you, precious Jesus. You are the center of it all!

"then God's wonderful peace that transcends human understanding,
will make the answers known to you through Jesus Christ."
Philippians 4:7 TPT

DAY 55

The term "but God" is found 50 times in scripture. Six letters that completely oppose the intimidating negative assault of problems, sicknesses, financial situations, relationship conflicts, business, or job-related challenges, and seemingly impossible outcomes that come our way. "But God" is the bottom line, the last word.

Israel was in Egypt, "but God" sent Moses. Goliath was bigger, better equipped, and more trained than David, "but God" used a slingshot and a rock to give him the victory. The Hebrew three were thrown in the fiery furnace, "but God" was with them and they came out without even the smell of smoke. Daniel was cast into a den of hungry lions, "but God" completely closed the mouth of the devourer.

All of us have "but God" experiences. I should have been "but God." I would have been "but God." This would have ended this way "but God." I couldn't see any way out "but God." The "but God" moments in our past give us hope that there will be even more and greater moments like that in our now and in our future. Life can be hard at times; the struggle is very real, "but God" is faithful and good. You may have weaknesses, "but God" has strength. You may have sin, "but God" has grace. You may have failed, "but God" remains faithful. You may have been ripped off, "but God" is the restorer. The enemy says defeat, "but God" says victory. The enemy says disease, "but God" says healing. The enemy says there is no way out, "but God" says I am the way. The enemy says you will go under financially, "but God" says I will bless you coming in and going out. But God yesterday, today, and forever.

"For sin's meager wages is death, BUT GOD'S lavish gift is life eternal, found in your union with our Lord Jesus, the Anointed One."
Romans 6:23 TPT

DAY 56

Luke 2:52 says that "Jesus increased in wisdom and stature, and in favor with God and men." God's favor in our life positions us for increased influence, supernatural turnarounds, past limitations to be broken, dreams awakened, missed opportunities redeemed, and wide-open doors of divine possibilities. God created us to live in expectation of His favor. When we do, even in the midst of dire circumstances, we can have the assurance that someway, somehow, something good is going to come out of it. Fear will cause you to fantasize about failure being your future. Favor will cause you to see a future filled with possibilities.

Just like Joseph in Genesis, our challenges can be our transportation into our best years! Joseph's enemies thought they were purchasing a slave, but they were giving him a ride to position him to become the Prince of Egypt. God wrapped Joseph in favor. Believe that God can be working on your promotion even when it looks like you're being demoted. Even when the only people that show up are slave traders, God's favor can turn it around!

Faith is prophetic foresight. It prophesies your descendants will inherit the promised land while you're still a slave. Speak to your future today. Declare with great expectation in the goodness of God, "My future is filled with favor. I expect the favor of God to be upon me, through me, and around me wherever I go and in whatever I do. I position myself to experience the immeasurable, unsurpassable, unimaginable favor of God!"

"Lord, how wonderfully you bless the righteous. Your favor wraps around each one and covers them under your canopy of kindness and joy."
Psalms 5:12 TPT

DAY 57

Don't be afraid of praying big prayers, moving past old boundaries and bondages, stepping forward, and stretching out your life and future to God in faith. You have seeds of greatness on the inside. Today could be the start of something amazing. Jesus came that we may have life and have it to the full.

So today, refuse to tiptoe through life in fear because God has made a covenant with you through the blood of Jesus. God didn't withhold His own Son; therefore, He will not withhold any good thing from you. Expect His best today and say so.

"Oh, Father, enable me to live every moment to the fullest totally involved in Your will. I will not allow fear, intimidation, and insecurity to decide my future. I am made in Your image, filled with Your Spirit, led by Your love. Great things are going to happen to me and through me. My life is directed by Your heart, Your purpose, Your plans, and Your words. Your voice will be louder and stronger than anything anyone has ever said to me or anything that has ever happened to me. What I've been through is nothing compared to what You have for me. I'm not a beggar. I'm a believer! I'm not a victim. I'm a victor! I'm not a loser. I'm a learner! I'm not who they say I am. I'm who You say I am! My due season is on the way. You are a God of increase and You delight to bless me! Hallelujah!

"He who did not spare his own Son but gave him up for us all, how will he not also with him graciously give us all things?"
Romans 8:32 ESV

DAY 58

Things aren't always what they seem or look like. No current condition can define God's intention for your life. You may wonder why you feel stuck in the seeming mundane while you dream of greatness, but your Father says, "I have not forgotten you! You are the one I have chosen!"

You may be like Ruth, who was picking up leftovers in a dusty field. Your circumstances may seem common, but your faith is not! God can bring extraordinary results from ordinary tasks. The world glorifies the finished product, but God glorifies the work in progress. He's in the "waiting," the "working through," and the "walking." You may be walking through hardship through fire or storm, but He has promised to bring you into victory. Our God is the arm that will hold you at your weakest and the eye that will see you at your darkest. Your Father in Heaven has walked with you through every season of your life. He has seen you in your darkest moment, seen you at your worst but continues to love you with His best. He caught every tear and soon you will be declaring, "Harvest is here!"

So, if you don't understand some things in your life right now, trust God and keep moving forward. In time, it will all become clear. This is still your season to see new growth, new opportunities, and new breakthroughs. Hear your Father saying today, "I am healing your perspective concerning where you are right now. I am giving you the courage to dream again!"

"The lovers of God who chase after righteousness will find all their dreams come true: an abundant life drenched with favor and a fountain that overflows with satisfaction."
Proverbs 21:21 TPT

DAY 59

When it feels like hope is gone, when it seems like there is no way, when all of the road signs say, "dead end," God can still make a way. Remember, you are God's idea. He chose you before the world began, before you were in your mother's womb. You might have gotten here through the portal of your mother and father, but you were conceived from the heart of God. I pray over you wherever you might be as you read this that the Spirit of God brings peace and hope where there is hopelessness. God is moving on your behalf. God's hand is still on you. His presence is around you. Nothing you feel or think can nullify the Holy Spirit's vow never to leave your side.

So today, get a fresh vision of your God that ignites a fire and a great faith in you for your future. Even in your wilderness, God is making a way. You will come out! Even in your struggle, God is turning your trial into triumph. You will overcome! Whatever it is, God is already on it! Psalm 138:8 says that He will accomplish those things that concern you. No problem stands a chance against God's plan. You will prevail!

You will go from ruins to restoration. You will go from problems to provision. You will go from depression to deliverance! Walls that have prevented you from moving forward are now destroyed! You will overcome! You will break past previous boundaries! You will breakthrough to abundant living! God will see you through!

"For the Lord God is brighter than the brilliance of a sunrise! Wrapping himself around me like a shield, he is so generous with his gifts of grace and glory. Those who walk along his paths with integrity will never lack one thing they need, for he provides it all! O Lord of Heaven's Armies, what euphoria fills those who forever trust in you!"
Psalms 84:11-12 TPT

DAY 60

"Heavenly Father,

Thank you for the gift of another blessed day. Your mercies are new each and every morning.

As the sun rises, thank You that the worries, frustrations, and anxiety of yesterday are diminished and defeated at the sound of Your great name.

Lord, I worship You because of who You are. You are my God, the lover of my soul, my righteousness, peace, victory, and joy!

I put my confidence and trust in Your love for me today and I thank You for Your unwavering faithfulness. Through the power of the Holy Spirit, I let go of any bondage that is holding back my progression. Thank you, Lord, that every chain is BROKEN!

Whatever challenges I face today, I trust in You Lord with all my heart, having the confidence to not lean on my understanding but in all my ways acknowledge You, for You will direct my path.

I release ALL doubt, fear, anger, confusion, and frustration. I will keep dreaming and keep pursuing You and what You placed in my heart. I am here, and my God's greatness is in me! I am here, and I will not compromise! I am here, and I will not quit! My boundaries are expanding. The increase is coming my way in every area of my life. Thank You for your strength to face any battles and emerge victorious through Christ Jesus my Lord."

"The faithful lovers of God will inherit the earth and enjoy every promise of God's care, dwelling in peace forever."
Psalms 37:29 TPT

DAY 61

Someone needs a word of love and encouragement today. Someone needs to know that God hasn't forgotten them and is doing something powerful on their behalf! Someone needs to know that the Father loves you and rejoices in calling you His own! You may be in a season of silence right now where you feel like you are hidden, but the silence does not mean God has forgotten about you. He has heard every prayer; He had seen every tear. God is not just preparing the blessing for you; God is preparing you for the blessing.

He hasn't forgotten you. He sees you. When others forget you, ignore you, or even work against you, God is for you, standing with arms open wide. You are loved!

You are a somebody that God has brought from somewhere and is taking you to a somewhere, a higher place in Him! I pray you experience God's presence and love rushing through you, filling every broken and hurting place with courage, strength, hope, and peace. So wipe those tears and lift your head! You belong to Him and He knows how to bring it to pass! He is faithful to you always.

"So do not fear, for I am with you; do not be dismayed, for I am your God. I will strengthen you and help you; I will uphold you with my righteous right hand."
Isaiah 41:10 NIV
"The father of a righteous child has great joy; a man who fathers a wise son rejoices in him."
Proverbs 23:24 NIV

DAY 62

I pray today that through divine connections, you move into the realm where the possibilities are endless in Christ, that your faith and vision discover unseen possibilities and opportunities as God opens doors you didn't even know were there! I pray you to experience His goodness and favor today in the name of Jesus! A flood of favor is coming your way. I pray anything that is burdening you be removed. That every yoke break and every burden be lifted in Jesus' name!!

I declare peace to you! I declare divine favor and uninhibited access to people and places that are connected to the fullness of the will of God for your life! I pray for success and blessing over you. You are sentenced to succeed! I declare success over you! In the name of Jesus. God has prepared something even greater than you could dream up for yourself! This is a time when a divine reversal begins. When all that has been stolen from the generations is given back and the set time of God's favor is released! I believe for you and your entire family to walk free during this season of breakthrough!

Say it, "This day I declare breakthrough in every area of my life. The devil is already defeated. I walk by faith in the victory that is already mine. I am seated with Christ far above all the power of the enemy. As Jesus is, so am I, in this world. I accept everything that Jesus paid for me to have, and I rule and reign with Jesus in life. I will never again submit to the rule, reign, or lies of the enemy. My chains are broken, and I am free! Spirit, soul, and body! Jesus has already won the victory in my life. Jesus has already won my battles for me. My fight is to believe. I refuse to stop believing. I walk by faith and not by sight. There are already more for me than those against me. I cast my care and trouble on God, and I am filled with peace! He is fighting for me. Jesus is interceding for me right now! I rejoice in the midst of my battles because no matter what things look like, it's a new day, a new season, and it's my time!"

DAY 63

What happens between praying and releasing your faith and believing that you will receive? Between the "already" and the "not yet?" A lot of patience and usually a lot of lies from the enemy. Never forget that things are happening behind the scenes that can't be seen on the surface.

The Christian journey is a process as well as a discovery. So, while you're waiting, remember your destiny and fulfillment is not just at the end of the journey. It's in the journey because miracles don't always mature us our journey with God does!

The power of God is never more apparent than when a believer is made strong by his or her relationship with God through the hard times. Staying patient during the journey allows God to make those forces that are aligned against us our footstools!

So when the enemy lies to you, just tell him to go home, and you know where that is! This we know for sure; our God will safely see us home. That promise is guaranteed. There is nobody like our God. He will see us through. Jesus is called the author and finisher of our faith. He's not only given you the grace to start, but the grace to finish!

"We look away from the natural realm and we fasten our gaze onto Jesus who birthed faith within us and who leads us forward into faith's perfection. His example is this: Because his heart was focused on the joy of knowing that you would be his, he endured the agony of the cross and conquered its humiliation, and now sits exalted at the right hand of the throne of God!"
Hebrews 12:2 TPT

DAY 64

The faithfulness and greatness of our God cannot be over-exaggerated. God has brought you too far to leave you where you are. He has something great in your future. The Lord's harvest is full of opportunities and introductions that will take you to new levels you didn't know existed.

I believe God wants you to know that He hears, and He sees, and you are not alone in your struggles. He is saying, "I am with you every step of the way, even when it feels like you're alone. Remain firm and stable, for I have your deliverance planned. You need to get ready. You're coming into acceleration! As you walk with, you will emerge from the fire without even the smell of smoke. You have no reason to fear, obsess, or panic. Your Heavenly Father has surrounded you with His presence and assigned angels to move with you!"

I am praying for God's perfect peace and love to embrace you now in the name of Jesus. I pray for strength to you in every area you feel heaviness. I pray this will be a successful week for you and the people that matter to you. While what you've been through may have been dark, messy, painful, and relentless, in Jesus' Name, God is miraculously making it work for your good! He is setting you free. He is not conspiring against your wholeness and happiness. He is your good, good Father! I pray something great, amazing, powerful, and miraculous happens to you, through you, and for you this week! Let's agree! Amen!

"So take courage! For I believe God. It will be just as He said."
Acts 27:25 NLT

DAY 65

Life isn't always a sea of tranquility. There are storms of adversity and negativity. It can feel overwhelming, but Jesus is our utterly dependable unchanging Rock. Faith and hope are essential.

Consciously choose to continue looking up, looking forward, and pursuing God's purpose for your life. Never let your problems silence what you've heard from God, and don't ever let anyone convince you that there's no hope for you or that it's a lost cause. Every adversity, every failure, every heartache carries with it the seed of an equal or even greater blessing. When the battle is over, you will not only come through it, but you will come out stronger and better than you were before.

Hear your Father say today, "As you find yourself in the middle of the struggle, conflict, and pressure, rest and trust, I am with you in all things. Even though there are hardships and difficulties, I am with you. I will not abandon you in the middle of your trials, for I am with you in all things. It may seem contrary to your mind, but I am making peace and comfort available to you even in the midst of storms. As you see, the waves rise high and feel the pressures continue to build, know I am with you, and know you can be comforted. I know what you have need of even before you ask. There is no mountain too big, no circumstance too hard, no obstacle too difficult that I cannot make a way for you. So, as you look down at your hands and see lack, trust that my hands have all you need, and I will provide and have even scheduled and orchestrated its release for you before you even know of it. I am El Shaddai, your all-sufficient God."

"They remembered that God, the Mighty One, was their strong protector, the Hero-God who would come to their rescue."
Psalms 78:35 TPT

DAY 66

I believe for those that are open to God's work in their lives that this year can be a year of innovation, advancement, progress, supernatural increase, and unexplainable blessings. It can be a year of expansion, opportunities, and empowerment to do great exploits. This year can be a year for favor to flow. But it will require an openness for transition and allowing God to interrupt our attitudes. The prophet Samuel allowed God to interrupt his frustration and grief over Saul in 1 Samuel 16.

"Now the LORD said to Samuel, "How long will you mourn for Saul, seeing I have rejected him from reigning over Israel? Fill your horn with oil, and go; I am sending you to Jesse the Bethlehemite. For I have provided Myself a king among his sons."
I Samuel 16:1 NKJV

What a powerful word for us today. How long shall we continue to be held captive by things God wants us to be free from? And the message to move forward is this, fill your flask with anointing oil and get going. Allow the Holy Spirit to penetrate and fill every place in our lives, to give us His perspective, to transform our thinking and decision making, and then live out of that. Go forth into our future with our horns filled with oil! You cannot get to your tomorrow while you are chained to your yesterday. Yes. Learn from your mistakes so that you're not a prisoner of them but always remember, my mistakes and failures and the mistakes and failures of others are not my God. They will not cause me to stay stuck in continual disappointment, regret, and condemnation day after day, bowing at the altar of the enemies of our destiny! Today let's all open ourselves to the transition God has for us fill our horns with oil and go! Go into our God-ordained future! Know that in the last part of that verse, God declares, I have provided! There's a provision as we go with our horns filled with oil!

DAY 67

I'm releasing these three words today over you- Restore. Recover. Reclaim.

For all who have suffered any kind of loss or setback, had the enemy steal from you, or have something you want back, God recently reminded me of this promise in Luke 19:10 *"For the son of man is come to seek and save that which was lost."* God specializes in finding lost things! I want to remind you of this powerful promise today, *"So I will restore to you the years that the locust has eaten."* Joel 2:25

Only God can restore years. The enemy wants us to dwell on our lack and losses, with a focus on our failures, Jesus always reminds us that He makes all things new and has overcome. God's plan is always bigger than your pain. He wants us to rise up, start fresh, and see the bright opportunity in each new day. Your next chapter will be more impactful than your last one and whatever the famine has been in your life, God is able to turn it into a feast!

"I am praying that your heart will soar with a fresh new expectation. I pray that new hope and grace will abound in you! I pray that you will rise up in faith. I pray that disappointment will not rule in your heart and mind and that our God will empower you to RECOVER ALL! I speak over you; God's goodness is following YOU all the days of your life!!! YOU will walk in His abundant blessing! In Jesus' Name, Amen!"

"Surely goodness and mercy shall follow me All the days of my life;
And I will dwell in the house of the Lord forever."
Psalms 23:6 NKJV

DAY 68

Many times, in life the attacks become greater because the blessing is getting closer. The anointing that's on your life attracts attacks. Don't look at it as only trouble; look at it as confirmation. You're getting closer and there's even greater beauty at the end of the struggle. Many times, your greatest ministry will be where your greatest warfare has been.

The chapters of your life are still being written by the hand of God, and in spite of the trials, transition is powerful, because it announces the fact that a new season of fruitfulness is on its way. Through it all, God is there to pull you out, carry you through, lift you up, bring increase to places of lack, lead you forward and get you through the attacks and storms. Let's rise up today and say,

"I'm not shrinking back, thinking back, or going back. I'm moving forward into God's destiny for my life. I won't be intimidated or back down. I may feel like I am standing at the gates of hell in my problems, but I won't back down. When my human mind cannot imagine a human answer to a problem, I will believe in my supernatural God to bring supernatural results to every place in my life. Things change, people change, but my God remains steadfast and true. Even when all else fails, my God will not!"

"God, your wrap-around presence is my protection and my defense.
You bring victory to all who reach out for you."
Psalms 7:10 TPT

DAY 69

Never surrender your destiny and future to other people's criticism and judgments. Don't allow the negative and cynical opinions of others to frame your world. A powerful truth I've discovered after years of life and ministry is people will find what they're looking for, good or bad. Perspective is everything in life. Never accept where you are as the basis for defining who you are. Do the thing you were created to do and go after the dreams God has placed in your heart. Wake up each and every day with a deep knowing that your inheritance is eternal, priceless, untainted, permanent, and secure, and no one can take it from you as long as you choose to follow Him. I mean absolutely no one!

The truth is anyone can be a critic. It requires no special skills. As long as you are arrogant, egotistical, hard-hearted, stingy, judgmental, or have a Facebook page or Twitter feed, you qualify. I don't believe I'm familiar with any monuments erected for critics, but I know of multitudes of changed lives that are a monument to those who encouraged and believed in someone else. So, you may have experienced some rejection and disappointments, but God will bring you out better off than you were before. For every unfair situation, every hurt you've endured, God is saying, "It's not the end. I have called and chosen you. My hand is on you, for you have been commissioned for this very hour and season. Everything the enemy has stolen, I'm going to restore: the joy, the peace, the health, the dreams, the confidence, the love. I have made you; I will carry you; I will sustain you, and I will rescue you. The waves meant to take you under will be the very waves you ride into your destiny!"

"That's where he restores and revives my life. He opens before me pathways to God's pleasure and leads me along in his footsteps of righteousness so that I can bring honor to his name."
Psalms 23:3 TPT

DAY 70

All of us have dreams that live in our hearts, things that we sometimes can't even fully articulate or share. I don't know everything God has placed in your heart, but I know He has a journey, a path, and a plan to bring it to pass. Just like Joseph in the book of Genesis, He has never forgotten you. Even when it seems it's getting further away if we keep our focus on Him, He has a way of making a way. His plans for my life are good. Better than anything I could imagine for myself.

Our current limitations do not determine our future. Breakthroughs are birthed when we believe, believe in the face of seemingly impossible odds. Our insufficiency is more than covered through His abundant provision. He told the apostle Paul, "My grace is sufficient..."

If you are walking through a hard time right now, God's grace and provision are calling your name. Grace is not only the power of the Holy Spirit to enable you to go through things that seem impossible, but the supernatural ability to accomplish and possess what seems impossible! His grace is sufficient for whatever we need every day. When my natural eyes can't see what's on the road ahead, can't understand all the parts of the journey, can't see what's around the next turn, that's when my heart rises up and says, I will not fear. My God will provide and lead me in the right direction. He is not just taking me somewhere; He's preparing there for me and me and me for there! Your breakthrough is coming. Hold on, stand firm in faith, He can work wonders when we trust Him!

"Give God the right to direct your life, and as you trust him along the way you'll find he pulled it off perfectly! He will appear as your righteousness, as sure as the dawning of a new day. He will manifest as your justice, as sure and strong as the noonday sun."
Psalms 37:5-6 TPT

DAY 71

"I declare victory, grace, and great favor over you, your projects, and your future. Every evil gathering and conspiracy against you be overturned. Let the enemies of God against you turn on each other in Jesus' name! Everything contending against your destiny has lost its power to stop you! You shall overcome, progress, prosper, and succeed in spite of obstacles and opposition. The Lord Almighty has made room for you in the realm of His greatness and He will crown the rest of this year with an abundant harvest. I pray any lying spirit of fear and dread is powerless against you. Expect the fulfillment of His promises. Absolutely nothing that the enemy unleashed will be able to stop the powerful move of God that you are walking into in Jesus' name. There is no scenario, situation, or circumstance in which you find yourself where there is no hope because you are a child of God. There was hope yesterday, today, and tomorrow. I speak peace over every fearful heart.

In the darkest hour, God's glory is going to breakthrough. When that wave of worry that seems so big you can't even see what's on the other side, tries to sweep over you, you know that your future is covered in God's faithfulness. He has overcome this world and made you an overcomer. Hear the Father say, "Right here, in this seeming delay, I am with you. I am guarding you and guiding you. The moment has come for you to perceive Me. Looking deeper into My word, seeing Me afresh and new, being transformed as you look into My face and see the radiance of My love for you."

"And everything I've taught you is so that the peace which is in me will be in you and will give you great confidence as you rest in me. For in this unbelieving world you will experience trouble and sorrows, but you must be courageous, for I have conquered the world!"
John 16:33 TPT

DAY 72

Even in the midst of times when it feels like the future is so unclear and uncertain, I will remain in relentless faith. Even when it looks like I don't have enough for what's ahead, I will remain in relentless faith. Even when my mouth wants to speak doubt and unbelief at the prospects which lie before me, I will speak out relentless faith. Even when others doubt me and look at me with skepticism, I will remain in relentless faith. Even when the temptation arises in my soul to doubt and question where He is, I will remain in relentless faith. Even when Pharaoh's army is behind me and the Red Sea is in front of me and complaining unbelieving people are all around me, I will remain in relentless faith. Even when the night feels long and dark and morning seems so slow to come, even then, will I sing a song in the night in relentless faith. Even when my feet grow weary and my steps unsure, I will keep my hand to the plow and not look back in relentless faith. Even when the love I give is not reciprocated or appreciated, I will continue to share it in relentless faith. Even when I don't understand and nothing makes sense, I will continue to worship in relentless faith.

Relentless faith that He is good when it feels like nothing good is happening. Relentless faith that He can take even the bad and make it work out for my good. Relentless faith that no matter who is against, He is for me. Relentless faith that every word He has promised me shall come to pass no matter how long it seems to take. Relentless faith that in all things, He will have the final say!

DAY 73

Most of the meaningful things in our lives aren't created instantly or overnight; they take time. They're not just the results of what we do in the spotlight but what we do when no one else is around to pat us on the back. May we be a generation that desires the secret place with God far more than the platform in front of thousands.

Consistency is staying with it and being faithful when no one sees, is so important. Consistency is to continually, rain or shine, day or night, in every season, no matter how we feel or what it looks like, show up every day simply doing what we're called to do, can create powerful and amazing things.

It is not just the big things, but the small things done consistently over time that can make a huge impact. Great blessings are a result of great perseverance. Great distances can be covered by small steps. Small things make a huge impact.

Remember that one of the greatest keys to success is to stay steady and keep your peace knowing and trusting that God is continually working on your behalf even when it doesn't look like it.

If you're feeling tired and weary from the hurt, disappointment, and confusion, I pray for a renewed energy and focus from the Lord to be released in your life that will empower you in the daily things. That no matter what knocks you down in life, you are going to get back up and keep going, one step at a time, one day at a time. Never give up!

"His lord said to him, 'Well done, good and faithful servant; you were faithful over a few things, I will make you ruler over many things. Enter into the joy of your lord.'"
Matthew 25:21 NKJV

DAY 74

LIFE. When I think about life-

I've lived, I've loved, I've lost, I've won, I've missed, I've hurt, I've trusted, I've made mistakes. But most of all, I've learned, not everything I need to yet, I'm still a work in progress.

In fact, life and time are the two best teachers. Life teaches us to make good use of time and time teaches us the value and preciousness of life.

A good life is when you smile, dream big, laugh, and even through the tears, realize how blessed you are for the people and things that you have.

So, no matter how good or bad you have it, wake up each day thankful for "your life." Keep the right perspective. One reason people give up in life is that they tend to look at how far they still have to go, instead of how far they have come!

So, don't give up. Stay positive, faith-filled, focused, and energetic. God always has something for you, a key for every problem, a light for every shadow, a relief for every sorrow, and a plan for every tomorrow! He came that we might have life, abundant life. He is a good, good Father!

"Keep trusting in the Lord and do what is right in his eyes. Fix your heart on the promises of God and you will be secure, feasting on his faithfulness."
Psalm 37:3 TPT

DAY 75

"Thank You, Lord, for another day. Thank you for new grace and mercy for today. Thank You for sending Jesus. Thank you that He paid it all for us. Thank you for dreams and visions of our future to flow as instruments of your love. Thank you that we are winners through You. Thank you that we don't have to be afraid. Your eyes are on us. We are not abandoned, and our situation is not hopeless. When Jesus is in the room with us, everything changes, and the possibilities are endless. We are Your masterpiece, created for Your own good pleasure, fearfully and wonderfully made in your image and likeness.

Dear Father, stir this in the hearts and lives of your precious people today! Let great encouragement and hope rise up in them! Thank you for the awareness that Your presence makes all the difference in their lives, that the Holy Spirit is with them, leading and strengthening them today. Touch every person who reads this today and give them hope for their future. Remind them there is never a moment that they are not loved by You. Remind them that they are not alone in this. You are with them and that You promised them that You would never let them down or abandon them. Remind them today that Jesus said, "My grace is enough; it's all you need. My strength comes into its own in your weakness. Amen."

"But he answered me, "My grace is always more than enough for you, and my power finds its full expression through your weakness." So I will celebrate my weaknesses, for when I'm weak I sense more deeply the mighty power of Christ living in me."
2 Corinthians 12:9 TPT
"I will never leave you alone, never! And I will not loosen my grip on your life!"
Hebrews 13:5 TPT

DAY 76

God didn't create any of us to live feeling hopeless, rejected, or defeated. He didn't make us to live in dread. We were created to live, love, reach, and anticipate His goodness! We are made to reflect God's glory!

So, no matter what your issues are, they don't intimidate Jesus! Your deepest secrets don't scare God. Your hidden pain doesn't bring Him shame. He will help you heal through it because He loves you. He can handle it! I declare over you today; God is going to increase your gifting, your boldness, your clarity, your calling, and your provision! Don't lose hope; God has a plan for your life! You may not understand it right now, but it's coming together in God's timing!

Dear God, "Thank You for this new day. Thank you for the precious people you love so much. Touch every person reading this today and give them hope for their future! Renew their vision and strengthen and refresh them with Your unfailing love. I pray an increase over them in favor, in harvest, in success. An abundance of God, overflowing, breaking forth, springing up, good measure, pressed down, shaken together, bubbling over, and setting free! In the name of Jesus, let it pour out on them and through them! May they abound in blessings! There is power in the name of Jesus! There is healing in the name of Jesus. There is provision in the name of Jesus. There is strength in the name of Jesus. There is freedom in the name of Jesus. Let every bondage be broken and your people walk in freedom today! Amen!"

"...I will strengthen you and help you; I will uphold you with my righteous right hand."
Isaiah 41:10 NIV

DAY 77

We are in a season of being loosed for God's glory! Don't believe the lies the enemy has been whispering to you. He tries to paint a hopeless, dark picture of your life, so you become discouraged, lonely, and depressed. You may be in a place like that right now, but God is causing new hope to arise in you. Old cycles are ending! You will no longer allow lies and misunderstandings to lead you to believe you are defeated, incompetent, unloved, undesirable, or incapable. A new season of breakthrough is here! The wait may seem more real than God's promises sometimes, but you are still on the path to victory!

Cycles of hopelessness, despair, and depression will no longer reign in your life. Be broken in Jesus' Name! Every wall that's been holding you back is going to come tumbling down! Every disappointment, every setback, every person who did you wrong, God is going to turn it around for your good and His glory!

"Lord, let freedom and liberty rule and reign in the hearts and lives of your precious people today! A new season of divine turnarounds and increase be loosed! New strength and refreshing in our lives birthed by the winds of the Holy Spirit, be loosed! We decree confinement be broken and great freedom, be loosed! We decree harvest multiply. Multiply now at levels never seen before, be loosed! Angels sent to minister on our behalf, be loosed!

We receive it and thank you for it, precious Lord!!"

"God is not man, that he should lie, or a son of man, that he should change his mind. Has he said, and will he not do it? Or has he spoken, and will he not fulfill it?"
Numbers 23:19 NKJV

DAY 78

When God exposes us to things we have never experienced, it's not to frustrate us, rather it's to inspire us to reach for a dimension that is now possible, which we previously thought was inaccessible. He wants us to reach out and stretch beyond where we are and believe to continually grow and expand. Our destiny is greater than our history.

Every one of us has a high calling on our lives and the question becomes, "Are we answering, 'our call'?" Are we answering our call or are we turning a deaf ear and looking in amazement at someone else's call? God wants to work in wonder and amazement in our lives! There is a greater harvest yet to come for you. There is a greater abundance in store for you.

I want to stir you today to arise to this powerful truth. You are a product of Heaven, bought with a high price, set apart for a great purpose, and your story is significant. He has a plan for your life. He bought you with His blood. You are significant, important, and special. Father God has destined you to be blessed, favored, fruitful, chosen, and set apart for a special purpose! Yes, you!

His work is continuing in you, not just for you. Allow Him to cultivate within you the beauty of His special calling that is yours alone. He loves you and chose you from the foundation of the world. Oh, how precious you are.

"And you are among the chosen ones who received the call to belong to
Jesus, the Anointed One."
Romans 1:6 TPT

DAY 79

God can! Two of the most powerful words ever spoken!

If "God Can" cause the cross, the painful tree of suffering and sacrifice bear eternal fruit, what can He do with the storms and adverse winds that come against us? It's not just about bearing them, it's about causing even the bitter to "bear" sweet fruit! He can turn it around. Yes, God can when no one else can! He has a new beginning for every loss and restoration for all that's been stolen. His plans for your life far exceed the circumstances of your day!

So, things might not have worked out the way you wanted or planned. But you still have so much to live for and believe for and every reason to keep moving forward. There is something in your future worth fighting for in your today. You were born to unleash God's glory for His purpose. Join me in declaring over your life.

"I commit to treasure the precious gifts God has given me that separate me from the masses and that has made me who I am, to believe I can bless someone else. To never cease to believe that I am an overcomer because of who I am in Christ Jesus. To not allow anyone or anything to diminish my faith, hope, and trust in You Lord or rob me of abundant life! As I daily trust in you and obey, I shall surely dwell in the land and be abundantly fed! My God is able!"

"That's where he restores and revives my life. He opens before me pathways to God's pleasure and leads me along in his footsteps of righteousness so that I can bring honor to his name."
Psalms 23:3 TPT

DAY 80

Many miracles are lost in the seemingly small and insignificant decisions. We must cultivate a lifestyle of being consistent in the monotonous and routine parts of our lives and not just when the world is watching. Our decisions to stay the course with diligence has great reward. MIRACLES ARE BIRTHED THROUGH MUNDANE MOMENTS.

We learn to say 'no' when we say 'yes' to the most important priorities of our lives. By answering the question, "What will I GIVE myself to?"

Think of your life like a wheel. The center of the wheel is the hub. The spokes of your life (which is your family, your career, your goals, your money, your relationships, etc.) come from that hub. We all build our lives around some sort of hub. The question is, will God be our hub? Will I make every decision in my life, even those that seem small with God's view and perspective in mind?

Proverbs 3:6 instructs us in being led to a secure path in life. "Become intimate with him in whatever you do, and he will lead you wherever you go." If we desire the outcome, we must also embrace the process. Jesus at the center of it all, every minute of every day, is the key to an abundant life and future. He knows what is best for us even more than we can know for ourselves. We say yes to You and Your plan for us today, Lord. Oh, how very good and loving and caring and gracious You are and how secure we can be with You at the center of it all.

"So above all, constantly chase after the realm of God's kingdom and the righteousness that proceeds from him. Then all these less important things will be given to you abundantly."
Matthew 6:33 TPT

DAY 81

Things change and life is constantly shifting. While our circumstances may have changed, our great God has not. His faithfulness still stands. His goodness still reigns. His love still overcomes. No matter what you are going through today or will go through tomorrow, your destiny is greater than your difficulty, greater than your dilemma, greater than your discouragement. God in Christ has given you everything you need to get there. Keep being your best, keep honoring Him, staying faithful in the seemingly small things.

While you're on your way, don't get caught up in continually comparing yourself to others, constantly feeling like you don't measure up. Don't compare your progress with other people. We all need our own time to travel our own distance. Life is not a contest; it's a calling.

Long before you were born and became a part of history, you existed in the heart of God. You are His special, unique, and precious child. Destiny is forged by your daily activities that flow out of knowing God loves and values you. May your activities be directed by God and built on the foundation of purpose. May you overcome all obstacles, defy the status quo, and fulfill His great and specific plans for your life. With our great God, all things are possible!

"His eyes of faith were set on the city with unshakable foundations,
whose architect and builder is God himself."
Hebrews 11:10 TPT

DAY 82

We need to regularly step back and take a deeper look. It becomes so easy to lose focus in the maze of life: the daily grind, the setbacks, the confusion, and the lies of the enemy that try to infiltrate our thought life. Sometimes we just sit on autopilot. Our minds start thinking and pondering all the natural reasons for what is going on and trying to figure out how we can fix it or how it's going to ever work out.

But we must always be willing to look deeper, past the shallow surface of what is happening and discern what is behind all of this. Could it be that there are forces that are working to cause us to lose our focus, to take our joy, to rob us of our peace and ultimately our destiny because there is a more sinister scheme being released?

Sometimes we have to move past the personalities and the people that seemingly always push our buttons and irritate us and awaken to the reality that our adversary walks about as a roaring lion seeking prey to devour. His ultimate goal for our lives is to get us to lay down, give up, roll over, and play dead so that he can have an easy meal. His ultimate goal is to get us to pay attention to the annoying gnats and forget about the beast. His ultimate goal is distraction. Next time you are tempted to start running around swatting gnats, remember it's a setup. Don't lose your focus. You are not at war with the gnats. There's a more subtle enemy whose greatest weapon is deceit, but we will not be taken captive!

Light a fire on the inside. Refuse to be intimidated! Refuse the spirit of compromise! You have the seed of Almighty God. Don't allow something small to keep you from God's best. I can allow life to create my attitudes or allow my attitudes to create my life. Keep your focus. The same spirit that came in the tomb and told Jesus to get up lives in believers. God lives on the inside of you. Let God arise and His enemies be scattered in your life today! Selah! (pause and meditate on this)

DAY 83

We can never be reminded too much of who our God is and what that means. Our God is a loving and giving Father. Savior. Love. Healer. King of kings. Lord of lords. Precious Lamb. Son of Man. Friend. Advocate. Cornerstone. Light of the world. Waymaker. Name above all names!

He will give truth to replace deception. He will give hope to replace impossibilities. He will give strength to replace exhaustion. He will give joy to replace heartache. He will give peace to replace despair. He will give healing to replace pain. He will give abundance to replace lack. He will give love to replace rejection.

He will give blessing to replace cursing. He will give power to replace weakness. He will give light to replace darkness. He will give freedom to replace bondage. He will give faith to replace doubt. He will give assurance to replace fear. He will give favor to replace betrayal. He will give calm even in the midst of the storm.

We say, Yes Lord! We celebrate who You are and all You provide and receive it today from the loving and giving hands of our precious Father. Thank you, Jesus, for all you have provided for us!

"Keep trusting in the Lord and do what is right in his eyes. Fix your heart on the promises of God and you will be secure, feasting on his faithfulness. Make God the utmost delight and pleasure of your life, and he will provide for you what you desire the most. Give God the right to direct your life, and as you trust him along the way you'll find he pulled it off perfectly!"
Psalms 37:3-5 TPT

DAY 84

Through everything that comes our way, it's so important to remind ourselves of the unchanging truth that reigns over us. Our lives are not ordered by what other people say or their timeline. I am a child of God and my steps are directed by Him! If God says I can, then I can, and I will not let anyone else convince me otherwise! Living in these realities helps us to settle down and steady ourselves and cast our cares on our great God. He will carry our burdens the rest of the way. Even when we don't see it, He's working things out for us. He never ever stops working. He is continually working for us and in us, processing us for something greater. I can rely on this reality no matter what part of my future may be held in mystery, but my Father, who is the Author of my story, knows what is up ahead and He is good!

Naomi experienced it when she set out on the road to Bethlehem (Ruth 1). Moses faced it at the burning bush (Exodus 3). The Apostle Paul experienced it when he was arrested in Jerusalem (Acts 21).

So, no matter how many unfair things happen to you, have happened to you, or if others do you wrong, God your Father hasn't forgotten you or His promises towards you. He hasn't been taken by surprise. There is life. There is wonder. There are divine appointments. There is healing and hope and fruitfulness up ahead. Thank you, precious Jesus!

"For I know the plans I have for you," declares the Lord, "plans to prosper you and not to harm you, plans to give you hope and a future."
Jerimiah 29:11 NIV

DAY 85

Things can improve and change for the better. We all need to live in that blessed hope. One day four lepers were waiting to die; the next day they are feasting in abundance. (2 Kings 7) Your breakdown today can lead to your breakthrough tomorrow. Your deepest need today can bring about His greatest provision tomorrow. Things can turn around for you. Always keep your hope alive. Psalms reminds us God can lead us through pathways we didn't even know existed.

"Your steps formed a highway through the seas with footprints on a pathway no one even knew was there."

Psalms 77:19 TPT

In faith and expectation of His goodness, I declare that "unexpected blessings are coming your way. You will move forward from barely making it to having more than enough. God will open up supernatural doors for you. He will speak to the right people about you. You will see Ephesians 3:20 in Jesus' name. God is guiding you into your greatest days. You shall overcome and prosper. Greater things are yet to come and greater things are still to be done in you and through you and for you! Hallelujah!"

"Never doubt God's mighty power to work in you and accomplish all this. He will achieve infinitely more than your greatest request, your most unbelievable dream, and exceed your wildest imagination! He will outdo them all, for his miraculous power constantly energizes you."

Ephesians 3:20 TPT

DAY 86

Power points for living

1. Motivation is what gets you started. Discipline is what keeps you going. Greatness comes when you start doing ordinary things in extraordinary ways, even on the days when you don't feel like it.

2. There is a difference in judging others and looking at the results of their actions. You might have to break it down to them like this, "I'm not placing distance between me and you. I'm placing distance between me and your behavior."

3. Sometimes we have to learn to live without the apology that was never given.

4. Gratitude is a great multiplier. So, say thank you for your life every single day. Gratitude can transform common days into thanksgivings, turn routine jobs into joy, and change ordinary opportunities into blessings.

5. Money can't buy happiness. But financial freedom brings greater opportunities and possibilities to not only bless you but also make a difference for others.

6. There is a balance between being open and not compromising. You can have such an open mind that there are no convictions or boundaries.

7. Maturity comes with experience, not just age.

8. The respect of your spouse and children should always mean more than the cheers of the crowd.

9. Life is about events and the process. We tend to overvalue the power of an event and undervalue the power of the process. We need both!

10. We seldom see the full results of our influence while on earth. But even when we feel a sense of failure, we must remember that our work for the Lord is not in vain. Keep on loving and caring and giving. You are making a difference

DAY 87

Stop beating yourself up. You are a work in progress, which means you get there a little at a time, not all at once. You can't reach for anything higher if your hands are still filled with yesterday's baggage or garbage. Today begin to live in the expectation that every one of your weaknesses will be swallowed up by the presence of Jesus, strengthened by His grace, healed by His love! Never allow your world to shrink down to nothing but a life of regrets! God's calling is greater than your falling! God is uprooting the root of rejection that has pulled you down and held you back. You are His beloved and accepted by Him!

Declare it to your day, "The voice of mercy is much stronger than the voice of condemnation in my life. His mercy is new this morning. I can go to God's throne of grace at all times. God's goodness and mercy are following me today. They are tracking me down, looking for me and are going to overtake me! God will accomplish what concerns me. He will finish what He started in me. He will not give up on me. He will right every wrong and God will restore everything the enemy has stolen from me! Therefore, I will not fail today because God's love never fails and that love is in me, with me, through me, and around me! I expect doors to open for me today that no one can close, for my God to make a way for me and for favor to surround me like a shield. Listen to me day, "God has brought me this far, He's not going to leave me now! No weapon formed against me or my family will prosper! His promises will not fail in my life! They are yes to me in Christ. He is watching over His Word to perform it! He will finish what He began!"

"Let us then with confidence draw near to the throne of grace, that we may receive mercy and find grace to help in time of need."
Hebrews 4:16 ESV

DAY 88

If we want to be all God wants us to be, we will face opposition. But feeling like you're alone in the battle is a lie. Know that God and others are there who love and care for you.

I am praying that God is giving you a second wind today. That He is causing hope to arise in you again, that you will see with your eyes the thing He has promised you. He has you in the palm of His hand. He knows every need, every struggle, and every desire. He has it all figured out. He's a supernatural God. He gives beauty for ashes. You will overcome this battle! There is nothing that can come against you that He can't make it come out for good in your life. He has already written our success story in His word. We only have to step out of ourselves into Him and seize it by faith!

Declare it today, "Thank you Lord for clarity, direction, provision, strength, favor, and freedom to follow You! Thank you that You are working in my, and I can trust You. No matter what, I am not abandoned, I am not forgotten, and I am not defeated! Thank You for bringing total provision to my life! You are worthy, O Lord. You are my miracle worker! No weapon formed against me and my family shall prosper! Great Is Thy Faithfulness!

"So we are convinced that every detail of our lives is continually woven together to fit into God's perfect plan of bringing good into our lives, for we are his lovers who have been called to fulfill his designed purpose."
Romans 8:28 TPT

DAY 89

You are never powerless when you serve the all-powerful God! I believe God is working on something amazing in your life! A divine shift orchestrated by the hand of God is taking place. He has all kinds of discoveries and breakthroughs just waiting to be released! So, refuse to tiptoe through the day and your life in intimidation and fear.

Don't let messed up, negative people hold you back and mess you up. Every day is a gift from God, and your time is too valuable to waste trying to please everybody. Whoever counted you out, can't count! God is greater, wiser, stronger, and exceedingly able to bring you through to victory! Even in the midst of hurt, He will work things for your good and His glory!

Declare it today, "I am more than a conqueror because of God's love. He defeated my enemies. The Lord is my avenger! He will carry me through. He will restore to me what has been lost. The Lord is my defender. No matter what I face or where I am, I am confident that I am surrounded by God's perfect love!

Even if others reject me, I Believe in God's perfect love for me. I'm accepted, loved, and free! Thank you, Lord, for filling my heart with love today. Your victory is mine, in Jesus' Name! Amen!"

"So we are convinced that every detail of our lives is continually woven together to fit into God's perfect plan of bringing good into our lives, for we are his lovers who have been called to fulfill his designed purpose."
Romans 8:28 TPT

DAY 90

Precious Ones, Let's begin our day with some powerful do not's.

1. Do not let the silly little dramas of each day get you down. For you are here to do great God things!

2. Do not fear life and live in dread. Situations can turn around for the better if you have faith and patience.

3. Do not quit because someone turned their back on you. Not everyone who starts with you will finish with you! That's okay! You're still on assignment. Keep going!

4. Do not let your mistakes come between you and God. God's love is bigger than your mistakes. Embrace Grace!

5. Do not let the opinions of others ruin your life. Not everybody is going to like you. Not everybody is going to understand you. Shake it off and run your race.

6. Do not allow hatred to consume you. They hurt you, yes, but don't allow that hurt to grow into hatred. Hatred doesn't heal you. It hurts you more.

7. Do not speak death over yourself or others. As you speak words of life, those words have resurrection power! Declare, "Death does not reign, life is here, and Life has overcome!"

8. Do not be deceived. Trust, but be wise and discerning.

9. Do not let people abuse you. Life is about balance. Be kind but value yourself, your time, your effort, and your love.

10. Do not stop improving yourself- Ever! You are worth the investment! Be content but continually growing! Keep the growing going!

DAY 91

Let's believe and declare together that, "Every obstacle between me and my destiny will be obliterated. Every weapon formed against me will not prosper; I will be all God has called me to be because I am more than a conqueror through Him. My haters and naysayers can't stop what He has for me. What God knows and says about me is more important than what others think and say about me."

I choose to focus on the greatness of my God, not the size or number of giants. The greater the obstacle, the greater the victory. God's timing is perfect. My seasons will shift. Weeping may endure for the night, but joy comes in the morning. My future is brighter than my past. The calling in front of me is greater than any chaos behind me. My God is an awesome, all-powerful, living, true, faithful, loving, magnificent, just, all-consuming, brilliant, God who is worthy of praise. He is for me, and He wants me to become everything He created me to be. He wants me to fulfill my purpose. He is birthing within me a new sense of destiny as He inspires me to expand my territory and will put new ideas, new goals, and new motivation for new and different outcomes and expressions before my eyes! I will keep the faith and trust Him! He has a great plan for my life, and it will come to pass! Thank you, Lord!"

"Don't be afraid, for I am with you. Don't be discouraged, for I am your God. I will strengthen you and help you. I will hold you up with my victorious right hand."
Isaiah 41:10 NLT

DAY 92

Don't make the mistake of putting yourself down and accepting the enemy's idea that you are so hopeless that nothing can work out for you. Life is too short to be continually depressed and unfulfilled. Learn to carve out your passion and purpose. Believe in your heart that you are meant to live a life that matters, and that is blessed. You have the favor of God on your life. You may have been enduring seasons of storms. These seasons may have ushered you into times of severe questioning. You are not alone! You're waiting, praying, and dreaming about the promise yet to come and feels like forever. But God is faithful! In this season of waiting and learning, you can be assured that you will come out having learned important lessons for the next season that you will step into. God is calling you to a deeper level of trust that you literally have to stop doing anything in your own strength and just wait for him, and simply be still and know that He is God. God sees what is to come, and He knows what is best for you. His plan for you is better than any you could imagine for yourself.

Say it, "I believe this year and my future will be filled with the goodness of God. God is on the throne. Jesus is interceding for me. The Holy Spirit is leading me and guiding me. I will keep my heart open to the work of the Holy Spirit and I will live the adventure. I will walk in my God-given purpose and passion and I will see the provision of the Lord! I am ready for divine possibilities, awesome God moments, life changing turnarounds, overcoming obstacles, favor coming my way, and a year filled with grace, glory, and the goodness of God!

"For the LORD God is our sun and our shield. He gives us grace and glory. The LORD will withhold no good thing from those who do what is right. O LORD of Heaven's Armies, what joy for those who trust in you."
Psalms 84:11-12 NLT

DAY 93

The spirit of intimidation comes against all of us in some way and form. Satan's target is our mind and his weapon is lies. The enemy challenged Jesus in Matthew 4 in different ways. Throw yourself from the temple, turn the rocks into bread, fall down and worship me and I'll give you the kingdoms of the world.

We need to be aware when we are dealing with this kind of spirit and handle it just like Jesus did. We need to fill our mind and our mouth with God's word. Every time the enemy talked to Jesus; Jesus talked back. Never let the enemy have the last word in your life or situation. In fact, right now, let's all proclaim, "God always gets the last word in my life and He gets the final say so! I declare, just like Jesus did, it is written!"

Remember, faith comes by hearing, not just what the pastor says or what other people say, but especially when what you are hearing is the words coming out of your own mouth from God's word! God's word carries God's supernatural power. It releases breakthrough, favor, ability, confidence, and God's goodness in extraordinary ways. If Jesus needed to do this, so do we! Words are a long-term investment. They will reap an abundant harvest in your future! Every lying spirit of intimidation is broken today in Jesus' name. You will overcome every obstacle, defeat every enemy, and become everything God has created you to be!

"Fear and intimidation is a trap that holds you back. But when you place your confidence in the Lord, you will be seated in the high place."
Proverbs 29:25 TPT

DAY 94

For all those who keep on keeping on through it all, your faithfulness will have a great reward. Your faith-filled steps of obedience are releasing extraordinary blessings to you. Heaven is holding conversations about you. All of your "behind the scenes" has been preparation for what God is releasing to you and where God is taking you. God is releasing clarity of vision that will cause great acceleration and take you forward to live the promise He has spoken to you. Just like Abraham, there is an Isaac in your future, a blessing that will bring no sorrow with it!

"The blessing of the LORD makes one rich, And He adds no sorrow with it."

Proverbs 10:22 NKJV

Insecurity births so many unwise decisions. Continue to stay faithful and make life decisions out of the security of knowing God is your Father. 1 John 3:1 proclaims, "What marvelous love the Father has extended to us. Just look at it—we're called children of God! That's who we really are!" Stay true to the God birthed you! No matter what you feel like, no matter what others do or don't do, say or don't say. You are a winner! God created you to conquer, to rule, and to reign in life. Remember, you are valuable. You are strong. You are loved beyond measure. You can do this because God is on your side. There are still great victories in front of you, especially over the remaining months of this year!

Let's say so today, "It's not too late for things to improve in my life. God is restoring lost years and opportunities. Where I'm weak, God is strong. Where I lack, God will supply. Where I fear, God's perfect love will overcome. All the chapters of my life have not been written yet. God is working behind the scenes. He is preparing me for more. He will make a way for me! Yes, Lord!"

DAY 95

This is a time and season when God is stirring the desire to do something bigger than yourself. A season when God's direction and purpose are awakening. We are here on this planet to live a life that causes our heart to come alive. But too many of us are not living our dreams because we are living our fears. Believe with all of your heart that you will do what you were made to do, that you will live a life of purpose. Even though there are places and areas of our lives where we feel "less than" or "not enough," know that God will complete your incompletion!

So today, let's declare-

"I refuse small and limited thinking that is intended to keep me oppressed, bound, or defeated. I will not allow the parameters of my thinking to be shaped by my past, my environment, man's system of thinking, religion, or silent belief systems that try to capture my thinking. There is greatness on the inside of me because there is a great God on the inside of me. I will walk in increased influence, inspired by the Holy Spirit and be led to an increased territory for Kingdom culture to touch people's lives and open up new possibilities in my life. I will embrace my godly significance and shine my light and prosper in everything I put my hands to. Hallelujah!"

"Yes! Look how you've made all your lovers to flourish like palm trees, each one growing in victory, standing with strength! You've transplanted them into your heavenly courtyard, where they are thriving before you. For in your presence they will still overflow and be anointed. Even in their old age, they will stay fresh, bearing luscious fruit and abiding faithfully."
Psalms 92:12-14 TPT

DAY 96

Everyone can experience a bad day, a bad week, a bad season, or turbulent times of life. It might come at us with a bad medical report, "there's no hope," "I want a divorce," "you're fired," "bankruptcy," or "I hate you and never want to talk to you again!"

In the midst of God raising you up, there will always be people trying to pull you down. You have to learn how to shake them off and keep ascending. But even when those who have been closest to us don't understand and give up on us, even when we feel bare and dry, or the losses pile up—there is a way through. God hasn't just left us here to struggle facing life on our own. Our God is passionate about us, not indifferent. He is not standing back with arms folded, making us feel unwanted and forgotten or ignored. No!

I want to release this powerful promise over you today. "He will make a way in that "wilderness" and rivers will flow in the "desert." The desert speaks of a time of need, any need- a lack of human supply. The river speaks of God's supernatural abundant and extravagant provision.

Rivers are coming to those who are expecting it even while everything around them is saying desert. I speak renewed hope over those who are in despair. I pray for supernatural joy in the very areas where you have experienced extreme heartache. He is the Great I Am. There is nothing too hard for Him. He is unchanging, powerful, redeeming, ever-present, love, grace, mercy, righteousness, justice, and holiness. Who or what can stand up to Him? Nothing and no one!

"Behold, I will do a new thing, NOW it shall spring forth; Shall you not know it? I will even make a ROAD IN THE WILDERNESS and RIVERS IN THE DESERT!"
Isaiah 43:19 NKJV

DAY 97

When Jesus came walking on the water in the middle of the storm, the Bible says he would have passed them by, but they cried out. They saw him walking on the waves. What was over their heads was under His feet. There is no one like Jesus. He can still calm storms. What caused them to panic caused Him to prophesy.

He never wrote a book, but He is the subject of the greatest book ever written. He didn't have a medical license, but He is the Great Physician.

Kings could not stop Him. Satan could not deceive Him. Death couldn't destroy Him. The tomb could not keep Him. Your current situation is no match for Him. He is walking on the waves of your storms today, speaking to the wind, "Peace be still!" If He made a way for you out of no way before, He is able to do it again! Your tears of mourning are now turning into tears of grateful deliverance. Much like the natural seasons change, your season has changed, and you are walking into new hope, new joy, new love, new peace, new mercy, new grace, and new favor! He is walking on the seas of your life today! Peace be still.

"The wind was against the disciples and he could see that they were straining at the oars, trying to make headway. When it was almost morning, Jesus came to them, walking on the surface of the water, and he started to pass by them. When they all saw him walking on the waves, they thought he was a ghost and screamed out in terror. But he said to them at once, "Don't yield to fear. Have courage. It's really me—I Am!" "Then he came closer and climbed into the boat with them, and immediately the stormy wind became still. They were completely and utterly overwhelmed with astonishment."
Mark 6:48-51 TPT

DAY 98

Some of our greatest battles in life will be fought within the silent chambers of our own soul, the places of our thoughts, emotions, hurts, fears, dreams, and desires.

During these times, we all need a God vision to guide our hearts and our thinking that keeps our lives anchored and sustained by an outrageous love that comes from Him. A love that never wavers no matter what is happening. God's love is the gateway to God's dream for your life. His love is the gateway to His destiny for your life. God is love. (1 Jn.4:16)

Your Heavenly Father wants to encourage and empower you today. He is not passive about you. There is never a moment when He is not pursuing you, never a time He is not thinking of you, and never a day He has forgotten you.

"Every single moment you are thinking of me! How precious and wonderful to consider that you cherish me constantly in your every thought! O God, your desires toward me are more than the grains of sand on every shore! When I awake each morning, you're still with me."

Psalms 139:17-18 TPT

Remember today. Love is the motivating factor behind all that God does. My faith is simply a response to the love and goodness of God. We are created to live victorious, walking in His extravagant love for us. Knowing God loves you heals the pain of others rejecting you. God's love for us is beautiful, bountiful, unchanging, and eternal. Knowing that really brings peace to our hearts and minds. You are loved outrageously and extravagantly.

DAY 99

I know you have some things you are believing for and waiting on. As you're waiting on it, God is arranging it. Never let someone convince you that waiting for God's best for your life isn't worth it. Give me the perfect will of God: Nothing more, nothing less, nothing else.

As He leads you and you see your path change and evolve, do not fret or worry, for it has not yet stopped or even delayed God's good plans for you! Hold your head up high and know, He has a perfect plan for your life!

You serve a God who can shift you from "waiting on it" to "walking in it," just like that! But sometimes it takes pressure on the outside to get us to listen on the inside. We need to be willing to let Him prepare us for what He's prepared for us. That situation brought the revelation that God has to be your strength. That there is so much we can never do on our own. Don't chase it. Chase him. Trust Him. We worship God, not the promise. Don't try to force it. Have the faith for it. God is still going to do it and bring it all together. The waiting season is never wasted season. Ishmael is evidence of impatience. God is saying I love you and want the best for you. There is an amazing future waiting for you that is beyond anything you can create for yourself. Stay steady and keep your peace. God is working on your behalf!

"And this is no empty hope, for God himself is the one who has prepared us for this wonderful destiny. And to confirm this promise, he has given us the Holy Spirit, like an engagement ring, as a guarantee."
2 Corinthians 5:5 TPT

DAY 100

The enemy will try to constantly remind you of your past failures, inadequacies, shortcomings, and imperfections to attempt to sabotage your future success. Don't buy it! Believe in the God of second chances!

If it wasn't too late for Sarah and Abraham, Peter or Paul, it's not too late for you! When the enemy brings up the past, remind yourself and others, "Yes, I have a past, but I'm not a prisoner of it! Don't judge me by my past. I've changed addresses and don't live there anymore!"

We all have areas we need to improve in, but as long as we're pressing forward, we can be assured that God is pleased with us. You're not a failure until you stop trying. If you have no other testimony, you have this one: "I'm still here!"

Remember, our daily focus is so important. The enemy wants us to dwell on our pasts with a focus on our failures. Jesus always reminds us that He makes all things new and has overcome. Rejoice and focus on His victory today, not your shortcomings. God's plan is always bigger than your past. Rise up. Start fresh. See the bright opportunity in each new day!

Today God is confirming His plans for you; reviving hope, affirming your desire to follow, love, serve, and accomplish. Ignore the chatter and what is unimportant. Focus your faith and energy to pursue and accomplish what really matters. As you move forward in faith, remember He is faithful!

"The one who calls you by name is trustworthy and will thoroughly
complete his work in you."
1 Thessalonians 5:24 TPT

DAY 101

Sometimes life can leave you feeling frustrated and confused. God doesn't expect you to understand everything that happens and everything He does, but He does want you to trust Him in the process.

Sovereignty doesn't mean that God causes everything that happens, but that He can use everything that happens and make it work for your good. He can breathe purpose and powerful meaning into painful seasons that would otherwise be pointless and wasted.

Remember, there is no problem in your life that God's presence can't solve, no mountain it can't melt, no brokenness it can't heal, or no situation that can't be reversed.

The great God of the Bible wants to remind you today that you are perfectly loved, filled with His presence, and led by His promises! You are stronger than you know, not because of your own strength, but because He sees His Spirit within you. His grace transcends your abilities and disabilities.

That Great God is at work today to right every wrong and finish what He started in your life. So keep trusting, keep expecting, keep believing, keep smiling, and prepare to be amazed. He is amazing!

"But he answered me, "My grace is always more than enough for you, and my power finds its full expression through your weakness." So I will celebrate my weaknesses, for when I'm weak I sense more deeply the mighty power of Christ living in me."
2 Corinthians 12:9 TPT

DAY 102

You are the child of a God of miracles, so when your deliverance is naturally impossible, remember your Father is supernatural! When your human mind cannot imagine a human answer to a problem, believe in the supernatural God to bring supernatural results. What He has for you is custom-made and specially planned and designed by Him.

Your hope today is in one thing, a person, who not only has forgiven you but also watches over you with eyes of love. The solution to our problems is a Person. The answer to our questions is a Person. Truth and Hope is a Person. Our deliverance is a person and his name is Jesus! And He has a habit of making the impossible possible! So, shake off your fear, rise up with courage today, knowing that God never calls you without going with you and providing what you need!

"So let's do it—full of belief, confident that we're presentable inside and out. Let's keep a firm grip on the promises that keep us going. He always keeps his word. Let's see how inventive we can be in encouraging love and helping out, not avoiding worshiping together as some do but spurring each other on, especially as we see the big Day approaching."
Hebrews 10:23 MSG

DAY 103

There is power in making declarations and decrees over your life that will align you with God's Word. Let's say something to these things, whatever they may be in your life!

1. God has brought me this far and He's not done favoring me! I am excited and expecting great things!
2. My eyes will see the goodness of the Lord in the land of the living! Psalms 27:13
3. I will not let lack, defeat, or doubt cause me to give up! If I fall down, I will try again, and I will win!
4. Things might not have worked out the way I planned, but this is a new day and I'm ready for the new things God has for me!
5. No matter what I'm going through, the truth is I'm blessed!
6. Whatever I undertake, I will start in faith, stay in faith, and finish in faith! He is faithful!
7. Father, I thank You for doors of opportunity opening for me and my family.
8. He leads me beside still waters and restores my soul! I have right standing with God, peace, and joy!
9. My God is bigger than any battle and greater than any enemy! No weapon formed against me shall prosper!
10. All of God's goodness is being poured out on me! I am walking in favor, walking in power, and walking in continual success. Even when things don't look good in my today, I can still smile because I know my God is already working on my tomorrow!

DAY 104

Folks, God didn't put us on earth to continually struggle, settle, or give up. He wants us to be humble, but also to prosper. Don't feel guilty for wanting more out of life! We can be content without being complacent. Don't let the enemy bully you today. Put the word you've heard to good use. The devil wants you to crawl into a corner and give up. But regardless of what your feelings are telling you right now, you must know that God cares and only wants the best for you. So, keep honoring God with your life. Trust in His timing and He will open doors no man can close! God's favor is greater than any opposition. When we leave everything in God's hands, we will eventually see God's hands in everything!

"For all my godly lovers will enjoy life to the fullest and will inherit their destinies."
Proverbs 2:21 TPT

DAY 105

Agree today that favor overtakes you, favor that will take you to divine appointments, favor that open doors of opportunity, favor that brings blessings with no sorrow added to it. Pray that you will enter a year when God will exceed all you expect. He will increase all you invest in every area, spirit, soul, and body.

Pray against every spirit of oppression against you. Any heaviness or weariness on you, let it be removed. Let every burden be lifted, every sorrow comforted, and every sickness healed!

Pray that He will cause you to live life at the speed of grace and favor, supernatural timing that He will work powerfully in you to accomplish His purpose in your life and future.

Every spirit of failure over your life and family is broken in the name of Jesus. You have victory by the Blood of Jesus! God's voice is the loudest and strongest in your life this year.

Pray that God will promote you like Joseph, intervene for you like Esther, restore you like Job, protect you like Daniel, and use you like Paul!

In JESUS' name, this is your year of breakthrough, restoration, and recovery! Amen, Lord!

"That's where he restores and revives my life. He opens before me pathways to God's pleasure and leads me along in his footsteps of righteousness so that I can bring honor to his name."
Psalms 23:3 TPT

DAY 106

We can all have labels that get attached to us. It can be hard for people who don't know your history to understand your perspective.

Sometimes people categorize us and determine our potential based on those labels and perceptions. Labels can cause us and others to live with assumptions that we can never be, won't be, shouldn't be, are incapable of being, or aren't worthy of being something.

We can let the labels that others give us define us- poor, spoiled, uneducated, inexperienced, young, old, troublemaker, dumb, loser, fat, ugly, hopeless, stupid, ignorant, criminal, weak, pitiful, and worthless. Those labels can stick, hurt, and damage us because we start to believe them. But we have a choice. We can choose to live according to God's design for us rather than the way other people define us. It's time to tear some of those old labels from the fabric of our hearts and decide to be defined by God's word and His reality in our hearts. Knowing and believing this becomes the launching pad into a new life!

Declare it today, "I am forever labeled. I am forgiven, a new creation, saint, His workmanship, a royal priest, completely accepted, totally secure, deeply significant, I belong, a child of God, a joint heir with Christ, blessed and not cursed, above and not beneath, more than a conqueror, an overcomer, a winner, highly favored, victorious, loved, redeemed, chosen, accepted, adored, wanted, free, favored, honored, forgiven, and I wear HIS label on my heart. I am His."

"Now, if anyone is enfolded into Christ, he has become an entirely new person. All that is related to the old order has vanished. Behold, everything is fresh and new."
2 Corinthians 5:17 TPT

DAY 107

Kingdom life is about continuing to grow and take new ground. The challenging places are where we grow the most. It's where we discover our wings so we can soar and become who we were created to be. But we tend to always want immediate answers and clarity. Sometimes God gives answers directly, but most often, He initiates a process, leading us to an experiential journey, not just a destination. The process itself keeps us dependent on Him and there's a promise wrapped up in the process. The times of mystery can be the times we make the greatest discoveries about who God is and who we are.

God is the unfailing, unlimited source of our supply in every area of our lives. We can never get so successful or blessed that we don't need Him. Even having questions that don't have easy answers keeps us connected to Him. Wisdom looks for listening ears and humble, dependent hearts.

Part of the growing and the process is God speaking to us about our future, calling us out like He did Abram, speaking to the manifestation of what He has placed in us we may not even know is there. Today, He is calling the greatness in you out so that it manifests in your life. Even if you fail or things go wrong, remember, Jesus is the bridge and the way back. He is the outstretched arm pulling you up out of the water like Peter. Trust Him in the process. He brought you this far. Get excited for where He's taking you next!

"So we are convinced that every detail of our lives is continually woven together to fit into God's perfect plan of bringing good into our lives, for we are his lovers who have been called to fulfill his designed purpose."
Romans 8:28 TPT

DAY 108

There is nothing selfish about desiring to see God's promises fulfilled in your life. God wants your life to be abundant and blessed. Life is meant to be lived with faith, hope, and expectancy, not fear, worry, or resignation. If a man can rise from the dead, anything is possible.

Don't let anyone guilt you into expecting nothing. Keep away from people who belittle your faith, hopes, and dreams. Small people do that, but the great ones make you feel that you can overcome and thrive. Be with someone who brings out the best in you, not the stress in you. I'm not going to take criticism from someone I wouldn't take counsel from. You have to learn who to ignore and who to embrace. Never let negative people turn you into one of them.

So, I'm standing in faith for you today that the Lord is turning that thing around that has been overwhelming you, and you will see a glorious demonstration of His victory over the situation you have been dealing with in private.

"God is moving in your life, bringing you to a place where you will fully become all He has created you to be. His way is perfect, and He brings with Him a great reward. I'm praying for you to prosper and increase so that you can live and give like no one else, so that abundant life is continually your testimony, and you are entering the greatest season of your life in every way."

"Drink deeply of the pleasures of this God. Experience for yourself the joyous mercies he gives to all who turn to hide themselves in him. Worship in awe and wonder, all you who've been made holy! For all who fear him will feast with plenty. Even the strong and the wealthy grow weak and hungry, but those who passionately pursue the Lord will never lack any good thing."
Psalms 34:8-10 TPT

DAY 109

I want to encourage all the faithful ones who do so much, who hang on so long and sometimes feel overwhelmed. Remember to sow seeds of love every day, even while you're believing for yourself. You may never know the full impact you have on someone's life. Keep on smiling, blessing, sharing, encouraging, loving, and being sensitive to what God wants to speak into others. One simple God Word can transform a person's life forever. Those who are faithful with their gifting, even in time of famine, will have great blessings and opportunities in their future.

"God himself will fill you with more. Blessings upon blessings will be heaped upon you and upon your children from the maker of heaven and earth, the very God who made you."
Psalms 115:14-15 TPT

For every emotional hardship, financial setback, and loss, I decree you will receive double. This is a season for exchanging sadness for joy, poverty for prosperity, helplessness for empowerment, and hopelessness for hope. I pray an increase over you in favor, harvest, success, and abundance of God! In the name of Jesus, let it pour out on you! Get ready to cross over into a new season of victory and promotion. You will no longer feel restricted, confined, helpless, or hopeless. The Lord himself is bringing you into a new, spacious place. The areas of your greatest disappointments will soon be flooded with a new life! Dream with God and declare, 'It's possible!'

DAY 110

Everyone encounters a time of futility in their walk, times when maximum effort doesn't produce maximum results. This happened to Peter. He fished all night using the expertise he had gained on the Sea of Galilee. But this effort produced no results. He did all he knew to do but came up empty. These times can be really frustrating. (Powerpoint- Don't be bitter because things did not work the way you wanted. Simply say, God has a better plan!) But it's at this point Jesus comes on the scene with divine instruction. (Powerpoint- You are one divine instruction away from a supernatural turn around.) Jesus gives Peter directions that will change everything. Luke 5:4 "When He had stopped speaking, He said to Simon, "Launch out into the deep and let down your nets for a catch."

Peter, get out of this shallow neighborhood and once more sail into the deep. I want to do something in you and show you something that is possible as you obey me. God is trying to get something to you, but He can't get it to you because the parameters of your thinking haven't been shaped by your God. They've been shaped by who you were born to, by your life experiences, and your environment. God is saying I can't do a big thing inside of something so narrow. There is greater calling us into the deep. God is saying if you'll come out, I'll carry you in. Our greatest times of growth are experienced in the deep.

While launching out can look different to each of us, one thing remains constant. In whatever way you launch out, do it with an expectation that God will meet you there. He will never call you to walk on the water and not be there to walk with you. He will never tell you to let down your nets without bringing a collision with an increase. Faith, not fear, must be the winds behind our sails. The expectation in the goodness and faithfulness of God gives us the courage to not only launch out but also let down our nets! The story ends with Peter catching so many fish other partners had to come in to share the bounty!

DAY 111

There is power in agreement. God gave us a mouth not just to communicate, to say what is, but to create, to say what can be, to bring forth life, to agree with Him. God is calling us to launch out into the deep with our words, to stretch beyond where we are and see through eyes of faith to where we can be. Prophesy! Tell forth in authority and anointing. Your words call things into alignment with God's more abundant life, into His provision and possibilities. A life of "more" is one that is greater than what is expected or needed. It's an increasing life that has more joy, satisfaction, dreams, faith, new beginnings, and possibilities. It is life abundant! Jesus paid too high a price for us to live too low a life.

Dead bones must live (Ezekiel 37). They cannot resist the word of God spoken in faith when it's believed in our hearts. Get in the habit of believing and saying. Believe you can. Believe you will. Believe you are favored. Believe that life abundant can once again cause the dry bones to live! New life is coming to your finances, your faith, your family, your relationships, your ministry, your business, and your health. New doors are opening. New opportunities are coming to you. I speak forth abundant life today to every dry and desolate place in your life. Come alive! Overflow with the goodness of God! Bring forth a testimony that will be a witness to the greatness of our God! Thank you, Lord!

"A thief has only one thing in mind—he wants to steal, slaughter, and destroy. But I have come to give you everything in abundance, more than you expect —life in its fullness until you overflow!"
John 10:10 TPT

DAY 112

Life can be hectic. Storms come and go. Obstacles arise on our journey. But our outward circumstances don't dictate our inner peace. We can't allow life to intimidate us. We can't live in fear of life or have a fear of praying big prayers.

Jesus poured out His blood so we could go to heaven, but He poured out His Spirit so heaven could come to us. Jesus came that we may have life and have it to the full, even in adversity.

So today, we refuse to tiptoe through life in fear because God has made a covenant with us through the blood of Jesus. He didn't withhold His own Son; therefore, He will not withhold any good thing from us.

So, when chaos is all around us, there's hidden wealth in inside us. God chose us, He called us, and He empowers us. He has purpose and intention for us, and we won't be distracted by the noise in life! What God has designed and spoken over us will come to pass as we cooperate with the Holy Spirit. Our lives are full of hope, fresh vision, and we will glorify God. Even when things go wrong it can be redeemed because He is our Redeemer!

"We are like common clay jars that carry this glorious treasure within, so that the extraordinary overflow of power will be seen as God's, not ours. Though we experience every kind of pressure, we're not crushed. At times we don't know what to do, but quitting is not an option."
2 Corinthians 4:7-8 TPT

DAY 113

Let's make a prayer and a declaration of agreement over our lives today!

"Father, we come boldly before Your throne to obtain grace to help in time of need. We have confidence in Your word, and we take hold of Your promises for our lives. Today is a new day and we choose what gives life. We choose what is good and we choose what produces blessing! Even though we have had setbacks in our yesterdays, our past doesn't define our future!!! Today is a new day!!! We choose what You designed for us!!!

Your word says that Jesus bore all of our sickness and diseases and He carried our sorrows. We receive it! We know and declare that Jesus is our deliverer and provider! We give You all the praise for providing everything we need to walk in wholeness. Thank You for satisfying us with long life and thank You that You are no respecter of persons. What You do for one, You will do for all who ask and believe by faith. You haven't forgotten us or abandoned us ever! You never will!

Satan, I declare to you in the Name of Jesus that you have no authority over us. According to Matthew 18:18, I bind you from operating successfully against us in any way. Our lives are hidden in Christ. You have no power to bring any part of the curse upon us! We take our stand as one who is redeemed from the curse. You must flee now! We rise up and take our place in God!!!

Father, we worship You. We give You reverence. We declare that Your Word will not return to You void. We praise You for Your protection and for Your goodness on our lives!!! Thank You for bringing total provision to us!!! Great is thy faithfulness!!! Through Jesus Christ our Lord, Amen!"

DAY 114

None of us live unto ourselves. So, respect other people's feelings. Behind every smile and every tear, there is an untold story. Even if it doesn't mean anything to you, it could mean everything to them.

We don't always need an intelligent mind that speaks, just a patient heart that listens and loves. Remember, it's better to be kind than to always win the argument. We don't always need advice. At times all we really need is a hand to hold, an ear to listen, and a heart to understand.

Sometimes all we need to know is there is someone, somebody, somewhere who actually cares. They don't have to have all the answers. They don't have to be able to magically make it all go away. They just need to love and care enough to make your laugh a little louder, your smile a little brighter, and your life a little better. They're the ones worth hanging onto and the ones who impact others the most. The people that speak into you, not about you! The ones who celebrate your future, rather than resurrect your past!

There are no words to express how precious it is to have people in our lives who are willing to pray for us. People who think about us. People who love us. People who genuinely care. We may not remember everything they said but we will always remember what they did and how they made us feel! Take a minute today to remember and give thanks for them.

"And the King will answer them, 'Don't you know? When you cared for one of the least important of these my little ones, my true brothers and sisters, you demonstrated love for Me."
Matthew 25:40 TPT

DAY 115

Let's make some proclamations.

1. I will not let anyone take away my joy today!
2. I have a "right standing" with God.
3. I will not bow down to fear!
4. Satan has no dominion over me!
5. I am more than a conqueror!
6. God is my protection and my strength!
7. No problem is too great
8. No dream is too big.
9. With God's favor, I can do amazing things!
10. I will praise You, for I am fearfully and wonderfully made!
11. In my Father's arms, my spirit is free to fly. Thank you, Holy Spirit!
12. God's grace is more than enough!
13. I know God can do what medical science cannot do. I know God made my body. Doctors can treat me, but only God can heal me!
14. My God will provide. He is a God of more! Not just a God of enough!

Write these down and make proclaiming them a part of your daily routine!

DAY 116

You are worth so much more than what others see or say sometimes. What kind of value did God place on you? His only son willingly walked the path to the cross. Remember, God's love says, I walked that road for you, suffered for you, went through it all because I valued you! I will be there for you no matter what, always!

So, while we may be overlooked by others, we are handpicked by God. God's will is for you to overcome your circumstances, whatever they may be, by trusting in His great love for you. But if you don't learn to love yourself in a spiritually healthy way, you will never be able to overcome and be victorious in the way that you should.

By the way, not only did He walk the path to Calvary, He walked out of the tomb! The same power that raised Him up lives in You! You have been armed with strength for every battle. The forces for you are greater than the forces against you! So, light a fire on the inside. You have the seed of Almighty God!

"But if the Spirit of Him who raised Jesus from the dead dwells in you, He who raised Christ from the dead will also give life to your mortal bodies through His Spirit who dwells in you."
Romans 8:11 NASB

DAY 117

The secret to discovering purpose and fulfilled destiny is to walk daily with God. We don't have to have a perfect and detailed plan for our future, just a plan to obey what God has shown us to do each day.

The greatest pursuit in this life is knowing God, spending our life seeking to know Him and to make Him known. We come to know Him more through the fellowship of His presence and His Word. The growth and understanding that we get from the Word of God should be matched with the empowerment and guidance we receive from fellowship with the Holy Spirit. They don't compete, they complete! It's in the walk of everyday life that God speaks, strengthens us, and shows Himself strong on our behalf.

We must find our identity in the Lord because there is no other person, activity, or accomplishment that will be a solid foundation. Our peace, joy, purpose, and destiny are secure "In Him," found in fellowship with His Spirit and His Word. And we can be secure in knowing no matter how we feel and no matter what is going on, God is still good and so are His plans for us.

"So here's what I've learned through it all: Leave all your cares and anxieties at the feet of the Lord, and measureless grace will strengthen you."

Psalms 55:22 TPT

DAY 118

How we respond to difficulty is so important. We all have opposition just as surely as we have opportunity. Sometimes opportunities are hidden in setbacks. When we encounter a setback, how we respond is vital. When there's something that seems to get in the way of your promise, it's called 'opposition.' But God can even use your opposition to build you up, to strengthen you, to change you, to mold you into a better version of yourself.

Do you know that the challenges and oppositions in your life can push you to places that, without them, you'd never get to? The book of Genesis tells us the story of Joseph. Joseph's own brothers sold him into slavery. The people who hated him and took advantage of him and literally gave him a ride to his destiny. It was slavery that took Joseph to Egypt. Egypt was his destiny. Promotion was his promise. And sometimes the people who are opposing you are the ones who are going to take you to your destiny!

Sometimes, we just have to deal with the fact that life doesn't always go our way and we have to choose to intentionally remain faith-filled and positive. Fulfillment and destiny are discovered in the defining moments you intentionally choose the will of God above all other desires and paths. When life knocks you down, roll over, look up at the stars, and while you're down there, pray to the one who created them! God always has something for you, a key for every problem, a light for every shadow, a relief for every sorrow, and a plan for every tomorrow!

"He heals the wounds of every shattered heart. He sets his stars in place, calling them all by their names. How great is our God! There's absolutely nothing his power cannot accomplish, and he has infinite understanding of everything."
Psalms 147:3-5 TPT

DAY 119

For those in the process of walking through the daily demands of life, remember, the grind of life can get grueling. The continual necessity for pressing through and forward momentum in the midst of not seeing with your natural eyes the things you've prayed and believed for can be a challenge, no matter how spiritual or faith-filled you are. But there is so much more still to be experienced, so much more still ahead. I believe our Father wants to have a personal conversation with us today.

"Lift up your head and your hands. Receive a touch of refreshing, a fresh outpouring from my throne. I am for you and not against you. My Spirit is moving in your life, bringing freshness and vitality to places that have been barren and hopeless. In so many ways, you have walked with me, grown so much, and come so far. But in many ways, you have also only just begun. In many ways, there is another lifetime of growth ahead of you, so much more still waiting for you, so much more. I have prepared something even greater than you could ever dream up for yourself. So, don't let the grind, drama, stress, and craziness of this world distract you from the beauty, goodness, love, and future I have for you.

Though you forget a thousand times, I will be there to remind you, and I will guide you time and time again. Though you fall a thousand times, I will be there to pick you up. I will refresh you so that you will be able to continue. I am your restorer. I am your strength. I am yours and you are mine. You were made from love and for love. Nothing in the past, present, or future will ever separate us, nothing. I am alive to you and you are alive to me, and we shall be together for all eternity. I have redeemed you. I have called you by your name. You are mine."

"For they have a mighty protector, a loving redeemer, who watches
over them, and he will stand up for their cause."
Proverbs 23:11 TPT

DAY 120

Stay a visionary throughout your whole life! What we visualize in our hearts is so important. Life with vision is powerful. Life without vision is perishing.

"Where there is no vision people perish"
Proverbs 29:18 KJV

Hopelessness is an indicator of sight challenges in our lives. The enemy operates in the kingdom of blindness. He is the prince of darkness. Many of the pictures that hang in the gallery of our mind need to be replaced. An eagle raised by chickens is still an eagle, but once he perceives his true nature. Once he is awakened to it, he can begin to live in his true nature. The ability to birth a new season in your life is based on your willingness to see yourself and your situation through God's eyes and perspective. We can never receive what we don't perceive.

God will give you a natural picture to birth a spiritual vision in your heart and mind. He told Abram when he was childless, look at the stars in the night sky, look at the sand on the seashore, so shall your seed be. Open yourself today to a God birthed vision for your life and future that is filled with hope and assurance. Biblical hope is more than optimism; it includes the expectation that our God is credible and will come through for you. Can you see it?

"By Myself I have sworn, says the LORD, because you have done this
thing, and have not withheld your son, your only son — blessing I will
bless you, and multiplying I will multiply your descendants as the stars of
the heaven and as the sand which is on the seashore; and your descendants
shall possess the gate of their enemies."
Genesis 22:16-17 NKJV

DAY 121

Jesus died for us, knowing we might never love Him back. He reached out because that's what God's love does. He loves us with an everlasting love. He wants to work for us just because He loves us. It's not based on our merit or our worthiness. He loves us in spite of ourselves. We don't deserve it and we really can't earn it. God's love is just a fact of life! Our lives are proof that God is an artist. He took our sin and we became a canvas for Him to paint images of love, grace, and glory on and in. Remember that "His" love surpasses all human knowledge, and it's challenging for any of us to grasp the width, length, height, and depth of it.

Today, you are so loved and treasured by Jesus, so loved. When we live out of that powerful reality, our lives open up with amazing possibilities!

Declare it today, "I am perfectly loved by God, filled with His presence, upheld by His promises! I am not what others call me. I am not my mistakes. My past can't hold claim to who God has called me to be. I'm redeemed! God has an amazing future for my life. Past hurts, pain, or shortcomings will not stop His plan for me! Something good is about to happen in my life! The famine is over, and I am about to get launched into the much! Yes, Lord! It's my time!"

"Now may God, the inspiration and fountain of hope, fill you to over-flowing with uncontainable joy and perfect peace as you trust in him. And may the power of the Holy Spirit continually surround your life with his super-abundance until you radiate with hope!"
Romans 15:13 TPT

DAY 122

You have not yet walked in your greatest days. As we wake up every day, we need to awaken in our hearts as well as our physical bodies. Lord, awaken within us the mighty warrior. Awaken within us the answers to the problems which we are created to solve. Awaken within us the desire to take possession of our purpose. Awaken within us the vision for our mission. Awaken within us Your kingdom of possibilities.

Our accomplishments are birthed out of our identity. When we take a deeper look, we realize there is something about our discovery of who we are that the enemy fears. While we may have been knocked down, lost our job, been rejected by someone we love, received a bad report, and many more things that may hurt or be unexpected, it doesn't take away our true value. Don't ever let anyone or anything, especially the enemy, rob you and take away your identity. You are so valuable and precious. When God speaks into our life, He speaks to our destiny, who and what He created us to be, even if it doesn't always look like it.

I'm speaking over us in faith today, "Nothing that's coming against us is going to keep us from our destiny. Nothing we've been through is going to hinder our future. All of it is setting us up for God to show out in our lives. We are stepping into the most powerful and productive season of our lives. The Holy Spirit is navigating us into the greatest days of our lives. Our great God will do the impossible!"

"So, what does all this mean? If God has determined to stand with us, tell me, who then could ever stand against us? For God has proved his love by giving us his greatest treasure, the gift of his Son. And since God freely offered him up as the sacrifice for us all, he certainly won't withhold from us anything else he has to give."
Romans 8:31-32 TPT

DAY 123

It becomes clearer every day that God has so much more planned for our lives than just managing our current circumstances and problems. God calls us, just like He called Caleb, to take our land, our promise, whatever that would be, to have a renewed passion for His purposes in our lives. People who are following God must learn to look beyond natural circumstances and believe in God's supernatural ability. You may not be able to see how it could ever happen in your life, but that's not your responsibility. That's God's responsibility. Your responsibility is to believe and obey. No matter how big the obstacles, there have always been people who believed God's promises and won. God gave Moses a stick and told him to split the Red Sea. David killed a giant and was propelled into his destiny. Daniel was thrown into a lion's den. The widow at Zarephath offered the last of her worldly possessions to Elijah. They obeyed in faith and mighty miracles happened. Abraham must have thought he missed God when he left his family and home to follow God only to immediately encounter a famine. He ended up in Egypt but also became very prosperous. So, it's past time for the spirit of heaviness to leave and for the goodness of God to arise. You can't spell good without God! He is working for you. Heaven is holding conversations about you. Angels have been assigned to you. When you are going through something that seems harder than you thought it would be and lasts longer than you thought it would last, it's going to turn out to greater than you thought it could be! Exceedingly abundantly above all we can think or imagine. He is our faithful God!

"May He grant you according to your heart's desire, And fulfill all your purpose. We will rejoice in your salvation, And in the name of our God we will set up our banners! May the LORD fulfill all your petitions. Now I know that the LORD saves His anointed; He will answer him from His holy heaven With the saving strength of His right hand."
Psalms 20:4-6 NKJV

DAY 124

Our God is a redeeming and restoring God. For every person who feels like your season of opportunity has passed you by, opportunities can still come your way. God is the God who restores lost opportunities. He did it for Abraham at 99. He can do it for you too!

Through God's grace, it's never too late for a turnaround. It is never too late to be all we can be. Sins, weaknesses, bad habits, even the ones we struggle to shake off are not greater or more powerful than God's love and grace. Our loving Father has always desired to restore us to Himself. He sent His Son, Jesus, to do just that and to heal our broken places. To grow up spiritually is not a process of trying really hard not to sin. It's a process of waking up to your righteousness in Christ Jesus and daily receiving His love. Our love for God is rooted in His love for us. Our love grows as we continually encounter His love. Center yourself in His love every day. Feel the Father's affection for you. Be more aware of His Spirit, which is in you and surrounding you always.

So, don't confuse your mistakes with your value as a person. Keep your head up and walk forward. God gives purpose to the years of question marks in our lives. God will give grace, strength, favor, and joy that lifts you, sustains you, and takes you through things that should have stopped you. I pray today is filled with redemption, favor, open doors, unprecedented blessing, and supernatural turnarounds in the name of Jesus! I declare divine strategies to be downloaded from heaven to you for the glory of God! I pray your life is overwhelmed with God's love. He loves you.

"And this hope is not a disappointing fantasy, because we can now experience the endless love of God cascading into our hearts through the Holy Spirit who lives in us!"
Romans 5:5 TPT

DAY 125

God is calling us out. Calling us out like He did Caleb. Drawing us out like He did Moses. Drawing us out of fear, insecurity, small-mindedness, comfort zones, and ways of life that we have built for our dysfunction to stay comfortable. Let's choose a Caleb attitude today and every day.

"But my servant Caleb has a different attitude than the others have. He has remained loyal to me, so I will bring him into the land he explored. His descendants will possess their full share of that land."

Num. 14:24 NLT

Our destiny is never discovered in comfort zones. Moses' destiny wasn't in a river. He first had to be drawn out! Moses didn't have a name. For three months he had no identity, just a child hidden, he just existed. God has more for you than just existing!

He was named Moses, which means *drawn out* by Pharaoh's daughter. He was drawn out of the womb, the water, the palace, the wilderness, Egypt, and step by step into God's great plan for his life! Today, God is drawing you out, step by step. He draws you out to take you from the lesser to the larger even when it doesn't look like it! Like a worm in the cocoon and then a beautiful butterfly!

We usually don't like it because it can be uncomfortable. Even if you feel like crying out, put me back in that water, that nest, that shell don't do it! It's time to find out who you really are in Him. I'm speaking over us today. We are being drawn out like Moses to go in like Caleb. New beginnings. Transition. Crossing over. New levels. A shift in perception and atmosphere into the fruitful land of increase.

DAY 126

I pray that as you go through your day and week that in your heart, you have such boldness and confidence in who you are in Christ. That you will not allow other people's negativity to stop you from having a great day and a great life. That they won't influence you, you will influence them! Shine that light!

I pray that you will have a year of hope, love, God surprises, miracles, and open doors that God has planned for you long ago. I pray that Father God will stir in you the gifts, talents, and abilities that He has placed in you before the foundation of the world! I pray that you will come alive like never before.

I pray that every daily need in your life is met with a daily wave of God's grace, his all-sufficient grace is, never lacking, abundant, and full for every challenge!

I pray that this promise will rise up in you like never before that God always provides a way OUT of whatever you're in; or a way in to wherever you've been left out. Thank you, Lord!

"...These things says He who is holy, He who is true, "He who has the key of David, He who opens and no one shuts and shuts and no one opens"
Revelation 3:7 NKJV

DAY 127

Are you facing a closed-door and wondering what to do? Replace "there is no way" with "My God will create a way!" Our Father never ceases to amaze us in His creative nature. He loves to create! His will for our life is that we will rise up and do all He has called us to do.

Today you might feel like you are the most unlikely person. You might feel ill-equipped. Still, God is saying, "I choose you! I'm calling you! He is speaking peace into that place in your life that concerns new beginnings, bringing freedom from pressure, and release from care. He is saying to you today, "I am imparting to you the fresh wind of my Spirit and new inspiration to continue to stay on course for what I have for you. I have not forgotten you; another opportunity lies ahead."

So, rise up and declare, "I will accept nothing less than my Father's intended outcome for my life! I am not defeated; I am more than a conqueror!"

"Yet even in the midst of all these things, we triumph over them all, for God has made us to be more than conquerors, and his demonstrated love is our glorious victory over everything!"
Romans 8:37 TPT

DAY 128

Remember to take life day by day and be grateful for the little things. It's easy to get caught up in what we can't control. But instead, focus on the good. A positive attitude gives you power over your circumstances instead of your circumstances having power over you! Be a prisoner of hope today and every day! While our life problems can be big, our God will always be bigger and greater.

Don't allow the situation to make you forget the God you serve. He's still able! Nothing is impossible with Him! God didn't bring you this far to leave you now. He has grace for you today. Grace to turn every trial into overflowing joy and every loss in your past into complete restoration!

So, I am believing today you will pursue, overtake, and recover all! God has amazing grace for an amazing day!

"Turn you to the strong hold, ye prisoners of hope: even to day do I declare that I will render double unto thee;"
Zechariah 9:12 KJV

DAY 129

Declare with me today-

1. I will always have more than enough, always blessed to be a blessing.
2. I will never lack anything good because the Lord is my Shepherd.
3. There will be doors of opportunity open for me and my family.
4. In Jesus' Name, I believe every need is met with heaven's best.
5. I will experience the maximum return on my giving because I give to promote the name of Jesus and the gospel on the earth.
6. Anything the enemy has stolen from me, God will pay me back with great abundance. Praying God will restore to me the years that have been wasted, damaged, or lost (Joel 2:25) This is my year to get back the lost years!
7. I declare every seed of hurt and bitterness planted by the painful past is dead in my life today, in Jesus' name! My life is a fruitful field!
8. I pray I will see and experience the tangible goodness of God in my life.
9. I pray I will experience an overflowing harvest full of opportunities, favor, and blessings that will take me to new levels of fulfillment.
10. That Father God causes me and my family to increase more and more in every area of life, spirit, soul, and body. That abundant life rules and reigns in me, around me, for me, and through me!

DAY 130

Stop comparing yourself to others. Stop constantly feeling like you don't measure up. Don't compare your progress with other people. We all need our own time to travel our own distance. Life is not a contest. It's a calling!

Before God promotes you publicly, He prepares you privately. There are times when you're in a season of transition versus a season of execution. The caterpillar must go through a process before it becomes what it is destined to be, a butterfly. What happens in us turns out to be the breakthrough for what happens for us.

I believe Father God would speak over us today, "Your preparation had already begun, even before you knew it. In the days ahead, I will be activating a new sense of adventure within you. Many have asked, "How long must I wait?" and "When will my day come to walk in my destiny?" Long before you were born and became a part of history, you existed in my heart. You are My special, unique, and precious child! I am moving, I am working, and I will finish what I have begun. Together we will see, feel, and experience all that is possible as you keep close to my side and remain with me. Hold onto me as I am holding onto you and in all things, we will surely overcome."

"God always makes his grace visible in Christ, who includes us as partners of his endless triumph. Through our yielded lives he spreads the fragrance of the knowledge of God everywhere we go."
2 Corinthians 2:14 TPT

DAY 131

Relationships hold the potential to bring such joy and satisfaction to our hearts and lives, but also pain and hurt. As they say, "It was the best of times, it was the worst of times." Anything that has the potential to cause you to love deeply also has the potential to cause you to hurt deeply. Nothing in life requires greater wisdom and understanding than managing our relationships. So always try to remember, success is determined by what we do when life hurts. Not everyone is going to love you, encourage you, rejoice in your victories and blessings, be thankful for you, or want the best for you. But God does all of those!

Even though we might have to shed a tear or two, we might have to catch our breath from time to time, we might have to have a talk with our self now and then, we may have to encourage and pat our own self on the back sometimes because no one else is, we always keep going and we always keep loving. We keep moving forward, no matter who and no matter what. If no one ever looks at you and says you're going to make it, look in the mirror and say these words to yourself. "Look who God loves. You're going to make it."

"Through your glorious name and your awesome power we can push through to any victory and defeat every enemy."
Psalms 44:5 TPT

DAY 132

God wants to be involved in everything concerning you. To walk with you through whatever life brings. He has so much more in store for you. While everything may not happen today, if He's spoken it over your life, it will happen. You could be one step away from your breakthrough.

There are times we desire a 'quick fix,' but God wants to take us on a journey of transformation in our character. Remember, it wasn't the first step but the last step that brought down the walls of Jericho. After spending a long night of failure, Peter went from empty nets to an abundant catch so great it had to be shared with others. The woman with an issue of blood first had to press through the crowds to get to that one step that set her free from 12 years of suffering. One step at a time, we keep moving forward to the good and acceptable and perfect will of God.

God spoke to Abram as he journeyed in faith toward God's promise for him. The Lord said to Abram, after Lot had separated from him: "Lift your eyes now and look from the place where you are; northward, southward, eastward, and westward; for all the land which you see I give to you and your descendants forever." (Genesis 13:14-15)

God gives you a picture of where you're going, not where you are. Lift up your spiritual eyes and look out from the place where you are. The ability to birth a new season in your life is based on your ability to perceive. In a world of uncertainty, our trust is in a faithful God who will always keep His promises.

"Lord, never forget the promises you've made to me, for they are my hope and confidence. In all of my affliction I find great comfort in your promises, for they have kept me alive!"
Psalms 119:49-50 TPT

DAY 133

The waves of life can try to crush all of us, but we must never abandon our promise during our season of pain.

In the midst of it all let's start agreeing with God and prophesying our future. We are made in the image of the creator of the universe. God made all things out of nothing. And if God can change our perspective, He can change our reality. Increase is what He has in mind.

May we never underestimate the power of our God to birth things in our lives, no matter how hopeless or impossible it might seem.

Israel's outlook was bleak. They had been kept in bondage and slavery for generations. But God brought them out. Psalm 105:37 shows us that God not only brought His people out of Egypt, but He also brought them out with prosperity and wholeness. He is doing that for believers now.

So, no matter where you find yourself today, your life, your today, and your future is filled with potential. It is filled with Kingdom possibilities. Your rearview mirror is a lot smaller than your windshield for a reason. Begin to live with a view toward the future that sees God's favor in it!

I agree with you today. I pray that great things are coming your way. I pray that God is working to give you fulfillment and the desires of your heart, for you and your family!

"Then prosperity and favor will be their portion, and their descendants will inherit all that is good."
Psalms 25:13 TPT

DAY 134

Are you fighting a battle? Don't give in to the temptation to roll over and play dead. You have so much to live for and believe for. The enemy feeds on weakness, but faith sends him and his minions running for cover, looking for the exit signs of your life. Heaven is cheering you on. Angels are dispatched on your behalf. Don't quit! God is for you. You're going to make it through this. You are going to make it through this better than you ever expected.

Today I'm praying you will be able to rest in the midst of it all through God's power, peace, and promises knowing He is faithful to complete all that He begins in you.

Even when it looks bad on a natural level, don't stop believing God for the supernatural. Don't stop believing God's promises over earth's realities. Don't stop believing He can make a way where there seems to be no way. Live in the assurance our great God can interrupt whatever is occurring and create whatever you need in your life and future right now. May the thoughts of our future be faith-filled and not fear-filled. Your situation may look impossible today, but don't ever rule out the goodness and favor of God. The impossible is possible with our God.

"You see, every child of God overcomes the world, for our faith is the victorious power that triumphs over the world."
1 John 5:4 TPT

DAY 135

When God begins expanding and increasing us, He challenges us. He will interrupt our world. Sometimes we would rather He just leave us alone in our defeat and loss. But Jesus confronted his disciples after a night of fruitless fishing and challenged them to let down their nets one more time. We need to realize the very things we don't want to deal with are oftentimes the very things God is confronting in our life. So much of the time, the obstacles to a blessed future aren't just out there, they are in here, inside our heads and hearts.

As we allow God to shape us, mold us, and remove things in us that don't belong, we become able to overcome! Freedom comes as we let go and let God! Remember the scripture that we quote that says, "Let God arise, and His enemies be scattered." Declare this not only for those things around us but also for anything in us that hinders His best for us.

Keep looking for opportunities to grow and develop. Stay alert, connected, and sensitive to God's voice so you can see how and where God is moving you and what He is saying. Just like Peter experienced, "I boldly confess that this will be a time where barriers are removed, nets are broken, and breakthroughs are manifested for you and your family! Increase and abundance in Jesus' name!"

"But Simon answered and said to Him, "Master, we have toiled all night and caught nothing; nevertheless at Your word I will let down the net." And when they had done this, they caught a great number of fish, and their net was breaking. So they signaled to their partners in the other boat to come and help them. And they came and filled both the boats, so that they began to sink."
Luke 5:5-7 NKJV

DAY 136

"Father, I ask that the eyes of our understanding being enlightened; that we may know what is the hope of our calling, what are the riches of the glory of our inheritance in the saints and what is the exceeding greatness of Your power toward us who believe! (Ephesians 1:18) Holy Spirit open our eyes to the possibilities You bring to our lives!"

I am praying and believing for God's divine favor for you. Favor is the award of grace. God gives favor to accomplish purpose, to move you into what you were created for.

One thing about the favor and blessings of the Lord, you might start out on the bottom, at the back of the line, outside of the circle, but favor won't let you stay there. Favor will open doors that have been closed. Favor will change people's mind about you. Favor will attract success and prosperity to you. Favor made Esther a Queen.

Your situation may look impossible, but don't ever rule out the favor of God. You have to believe, no matter what has come against you, no matter how unfair it was, things are shifting in your favor. What the enemy stole from you, God knows how to pay you back with great abundance. The hand of God is shifting you to a new level of your destiny. Get ready; there's breakthrough ahead. God's favor is on your life.

"I know you are about to arise and show your tender love to Zion. Now is the time, Lord, for your compassion and mercy to be poured out— the appointed time has come for your prophetic promises to be fulfilled!"
Psalms 102:13 TPT

DAY 137

In the midst of all life brings, we must continue to believe and proclaim that God's goodness and mercy are following us. We must proclaim that no matter what's happening, His plans are to bless us and prosper us, not to harm us. May we never allow the faith-filled fire in our soul to go out. In fact, let's stir the embers and fan the flames! Stir it up today!

Declare it, "Father, today I speak victory and increase in not only my life but my family's as well. The hand of God rests upon me and my household, the blessing permanently dwells upon us. We are walking in glory, strength, victory, success, and prosperity.

I declare that we have redemption over the lies of the enemy. We are overcomers and more than a conqueror, the head and not the tail, above and not beneath! I declare our freedom in Christ from anything that has bound or limited us. I declare today, HIS mercy is unlimited, HIS grace unhindered, HIS forgiveness unmatched, HIS love unconditional, and HIS faithfulness unending! We are positioned for divine possibilities, awesome God moments, life-changing turnarounds, obstacles overcome, and divine favor coming our way.

We will keep standing, keep believing, keep trusting, and keep saying doors are opening for us that no one can close, and God's favor surrounds us like a shield. We will not be left alone in the wilderness or humiliated. The enemy doesn't have the final say; my God has the final say. And He says, 'I will ALWAYS cause you to triumph.' I will stay in the game and my God will make the rest of my life the best of my life!"

"For the natural realm can only give birth to things that are natural,
but the spiritual realm gives birth to supernatural life!"
John 3:6 TPT

DAY 138

I am grateful for today. Every day doesn't have to be perfect to be good. Remember, we smile not because everything in our life is perfect; we smile because we are grateful for the imperfect life we have. It's a blessing to be alive, to breathe, to be loved, to give love, to work through it all and grow. If you have a family that loves you, a few good friends, food on your table, and a roof over your head, you are richer than you think. Small blessings add up to a big beautiful life. In spite of life's imperfections, we have to learn to live being grateful for the opportunities each day affords.

Today, let's appreciate all the good that has come our way. We only have one life, let's do everything we can to make sure we enjoy it, not dread it! It takes a lot of energy to live in fear and dread.

So, let's not spend our lives focusing on why things seem so good for everyone else. Let's not spend today wishing you had someone else's life, always feeling like there's something missing. Living like this causes us to miss out on what we already have. You don't have to be a math major to remember this, "Always count your blessings and make your days count."

Give thanks for what you have at this moment.

Let's say it, "Thank you, Lord, for this precious gift called life, my life!"

"A thief has only one thing in mind—he wants to steal, slaughter, and destroy. But I have come to give you everything in abundance, more than you expect —life in its fullness until you overflow!"
John 10:10 TPT

DAY 139

"Lord, as I look toward my day, I am filled with hope and expectation because You have spoken to me and said that You know the plans You have for me and I rest in that promise because I know those plans are good because You are good.

Holy Spirit, I ask that You lead me and guide me. Help me to believe and know You are working even when it seems things aren't working out. Thank You, Jesus, that you are interceding on my behalf right now and no matter what things look like I will overcome!!!

I pray that my eyes will stay fixed on You and not my obstacles! I pray that the eyes of my spirit would see the unlimited number of possibilities that surround me today and this week, as well as the ones headed my way this year! By your Word and Spirit, I am prepared, focused, and ready. I am a person of destiny handpicked by Father God. My God will see me through!!!"

"So cheer up! Take courage all you who love him.
Wait for him to break through for you, all who trust in him!"
Psalm 31:24 TPT

DAY 140

There is nothing selfish about desiring to see God's promises fulfilled in your life. God wants your life to be abundant and blessed. He wants you to be victorious. Don't let anyone guilt you into expecting nothing. Keep away from people who belittle your faith, hope, and dreams. Small people do that, but the great ones make you feel that you can overcome and thrive! Be with people who bring out the best in you, not the stress in you! Appreciate those who appreciate you and never let negative people turn you into one of them.

So, in this season, don't allow anything to pull you away from God's plan and purpose for you: no offense, no hurt, no division, anger, no pain, no disagreement, or disappointment. It's not worth it. God has planted greatness in you. Let today be the beginning of a great adventure as you step into the gifts He's given you.

Meditate on God's word. Activate your faith and know that greater is He that's in you than he that is in this world. If God promised it in His Word, you can believe it in your heart and expect to see it fulfilled in your life!

"Each believer is given continuous revelation by the Holy Spirit to benefit not just himself but all."
1 Corinthians 12:7 TPT

DAY 141

The scripture in Psalms talks about a "Selah." A moment to pause, reflect on what God is saying to us, and give praise. Let's do that today!

Today I give God first place in my life. No matter how I feel, and no matter how it looks, I will see God's promises fulfilled in my life! I am who God says I am, and I will do what God says I will do!!! Selah.

I refuse to feel down, go down, or stay down. I am getting up, growing up, and going up today! God's grace is sufficient for me. His power is perfected in my weakness. Selah.

I am valuable. I am strong. I am loved beyond measure. I can do this because God is on my side! Selah. I won't give up. I won't give in. I will Keep going. Selah.

With my God, what is broken can be fixed, what is closed can be opened, what is lost can be recovered, and what seems hopeless can rise again. He gives beauty for ashes and the oil of joy for mourning! Selah.

There is no prayer too big for my God to answer, no problem too large for my God to solve. There is no disease my God cannot heal or heart my God cannot mend. There is no bondage my God cannot break, no need He cannot meet. There is no enemy He cannot defeat or mountain He cannot move! There is nothing my God cannot do! Selah.

"For the LORD is the great God, And the great King above all gods."
Psalms 95:3 NKJV

DAY 142

If you have been knocked down, experienced disappointment or loss, loneliness, defeat, rejection, or anything else that life throws at us, I want to remind you that things can change! The greatest enemy of our "due season" is fainting, giving up, or growing weary.

It can be tempting to begin to listen to the lies of the enemy when he shouts, "Give it up, just forget about it. Who do you think you are anyway? Why should God do this for you? You're nothing special." But I have a simple but powerful revelation for you today; the devil is a liar!!!

When Peter faced the greatest test of his life, Jesus said to him,

"Simon, Simon, behold, Satan hath desired to have
you, that he may sift you as wheat: but I have prayed
for thee, that thy faith fail not"
Luke 22:31-32

Simon means "flesh, weak, water," and it is evident that Jesus knew that Peter would fail in his flesh. But Jesus declared that the Word activated on the inside of him, faith, would not fail. In the fires of the trial, remember that God's Word will stand, it will not return void!

If you are going through something you don't understand, I'm praying for you. Keep holding on to faith. Don't give up on God. You may be down, but you're not going to stay down! When tough times come, don't let go of your faith and don't let go of the Faithful One. You can and will make it through! The gates of hell will not prevail when God is ruling and reigning in your life!

DAY 143

There is something in your future that is worth fighting for in your today. Joshua 1:3 says, "Every place that the sole of your foot will tread upon I have given you." It's great to know that we've been delivered from Egypt, but it shouldn't stop there. I've been brought out to go in. I've got Canaan potential! Stop praying to become a better slave in a place where you're not supposed to be a citizen. Guard your freedom. Stop praying for a better Pharaoh. The enemy will try to yoke you to things that are not of God. Things that are designed to crush you, bind you, limit you, but Jesus came to set you free!

"Then Moses and the children of Israel sang this song to the Lord, and spoke, saying: I will sing to the Lord, For He has triumphed gloriously! The horse and its rider He has thrown into the sea!"

Exodus 15:1 NKJV

God allowed Israel to see with their eyes the defeat of their enemies so they could know that they no longer had power over them. Our enemy has been defeated. We no longer have to fear a drowned army. But Israel still faced an enemy within the way they perceived themselves. Many died in the wilderness because of what they believed. The way Israel perceived themselves is ultimately why they died in the wilderness. They had come out of Egypt, but Egypt had not come out of them. They had left physical slavery, but not mental slavery. Let's be like Caleb. Numbers 13:30 says, "Then Caleb quieted the people before Moses and said, "Let us go up at once and take possession, for we are well able to overcome it." Overcomers move past the group dynamic, the limited opinions, the unbelief, the feeding frenzy, and bad energy-that negative talk and wrong believing produces. Let's make up our minds that we are not going to quit until we see the fruit of everything God has placed within us. Declare it today, "No more wilderness mindset!"

DAY 144

Our word today is for those who have experienced or are experiencing a season of waiting. We can look at waiting as a time of anxiously patting our feet and saying hurry, hurry, hurry or when, when, when or the opposite, being passive and disengaged. But scripturally, it is so much more than that. The Hebrew word most commonly translated as wait (wait upon the Lord) is "qavah," also means to tie together by twisting, entwine, or wrap tightly.

This is a beautiful concept of waiting upon God, not as something passive, not as being overly anxious, but entwining our lives and hearts with Him and His purposes. Scriptural waiting is living with our lives so entwined with God that we are continually aware that while we are waiting, He is working. It's continually seeking His face daily and living in expectation of His ability to do what we can't. It's living with lives so wrapped up in Him that we always take into account His ability to show up in our lives and turn it around. It's walking in what we do know and understand and not being consumed with we don't know and understand.

Just because life hasn't unfolded with the timeline we laid down doesn't mean it's over. You may have a situation right now that looks like it will never work out but wait with the expectation that God is about to show out in your life. He's about to turn some things around. As I live my life wrapped in His, His presence in me is greater than the problems around me. God is my avenger! He will right every wrong. He will turn things around for my good! While I'm waiting, I'm remembering, my Redeemer lives!"

"They remembered that God, the Mighty One, was their strong protector, the Hero-God who would come to their rescue."
Psalms 78:35 TPT

DAY 145

W-A-I-T-I-N-G can be hard. But if things aren't happening as quickly as you thought or hoped, don't get discouraged. Sometimes the path that leads to our breakthrough is much different or longer than we imagined. God never lets us down but there have been plenty of times when He has had to let us learn! He can take the years of disappointment and turn it around. A God thing is something worth waiting for.

As we stay faithful in the mundane, God is faithful in the miraculous. As we stay faithful in the daily, He is faithful in the deliverance.

Preparation always precedes promotion, so stay diligent. Engage in what you can do while you're dreaming about what you will do. Love larger, laugh harder, live fuller in your today.

Keep dreaming and believing for the future while making your today better than your yesterday by using the gifts and talents God has blessed you with. Don't hold back waiting for everything to be perfect or for a bigger stage or audience. Be faithful in the moment. Move forward. Keep going. Keep trusting God. He knows where He's taking you. God is preparing you for all He has prepared for you!

"He did not waver at the promise of God through unbelief, but was strengthened in faith, giving glory to God, and being fully convinced that what He had promised He was also able to perform."
Romans 4:20-21 NKJV

DAY 146

The Holy Spirit is birthing a vision in the body of Christ for coming into a new measure of "increase," flowing from the heart of God. People can be pursued by debt collectors or negative situations. Let's turn it around. I believe that God is speaking in this season about us being pursued by the goodness of God that brings blessing and prosperity to our lives. God is desiring to develop a mindset within us that is aware of His leading us to green pastures and still waters. Green pastures speak of bounty and lushness. Still waters speak of refreshing and peace. This is where God wants to lead us, to a place of living out of the blessings He brings so that we can fully come into the call that is on our lives and we can help others come into that place in their lives as well.

Prosperity means not having to tell your divine purpose, maybe someday. Think about all the times you've wanted to give but were limited because of lack. "Oh, Father raise up a people who will live in the abundance you have promised us so that we can give out of the abundance you have given us to be difference makers and world changers! May we never settle for anything or any place less than the best you have for our lives. As we go after You, thank you that Your promises will come after us. May You always be first place in our lives and may everything that we experience flow out of our relationship with You. Speak to us, lead us, guide us and take us forward into all that You have for us!

"The Lord is my best friend and my shepherd. I always have more than enough. He offers a resting place for me in his luxurious love. His tracks take me to an oasis of peace, the quiet brook of bliss. That's where he restores and revives my life. He opens before me pathways to God's pleasure and leads me along in his footsteps of righteousness so that I can bring honor to his name."
Psalms 23:1-3 TPT

DAY 147

I believe many today are on the threshold, the place of transition that can be so uncomfortable, yet filled with promise and potential. Change often exposes things in our lives that we don't want to face, deep-seated doubts and suppressed fears. But there's a great reward for the willingness to be uncomfortable for a season. If we can trust God through some temporary discomfort and step out, it can take us to an extraordinary place and reveal the next chapter in our story. Now is not the time to draw back in fear. Never allow your doubts and regrets to shatter your dreams. The next chapter of our lives can be filled with redemption, restoration, and renewal. Even our scars can tell a story that will bring God glory and make us stronger.

As we journey through transition, let's meditate on God's word and goodness. This enables us to see the future which the Holy Spirit has placed in our hearts and to be energized for what's ahead, for God to stir a passion and strong desire to fulfill something in our lives, to step into a chapter of hope, a kingdom of possibilities. God can take the years we have left and fill them with a quality of life greater than anything we've ever lost or experienced before. Restoration and recovery are His specialties. The breath of God is blowing on you and it is launching you into a new realm of revelation, divine wisdom, insight, and favor. A new chapter is opening over your life filled with increase and prosperity and it will look like no other.

"Now, Lord, do it again! Restore us to our former glory! May streams of your refreshing flow over us until our dry hearts are drenched again. Those who sow their tears as seeds will reap a harvest with joyful shouts of glee. They may weep as they go out carrying their seed to sow, but they will return with joyful laughter and shouting with gladness as they bring back armloads of blessing and a harvest overflowing!"
Psalms 126:4-6 TPT

DAY 148

INCREASE. Increase in finances, physical health, mental health, emotional health, understanding, increase in all the good things of God. Who is this for? This is for people who will rise up and say, "You know what? That bears witness with my spirit. By faith today, I will take hold of it." Say it today, "God has a purpose and intent for my life, and it's good, better than I could do for myself. Increase is the will of God." God wants us to prosper and increase us in whatever we do so that we can glorify Him and be equipped to help accomplish His will in the earth, not only concerning the gospel and showing His love, in invention, in innovation, and all that benefits and blesses mankind. Even Jesus walked in this.

> *"And Jesus INCREASED in wisdom and stature,*
> *and in favor with God and men."*
> *Luke 2:52 NKJV*

3 John 2 declares, "Beloved, I pray that you may prosper in all things and be in health, just as your soul prospers." The word "prosper" means: to get help on your journey, to succeed in the business of what you put your hand to. We all need help on our journey.

That pretty much sums it up. God blessed Abraham in all things. You cannot get more than all! So, "I speak Increase over today. May the goodness of God be on display in your life greater than ever before. Father, we thank you that every hindrance that has held back increase in our lives is broken. Father by your Spirit, open our eyes so that we can dream, envision, see, and imagine. Increase us and take us past old boundaries and launch us to a new level in You, in our personal lives, families, jobs, business, relationships, finances, and health. No shrinking back, thinking back, or going back! We are moving forward into God's destiny for our lives and increase is on the way!"

DAY 149

Too often in life, we focus on the broken pieces of yesterday. Yes, there is an appropriate amount of time and way to deal with rejection, grief, and loss. God can use persecution, rejection, and loss to help us to change. He's not trying to make us miserable; He's leading us even deeper into His purpose, helping us realize how very dependent on Him we really are. But there is also a time to look in a new direction.

Through it all our hearts must remain focused on God's great love for us, not the things we don't understand, or we will become slaves to the treadmill of pain from yesterday.

The love of God brings light to the darkness, hope to the hopeless, and healing to the broken. Jesus was a man of sorrows and acquainted with grief (Isaiah 53) but He didn't stay there. He is risen and seated at the right hand of the Father, making intercession for us. Through it all, He desires to say to us, "I know your loss, your hurt, and your pain. I'm your Comforter, Healer, Deliverer, and the Strength to see you through."

It's time. Time to let go of disappointments and setbacks in your life and hang on to the promises of God for your future! Everything in your life may not have turned out as you wanted, but God. But God has a new beginning for every loss and restoration for all that's been stolen. You still have so much to live for and believe for and every reason to keep moving forward.

"It won't be long now." God's Decree. Things are going to happen so fast your head will swim, one thing fast on the heels of the other. You won't be able to keep up. Everything will be happening at once and every-where you look blessings! I'll make everything right again."
Amos 9:13-15 MSG

DAY 150

Don't let your troubles convince you things will never get any better. The voice that is telling you to quit, stop, give up, admit failure, you're too weak, it's too late, that voice is a liar. Carry on. Don't quit, don't give up, don't give in to discouragement. Your breakthrough is coming to pass. There is no promise too hard for God to fulfill. No prayer is too big for Him to answer. No problem is too large for Him to solve. There is no disease He cannot heal or heart He cannot mend. There is nothing God cannot do.

You are made for more and you have seeds of greatness on the inside. It doesn't matter if you are moving inch by inch or foot by foot. The key is to keep moving in the right direction. Ask Father God to order your steps and stay in faith.

Remember, something good is happening in your life even when you can't see it yet. God has lined up solutions for you. That very thing the enemy has stolen from you is what God is going to use as a powerful weapon. He is the God of the turn-around. The Lord of breakthrough is your Father, and your harvest is being released! Let God do the revealing in His timing. And through it all, He is always there for us in every season. He is our Father, Provider, Healer, Counselor, Way Maker, Strength, Hope, Peace, Beginning, End, and all that's in between.

Our everything!

"So here's what I've learned through it all: Leave all your cares and anxieties at the feet of the Lord, and measureless grace will strengthen you."
Psalms 55:22 TPT

DAY 151

Life Lessons and Confessions.

Life is about balance. Be kind, but don't let people abuse you. Trust, but don't be deceived. Be content, but never stop improving yourself. Life will challenge us every day. But God commands us to be courageous, so be confident in all you do. He's with you!

Never speak anything over your life that you don't want to come true. Each word we speak either waters the seed or destroys it, so let's speak life! Scripture says, "You will eat the fruits of your words!" So, let's make some life confessions!

"This is my time to love and be loved. In every season of my life, I am loved!!! I believe God has all the divine interventions that I need in my life to position me to do His will and fulfill my destiny. God is for me. God loves me and works on my behalf. God is good and I can expect good things in my future.

This year will be a year of expanded opportunities! I choose the path of faith to step into a higher place exceeding anything ever before in my life! My prayers are going to avail much today because I am the righteousness of God in Christ!"

> *"...The effective, fervent prayer of a righteous*
> *man avails much."*
> *James 5:16 NKJV*

DAY 152

One of the keys to success is having the discipline to do something, even when you don't feel like doing it. Don't allow the way you feel to dictate to you what is real. Feelings are up and down, but God's word and love are everlasting.

So, don't wait until you feel powerful to speak God's word. Speak God's word because it is power! The word of God is alive and powerful! It will set you free, comfort you, heal you, feed you, and bring understanding to your life.

Say so today, "God has given me the grace to live victoriously today. I live from the strength that He supplies, in Jesus' Name! I believe in God's perfect love for me today. I am accepted. I am loved. I am free from loneliness, rejection, fear, and dread. God loves me today! Therefore, I will not fear. He has won my battles at the cross. His victory is mine, in Jesus' Name!

"Love never brings fear, for fear is always related to punishment. But love's perfection drives the fear of punishment far from our hearts. Whoever walks constantly afraid of punishment has not reached love's perfection. Our love for others is our grateful response to the love God first demonstrated to us."

1 John 4:18-19 TPT

DAY 153

Some days you may not feel loved and appreciated, but know that God cares about you, your circumstances, your pain, your future, your dreams, and your passions. If you aren't really sure how God feels about you, you'll believe what everybody else feels about you. So, no matter who excludes you, God will always embrace you.

But most times, He does His best work behind the scenes, in the quiet, in unknown ways, where it's not always obvious. He has amazing plans for you in the future. He'll never give up on you, not today, not tomorrow, not next week, not ever!

Whatever our today looks like, let's make Him the center of it. Let's remove the problems from the throne of our hearts so God can take that seat. Because even on our worst days, He still reigns over our issues. He will reign, always and forever. Keep trusting in Him!

"For He must reign till He has put all
enemies under His feet."
1 Corinthians 15:25 NIV

DAY 154

Sometimes the only way to get where you're going is to walk through something you don't want to go through. Who would have thought that the cross could have had any kind of divine purpose? Crosses were for criminals, not the Son of God. The reality is that life sometimes goes in the opposite direction we're expecting. That is when we can learn to just be with God. We can decide to trust God, or we can decide to be miserable.

God is going to take your season of pain and make it a season of purpose, your mess a message, your test a testimony! That's who He is and what He does!

Our greatest strengths can be found while trusting God through our greatest obstacles. The Christian faith is meant to be lived moment by moment. It isn't some broad, general outline. It's a daily walk with a real person.

So, remember to go through hard times the same way you went through good times. Trusting God, thanking Him, praying, believing, and knowing He will get you through.

"Lord, I praise You because You are my strength, my beginning, my end, and everything in between! In every season, You are faithful, unfailing, perfect love. In every situation, in every circumstance, You are strong and well able to see me through, and you will see me through! So, I won't give up. I won't give in. I won't lose heart. I won't lose hope! I will walk the path; I will run the race, trust in Your great love for me, and rest in what You have for me in spite of temporary paradoxes and contradictions that show up in my life. I refuse to get caught up in the how's, when's, and whys. I am caught up in trusting and loving You! You are good!

DAY 155

I know that many reading this are believing to experience great breakthroughs. God knows how to get you to where He wants you to be. Remember, promotion doesn't come from people. Promotion comes from the Lord! So, if He is all you have, you have all you need.

While each season of life has unique challenges, each season of life has unique grace! God has something for us in breakthrough which will deliver us into the next season. There is nothing that can come against us that God can't make come out for good in our life. When the Father speaks to us of the future, it has already occurred in His heart.

The Father speaks to you today, "Do not give up as you reach out to me; I will encourage your heart. I will inspire hope again. I will grant you the strength to continue. I will give you all you are lacking, and even more!"

Today may the force of God's favor bring great provision, open doors and an unprecedented season of success, increase, favor, and wisdom for you and your family! You will know what to do and when to do it!

Don't lose hope. People who trust in self are limited by self. People who trust in God are limitless! The Lord gives power to the faint and to them that have no might He increases strength. Remain confident that you will see the goodness of the Lord!

By faith, declare today, "Jesus is leading me by the hand today into His perfect will. I will not be dominated by fear and insecurity. My trust is in Him!"

"But thanks be to God, who gives us the victory through our Lord Jesus Christ."
1 Corinthians 15:57 NKJV

DAY 156

In the photo album of our life experiences, there are pictures of success and failure, hurts, heartaches, broken dreams, and ships that didn't make it to shore, along with blessings and breakthroughs and mountain tops. Through it all, our faithful God remains our rock and our cornerstone.

Wherever you may find yourself in your journey, remember, God knows you better than you know you. He knows every hair on your head, every dream in your heart, and He is constantly working things together for your good. Sovereignty doesn't mean that God causes everything that happens, but that He can USE everything that happens and make it work for your good. He can breathe purpose and powerful meaning into painful seasons that would otherwise be pointless and wasted. Every adversity, every failure, every heartache carries with it the seed of an equal or even greater blessing.

I hear Him reassuring you today, "When the battle is over, you will not only come through it, you will come out stronger and better than you were before. By faith, today, look up and see the rainbow in the clouds. Never let your problems silence what you heard from Me and don't ever let anyone convince you that there's no hope for you or that you are a lost cause. My Spirit is brooding over your life, reversing the things the enemy has plotted against you. No weapon formed against you can prosper. I'm birthing a year of hope, love, God surprises, miracles, and open doors. You are honored and I love you."

"Every single moment you are thinking of me! How precious and wonderful to consider that you cherish me constantly in your every thought! O God, your desires toward me are more than the grains of sand on every shore! When I awake each morning, you're still with me."
Psalms 139:17-18 TPT

DAY 157

For everyone who ever has or is currently going through a really tough battle or ever felt like you've lost so much, it can never be restored; I want to proclaim over you today your turnaround and time of restoration, yes, your season of blessing is not nearly as far away as the enemy wants you to think it is.

When David stood in the ashes and criticism at Ziklag having lost everything, including his family, he was three days from a double portion and six days from being King.

After slavery had been abolished, a former slave saved his wages and bought a small farm. He planted his crops, but a storm came and washed them all way; his crops were lost. As he surveyed the desolation, he saw a large gold-colored rock. It was a chunk of gold. The same storm that had destroyed his crops had uncovered a gold mine. Don't curse your storm; believe God that increase is coming even through the wind and rain.

Never let the pain of the past, the pressure of the present, or the fear of the future make you abandon God's prophetic promises for your life. Midnight only lasts 60 seconds. Then a new day is born. This is your time. This is your moment. This is your season of increase. Your destiny is calling. The Lord will perfect everything that concerns you. None of His plans for your life will fail!!! You are so loved!!!

"Though the mountains be shaken and the hills be removed, yet My unfailing love for you will not be shaken nor My covenant of peace be removed," says the Lord, who has compassion on you."
Isaiah 54:10 NIV

DAY 158

Even through the mistakes and disappointments in life, there's no expiration date on you fulfilling your purpose. If you're still breathing, there's still hope and time to walk out God's plan and purpose for you. While you're walking and waiting and sometimes weeping, He's working. Even while you sleep, He's not!

Through it all, it's so important to believe that no matter what is happening right now, it can be redeemed, yes even the middle of the night, in tears, and the roar of the silence. Father God wants you to know today, "I see you. I hear you. I love you. I haven't forsaken you. I still have a grand purpose for your life. As you continue to trust Him, you can be assured that circumstances are being lined up and favor is being released for your life and what lies ahead. Trust Him for the outcome and continually acknowledge your dependency on Him. He can put it together in ways we never could!"

Today I declare that God's face shines on you with irresistible favor. His blessings, favor, and grace abound in your life. I pray you see the tangible goodness and provision of God and instead of all hell breaking loose against you, it's turning around, and all heaven is breaking toward you and for you. The fresh wind of the Holy Spirit is blowing through your life and circumstances. Hallelujah!

"Be alert, be present. I'm about to do something brand-new. It's bursting out! Don't you see it? There it is! I'm making a road through the desert, rivers in the badlands."
Isaiah 43:19 MSG

DAY 159

Everyone has a history. Some of the godliest people we know don't always have a godly past. Where we are now isn't always indicative of where we have been. Just like so many in the scriptures, we are all a "glory story" in some way.

While we can't change a painful past, we can change how we view it, how it affects us, and how it can help someone else. We can't control how everyone views us and sees us. Some will always see us how we were "then" as opposed to how we are "now."

But no matter what our past, our present can be focused, faith-filled, steadfast, and hopeful. In spite of how some people may see us, our God sees us through the eyes of His son Jesus.

So, keep on walking. God will give you strength for each step. He strengthens the weary and gives courage to the discouraged. Just like Ruth, who came from Moab, a people of idol worship and paganism, we don't have to have a perfect past to have a future marked by grace and favor. I didn't earn it. I don't deserve it. I don't understand it. But I got it. Now everybody else can just get over it! I'm redeemed and renewed and living a life marked by the goodness and favor of God! Thank you, Lord!

"I don't depend on my own strength to accomplish this; however I do have one compelling focus: I forget all of the past as I fasten my heart to the future instead. I run straight for the divine invitation of reaching the heavenly goal and gaining the victory-prize through the anointing of Jesus."
Philippians 3:13-14 TPT

DAY 160

Life will continue to be a rush and you will face storms, obstacles, and hardships, but don't let your outward circumstances dictate your inner peace. As long as your heart is connected to God's authority and His love, His peace will surround you. Sometimes we as believers forget what we already have! We don't have to seek what is settled. We don't have to pursue what we possess. We don't have to ask for what is already authorized. We don't have to break through what we rule over. We are victors, not victims. We have treasure in earthen vessels.

There is nothing we go through that God has not already made a way of escape. Our God is a mountain mover. I believe that every mountain and stronghold that is delaying our promises is under your feet. I hear a word rising up for us today, "Prepare for what you have been praying for. The blessings are about to overtake you one by one. I believe this is our season of increase. This season will be "life-changing." God has awakened our spirit to "suddenly" as our great God is answering prayers from the past. He will bring us out! Thank you, Jesus!

"We are like common clay jars that carry this glorious treasure within, so that the extraordinary overflow of power will be seen as God's, not ours. Though we experience every kind of pressure, we're not crushed. At times we don't know what to do, but quitting is not an option."
2 Corinthians 4:7-8 TPT

DAY 161

We have to decide how we are going to respond to the tough times in our life. Life is not always fair. You will have problems and hurts that will make you better or bitter. You will either grow up, blow up, or give up. You will either become who God wants you to be, your heart will become hard, or you will shut down.

If we want to be overcomers, we need to look at every problem from God's viewpoint. Victorious people have a larger perspective. They see the big picture. When you don't see things from God's point of view, you get discouraged, frustrated, and unhappy.

When we face adversities, one of the most powerful things we can do is simply stay calm. When you are at peace, you are displaying your faith in God. Your peace is acknowledging that God is bigger than your problems. Your peace understands that God is good! Have faith and see the good things God has in store for your future. Thank Him for what He has done, what He is doing, and what He is about to do. Thank Him for divine connections because He is ready and willing to fulfill every desire that He has placed within your heart according to His promises. Remember, no matter what you are going through today, God has not given up on you, so don't give up on yourself. Stay encouraged by deciding to see beyond the present moment. God has a wonderful plan and place for you. Your future holds great promise! God said so.

"Don't be pulled in different directions or worried about a thing. Be saturated in prayer throughout each day, offering your faith-filled requests before God with overflowing gratitude. Tell him every detail of your life, then God's wonderful peace that transcends human understanding, will make the answers known to you through Jesus Christ."
Philippians 4:6-7 TPT

DAY 162

"I pray every chain restricting you, every bondage, every weight containing you is lifted, removed, and destroyed in Jesus' name! I pray for favor, wisdom, blessing, love, and goodness to be unleashed in your life. I pray that the blessings of the Lord overtake you. I pray that Jesus is your Jubilee, that God will provide every blessing to you in abundance, that You will overcome every obstacle, that You will outlast every adversity. You are victorious in the name of Jesus!

I pray for a release, a flood of His power and grace, not a trickle, not a stream, not a river, but a flood of increase, a tidal wave of His goodness and glory. You will break out from the valley of barely making it (mediocrity) to the land of more than enough! You are harvest is coming! Blessings are being released!

I declare the God of peace will crush Satan under your feet. Every work of the enemy shall come to naught. I pray for the peace of God, which surpasses all understanding to guard your heart and mind. In times of trouble, His peace covers you. You will not be overcome with anxiety or fear!

I pray that God will order your steps. He is surrounding you with the right people and delivering you from the wrong ones today. His angels are around you.

I pray the Lord bless you and keep you, the Lord smile upon you, the Lord watch over you, the Lord be gracious to you, and the Lord bless you coming in and going out, and everything your hand touches in Jesus' Name, Amen!"

"So lift your hands and thank God for his marvelous kindness and
for all his miracles of mercy for those he loves."
Psalms 107:8 TPT

DAY 163

Everyone encounters storms in life- financial storms, physical storms, emotional storms, mental storms, relational storms. Storms come to the just and unjust. Some storms we speak to and some we walkthrough. Paul prayed, fasted, was visited by an angel, and shipwrecked. It says no matter what he did, the storm kept coming. (Acts 27-28) But remember, every storm eventually runs out of wind and rain. When we look at the storms of life, we tend to feel fear and anxiety. But when we look at Jesus, we find peace and strength and the storms lose their power over us. Matthew said the house built on the rock would outlast the storm. Make up your mind to still be standing when the rainbow signals the sunshine. Noah survived and so will you and I.

If you are in a storm, Jesus is the master of the wind. The size of the storm doesn't determine God's ability to deliver. And the storm is not just the place you face your enemy; it's also the place you have a deeper revelation of your God. God can prepare you for the conditions you are walking through. Every storm eventually runs out of strength, but what you learned through it will last a lifetime!

Refuse any theology that calls our God a loser. Never allow your current condition to define God's intention for your life. Your current situation is no match for Him. He is walking on the waves of your storms today, speaking to the wind, "Peace be still!" If He made a way for you out of no way before, He is able to do it again now! Through the fire or storm, He'll bring us into victory!

"We've passed through fire and flood, yet in the end you always bring us out better than we were before, saturated with your goodness."
Psalms 66:12 TPT

DAY 164

Today agree that every evil gathering and conspiracy against you is overturned. Let the enemies of God against you turn on each other in Jesus' name! Pray that any lying spirit of fear and dread is powerless against you from this day forward! Expect the fulfillment of His promises!

Absolutely nothing that the enemy unleashed will be able to stop the powerful move of God that you are walking into in Jesus' name. There is no scenario, situation, or circumstance in which you find yourself where there is no hope because you are a child of God! There was hope yesterday, there is hope for you today, and there will be hope tomorrow. Speak peace over every fearful heart.

In the darkest hour, God's glory is going to breakthrough! And when that wave of worry that seems so big you can't even see what's on the other side tries to sweep over you, know that your future is covered in grace!!! God will restore you. He will turn it around. He will vindicate you! This is the glorious promise you have in Christ. He has overcome this world and made you an overcomer!

"And everything I've taught you is so that the peace which is in me will be in you and will give you great confidence as you rest in me. For in this unbelieving world you will experience trouble and sorrows, but you must be courageous, for I have conquered the world!"
John 16:33 TPT

DAY 165

God hasn't changed His mind about you. He hasn't put you to the side or on hold. Things are still happening. His promises still stand! He loves you and wants the best for you. He is working for you!

When you go through deep waters, God will be with you. Whatever you're facing, you will get through it. You will not drown or be swept away! Though the waters get deep, it will not overwhelm you! He is moving you to the next level spiritually, physically, financially, and relationally. Heaven is holding conversations about you today. Angels have been assigned to you! What God is about to do in your life is going to cause people to want to know the God you serve.

The barren areas of your life are about to begin producing fruit!

So, don't you dare give up, don't you dare quit, don't you dare give in, and don't ever stop believing. The same power that calmed a raging sea lives in you!!! Yes, in you!

"Let us not become weary in doing good, for at the proper time we will reap a harvest if we do not give up." And don't allow yourselves to be weary or disheartened in planting good seeds, for the season of reaping the wonderful harvest you've planted is coming!"
Galatians 6:9 TPT

DAY 166

The end of one season marks the beginning of another. Winter is over. Spring is here. A new season that is full of beauty, freshness, new life, and hope. But maybe you had some unfair things happen in your last, and "offense" is trying to hold your heart. Offense is a trap, a vicious circle. Never leave a season of your life bitter or full of hate. If you do, the way you end one season is the way you'll start the other.

There can be beauty and opportunity all around you, but you'll miss it because of the pain and unfairness of the past. If you have come through a difficult season, be encouraged today. You are immensely precious to God. You can trust Him as an absolute good, loving Father who desires the very best for you! He has a way of blessing those who have been taken advantage of and mistreated.

In this new season, He is going to restore what should have been yours in abundance!!! Yes, God is going to restore what should have been yours in abundance! There is nothing God cannot turn around!

Our God is a God of restoration! He has healing for your pain and compensation for your faithfulness. Never give up. Not on yourself, not on your vision, not on life, not on love, and especially not on God. Never give up. Don't give up! Spring is in the air!

"The LORD is the one who goes before you. He will be with you, He will not fail you or forsake you. Do not fear or be dismayed."
Deuteronomy 31:8 ESV

DAY 167

Life is too precious for us not to live a full life in Christ. Living in fear that things can't and won't ever improve can be paralyzing. The enemy doesn't show up in our lives in spandex and a pitchfork with horns. He is seen as a serpent in the garden, as a dragon in revelation, but in between, he's seen as a thief and the father of lies. The weapons the enemy uses most against believers is worry, discouragement, lies, and the temptation to give up.

During these seasons, our thinking and our speaking are so very important. Just because it came in your head doesn't mean it needs to come out of your mouth! Speak the powerful living Word of God! Remember that the enemy is a terrorist. He is not okay with anyone being at peace because he is not. He fights to get your soul out of a place of rest in God's love because he lives in fear and terror.

But you are a child of the most high God! You are created in His image and likeness! You are God's workmanship in Jesus! You are hidden deep in Jesus! You were never created to live defeated, hopeless, depressed, guilty, condemned, ashamed, or unworthy! You were created to live victoriously! Not only has your past been paid for, but your future has been provided for. Wherever you are right now in this journey called life, remember this is just one page, one chapter in the book, but it isn't the end! Your God has the final say!

"He laid hold of the dragon, that serpent of old, who is the Devil and
Satan, and bound him for a thousand years;"
Revelation 20:2 NKJV

DAY 168

Everyone in one way or another has experienced hurt and disappointment. What do we do when we've been hurt? How do we heal? Healing from hurt doesn't mean the damage never existed. It means getting to the place where the damage no longer controls our life. But healing takes more than time. It takes being intentional. It takes the humility and courage to call what hurts by its name and the resolve to do the work that healing demands. It means being willing to let it go and being willing to love and be loved again.

Love can melt the hardest heart, heal the wounds of the brokenhearted, and quiet the fears of the anxious heart. Healing comes as we stop resisting God's affection for us and allow Him "IN" to the deepest places of our hearts, letting God lavish His goodness and grace upon us.

Life in abundance comes only through love and forgiveness. Take these away, and our world is a tomb, and it gets smaller every day. If your enemies consume your thoughts, your talk, and your time, they have won. Let them go and give yourself permission to love again and to really live again beyond the pain.

God wants to put a new song in your heart. He wants to fill you with strength and joy for the journey of life. Open your heart to Him and let Him pour His goodness into you. He has infinite understanding of everything we need to be truly free.

"He heals the wounds of every shattered heart. He sets his stars in place, calling them all by their names. How great is our God! There's absolutely nothing his power cannot accomplish, and he has infinite understanding of everything."
Psalms 147:3-5 TPT

DAY 169

Jesus told Mary and Martha; Lazarus is sleeping. Sometimes the thing you thought was dead is just sleeping. The dream is not dead, it's just sleeping. The promise is not dead; it's just sleeping. When you serve the God of the resurrection, He can awaken and resurrect every dream you thought was lost and every promise that seemed to have failed to come to pass.

I declare over you today, "What you've been through will not interfere with what and where you are going to. I pray that the eyes of your spirit would see the unlimited number of possibilities that surround you today. God has prepared something awesome for you in your future and has scheduled a head-on collision for you with greatness, success, prosperity, and blessing. Father God is your Alpha (beginning), Omega (end), and everything that takes place in the middle! He will continually provide and care for you diligently. He will come through for you in amazing ways! Thank you, Lord!

"Blessed be our Lord God forever and ever. And let everyone everywhere say, "Hallelujah!" Amen! Faithful is our King!"
Psalms 106:48 TPT

DAY 170

"But God," two small words with such powerful and life-changing impact. We can get tired and weary and worn in body and soul and sometimes wonder if we can continue, but God is not like us, His power is inexhaustible, His commitment to us is unshakable and so our hope in Him is secure.

God is greater than our anxiety. God is greater than our fears. God is greater than our depression. God is greater than our past. Even though our hurts are very real, they are small in comparison to the greatness of who God is and all He will do in our life. A lot of things may come against us, "But God" is greater!

You might have experienced the goodness of God already, but God says today, "there's even more in store for you in your future!" God hasn't let you go; won't let you go. and will never let you go. Trust Him. He is doing something bigger than you can see.

Your disappointments are merely your soul's reactions to what your natural eyes present to you as so-called "evidence." He never leads you where He can't keep you. His grace is always sufficient for you in any and every circumstance of life. You will make it. He will see you through!

"My flesh and my heart fail; BUT GOD is the strength of my heart and my portion forever."
Psalms 73:26 NKJV
"Lord, so many times I fail; I fall into disgrace. But when I trust in you, I have a strong and glorious presence protecting and anointing me. Forever you're all I need!"
Psalms 73:26 TPT

DAY 171

There are some of us today that have let life push us down. We're not experiencing the quality of life that God has for us. But God is saying to us, "It's your time!" God wants to demolish all bondage and unauthorized limitations in our lives and thinking today. As believers, freedom is our birthright. We do not have to live our whole life enslaved, praying to get comfortable in a place we don't belong to. For every believer and follower of Jesus today, I have a reminder and a declaration.

There is greatness on the inside of you, things for you to do and places for you to go, and you will not die and go to the grave with your destiny locked up inside you. There is a great blessing in your pipeline, in your God future!

By faith today, I declare you will not have any aborted or missed moments or seasons. You will not settle in a place you're supposed to just pass through. You will experience divine appointments and favor that will open doors and you will see the goodness of the Lord in the land of the living!

"So celebrate the goodness of God! He shows this kindness to everyone who is his. Go ahead—shout for joy, all you upright ones who want to please him!"
Psalms 32:11 TPT

DAY 172

Everybody faces storms in life. When we look at the storms of life, we tend to feel fear and anxiety, but when we look at Jesus, we find peace, strength, and the storms lose their power over us. Every storm is temporary; Jesus is eternal. Don't let what you see make you forget what God said. Remember, strength to keep going doesn't come from willpower alone but from the assurance that you will see God's goodness.

Say It Today:

"I look up, expecting to receive the best of what God has for me. I abide in unswerving faith, unlimited hope, and unending love today in Jesus' Name!

I forget NONE of His benefits. He forgives all my sins. He heals all my sicknesses, redeems my life from destruction, crowns me with loving-kindness and compassion, and satisfies my years with GOOD things, in Jesus' Name! I walk in the blessings of the Lord God; His favor shines over me, I am rooted in faith and I am blessed!

My God...

Is all-powerful, is all-present, is all-knowing, is love, strengthens me, helps me, upholds me, heals me, provides for me, fights for me, is my shield, forgives me, remembers me, protects me and my family, and is my Mighty God!"

"By His grace I am improving every day in every way. He is with me. I am dearly loved, and His supply is more than enough. I hear Him say, "Child, you are always with me, and all that I have is yours."

DAY 173

Let's pray.

"Heavenly Father, thank you, Lord, for loving me in the way only You can do. I know my life may not be perfect, but I still want to thank you for everything you have given me. In the toughest of times, I can be comforted with just the thought of You, my God.

Father, You are my comfort. You are my strength and my protector. Thank You for the release of Your empowerment when I feel weary in well-doing. I choose today to focus on Philippians 4:8. I will think about things that are true, pure, noble, lovely, and worthy of praise. I will think the right thoughts, say the right words, and make the right decisions in every situation I face today. I have the wisdom of God today.

I speak to the raging waters in my life, peace, be still.

I say to my emotions, peace, be still.

I say to my mind, peace, be still.

I say to my body, peace, be still.

I say to my home, peace, be still.

I say to my family, peace, be still.

No matter who or what made me feel degraded, rejected, unaccepted, or less than I am who You say I am. In every situation, in every circumstance, my God is strong and well able to see me through. He will see me through!"

"May undeserved favor and endless peace be yours continually from our Father God and from our Lord Jesus, the Anointed One!"
2 Corinthians 1:2 TPT

DAY 174

Handling the letdowns and disappointments in life, the places and events we don't understand can be difficult. We've all been there.

Our focus is so important during these times. Thoughts are medicine or poison. We need to identify negative thought patterns, turn them around and use thoughts as a source of empowerment instead of self-destruction. God wants us to wake up every morning with the idea that something good and life-changing for the better is possible.

As hard as it can sometimes be, never underestimate the power of expectation. Expect God to strengthen you; expect to be led by His Spirit and be willing to believe big. He will give us His strength to walk the path He's called us to walk. Hear your Father saying, "Salvation is my gift to you. Faith is my gift to you. Righteousness is my gift to you. Peace is my gift to you. Hope is my gift to you. Joy is my gift to you. Victory is my gift to you. All that I am, I give you willingly and freely." So, let's forge a partnership with the Holy Spirit and embark on an adventure of discovery. Look in the mirror and declare, "Look who God loves. I am working *from* a place of favor, not *for* a place of favor. I am redeemed and I will not spend the rest of my life poor, hurting, frustrated, defeated, miserable, and beat down. I declare I am salt and light, a city set on a hill, and my life and testimony will bring God glory!"

"Trust in the Lord completely, and do not rely on your own opinions.
With all your heart rely on him to guide you, and he will lead you in
every decision you make. Become intimate with him in whatever you do,
and he will lead you wherever you go."
Proverbs 3:5-6 TPT

DAY 175

"First of all, I bless you! I declare doors are opening for you that no one can close, and God's favor surrounds you like a shield. You will not be left alone in the wilderness or humiliated. God has seen every struggle when others didn't. He is fulfilling every promise. You will see the fruit and the fulfillment of the promises you've been holding onto through fierce winds and waves of warfare. God is the promise maker, not the promise-breaker.

You will not align yourself with what the lying spirit of fear and dread is saying. You will not fret or give into the spirit of intimidation. Nothing can stop what God is releasing into your life. The future belongs to those who belong to the One who holds the future. He is holding you up and making a way for you to come out in complete victory. I speak prophetically into your life and into your situations:

Your household is blessed, Your health is blessed, Your relationships are blessed, Your finances are blessed, Your businesses are blessed, Your income streams are blessed, Your ministry is blessed, Your children are blessed, Your grandchildren are blessed, And, there is a fire, a fresh determination being released and it is pouring through your spirit. You're on the threshold of an incredible breakthrough! This isn't the end; it's the transition, the start of a new beginning!" Thank you, Jesus!

"And the LORD spoke to Moses, saying: "Speak to Aaron and his sons, saying, 'This is the way you shall bless the children of Israel. Say to them: "The LORD bless you and keep you; The LORD make His face shine upon you, And be gracious to you; The LORD lift up His countenance upon you, And give you peace." So they shall put My name on the children of Israel, and I will bless them."
Numbers 6:22-27 NKJV

DAY 176

"Lord, today, I stand in awe of Your faithful and merciful hand upon my life. Day after day, year after year, You are my hope, my future, and my anchor in the storms. I believe Your word that says Your eyes are always upon me and upon my year and years to come. Thank You that you fill me every day with Your presence and my decisions are led and protected by Your grace and mercy. I know You have planned great things for my life and my future is blessed because of You. I thank You, Lord, for the courage to stand on my faith and to use my faith as You create power in and around my life. Thank you for giving me courage in standing on Your word, confidence to take heart in the dark hours of life, and faith to persevere against all odds. Let me look in the face of obstacles and be persuaded that You are able to do exceedingly, abundantly, above all that I ask or ever imagine according to Your power that works in me. Thank you for a faith that receives everything I need, faith that triumphs over everything I face, faith that finishes the race You have set before me, and faith that takes me into the fulfillment of every promise You have given me. Father, I thank you that You have delivered my soul from the lies and attacks of the enemy that would sow wrong thoughts or wrong thinking that causes a wrong perspective in my life and future. I know that even my worst days are never so bad that you cannot reach into my circumstances and change them and change me. Even when it seems nothing is happening, I keep the eyes of my heart fixed on You, the author and finisher of my faith, my great God and King. You are forever faithful! In and through the mighty name of Jesus, our Lord, Amen."

"For he alone is my safe place. His wrap-around presence always protects me as my champion defender. There's no risk of failure with God! So why would I let worry paralyze me, even when troubles multiply around me?"

Psalms 62:6 TPT

DAY 177

Living a life of fullness and abundance does not exclude us from having to navigate challenging circumstances. Life is going to happen, but we must trust God and follow His voice to move forward. When life gives you a hundred reasons to cry, remember that God has given you a thousand reasons to smile. When uncertainty about your future scares you, you can always be certain of God's love for you. Everything you need, you have in your God. He is your strength and help when you're weak and unsure. He is your safe place and your confidence when you're uncertain. You can trust Him with everything you've got because He is everything you need. We need to know that as we trust God in faith that tough times won't stop us, they will promote us! No matter what, God is still God. You are still blessed, you will get through this, and you are loved deeply by Jesus. Your biggest battle can lead to your greatest blessing.

"Lord give me the grace to remember that although I can't see into the future, You can and that You will prepare the way for me before I get there. By faith, I declare, my future will be filled with the goodness of God. My God is on the throne. Jesus is interceding for me. The Holy Spirit is filling me with power, gifts, and fruit. My name is written in the Lamb's Book of Life. I will keep my heart open to the work of the Holy Spirit and I will live the adventure. I will walk in my God-given purpose and passion and I will see the provision of the Lord! Thank you, Jesus."

"Who is to condemn? Christ Jesus is the one who died—more than that, who was raised—who is at the right hand of God, who indeed is interceding for us. 35 Who shall separate us from the love of Christ? Shall tribulation, or distress, or persecution, or famine, or nakedness, or danger, or sword?"

Romans 8:34-35 ESV

DAY 178

Join me in a prayerful declaration.

"Father, today I stand in limitless faith that gives me peace even when the odds are against me. My God will make things happen that I couldn't make happen. I didn't earn it; I don't deserve it. But I'm trusting in the goodness of God, showing His favor in my life and family. Thank you, Lord, for supernatural strength today and every day for every place in my life, especially for any place of struggle, in the name of Jesus. Through You, I will prevail in all things.

I declare household blessing over myself, my family, and future generations. Thank you, Holy Spirit, for leading us, teaching us, filling us, inspiring us, empowering us, and gracing us to do Your will today, every day, and throughout our lifetime. I pray supernatural and superabundant increase over us, an overflowing harvest marked by good success, marked by favor, divine possibilities, awesome God-moments, life-changing turnarounds, and abundant opportunities to touch others' lives and make a difference. Let us leave a legacy of your Lordship and goodness for all to see! Through Jesus, our Lord, Amen!"

"Yes, the LORD will give what is good; And our land will yield its increase."

Psalms 85:12 NKJV

DAY 179

Let's remind ourselves today of these powerful truths, especially as we encounter low places, and it sometimes feels as if all the lights are out. Things can get really complicated so easily by one thing, overthinking about the wrong things. Dark thoughts lose their power in the presence of *God thoughts*. We have to stop, take a moment, and realize that God knows our name and He is working in us and for us. God has given us a new day today.

Our God is our help, strength, power, glory, wisdom, provision, and love. He loves us and wants our hearts and hands to prosper. He is faithful and is filled with tender loving-kindness and grace toward us. His favor is causing our names to be spoken in conversations, rooms, and places we haven't even entered or been to yet. I speak favor over you now, divine possibilities, awesome God-moments, life-changing turnarounds, and obstacles overcome. I declare divine favor and uninhibited access to people and places that are connected to the fullness of the will of God for your life and for your soul to be overflowing with the (shalom) peace of God. Just in case you've forgotten it today, God's not finished with you yet. His strong hand is on your life and future! You are special! You are loved! You are precious! Declare it today, "My redeemer has spoken, and so shall it be unto me!"

"He will be standing firm like a flourishing tree planted by God's design, deeply rooted by the brooks of bliss, bearing fruit in every season of his life. He is never dry, never fainting, ever blessed, ever prosperous.
Psalms 1:3 TPT

DAY 180

You may be experiencing difficulties or just going through a lot right now, but remember, you have a God who loves you, a Savior who chose you, and the Holy Spirit who is with you. I hear our Father's assurance today for you, "I have been present with you in the journey and I will be faithful to fill you, fill your hands, fill your storehouses, and bring provision in this new season to give you a resurrection harvest. Restoration is coming; new beginnings are coming, breakthroughs, abundance, and victory is coming. My favor will take you to where you could never go on your own. I know what you need, when you need it, and who you need for your next level, so keep trusting My plan and timing."

We don't have to know how; we just have to know God will. No matter what it looks like in the natural, always remember, as a child of God, you are greatly blessed, highly favored, and deeply loved. So, when change and fear of the future try to capture you, remind yourself *whose* you are. You are a child of the God of the universe and He calls you His own. Press into His love. Think about it. Feel it. Meditate on it. God's love is far more powerful than fear. Your future is full of supernatural help, supernatural provision, miracles, and God birthed surprises! There is grace for your future!

"But he answered me, "My grace is always more than enough for you, and my power finds its full expression through your weakness." So I will celebrate my weaknesses, for when I'm weak I sense more deeply the mighty power of Christ living in me. So I'm not defeated by my weakness, but delighted! For when I feel my weakness and endure mistreatment—when I'm surrounded with troubles on every side and face persecution because of my love for Christ—I am made yet stronger. For my weakness becomes a portal to God's power."
2 Corinthians 12:9-10 TPT

DAY 181

God doesn't want you to define your life by your present circumstances. Don't accept that the way things are is how they will always be! This world and its troubles and trials will try to confine you and box you in until you feel hopeless, but remember, because of God's great love for you, you are a blessed person who knows and feels God's affirmation, acceptance, and approval! You are chosen, cherished, and valued!

Expectation is the key to manifestation! Miracles happen in an atmosphere or soil of expectation. Surely goodness and mercy will follow you all the days of your life. God doesn't want you to give in to your fear, defeat, or hopelessness! There's a new chapter about to open up this year that God is writing for you!!!

The next time you are tempted to feel overwhelmed, don't forget how big your God is! The sky is not the limit. People have walked on the moon! Today walk with your head up and your shoulders back in the confidence that only God can give you.

"Surely God is my salvation; I will trust and not be afraid. The LORD, the LORD himself, is my strength and my defense; he has become my salvation."
Isaiah 12:2 NIV

DAY 182

Sometimes life comes at us hard but just when life tries to overwhelm us, God's grace is there to pick us up! We didn't expect this trouble, but this trouble didn't expect this fight! Let's rise up today and confess, "I am in for an abundant supply of grace that is headed my way! I am hearing a sound of grace, a sound of hope, a sound of forgiveness, restoration, new beginnings, healing of broken places, rescuing me from every dark valley. I don't have to stay where I am!

I refuse to be a victim of my circumstances because I am a victor over my circumstances. I am not what happened to me. My history is not my destiny! I am not who they say I am. I am not the label others and life tried to put on me! I am loved and valued by the creator of the universe!

So, I 'm not shrinking back, thinking back, or going back. I won't stop learning, growing, reaching, or increasing. I am moving forward into God's destiny for my life!"

"As for us, we have all of these great witnesses who encircle us like clouds. So we must let go of every wound that has pierced us and the sin we so easily fall into. Then we will be able to run life's marathon race with passion and determination, for the path has been already marked out before us."
Hebrews 12:1 TPT

DAY 183

It's a great day to renew our confidence in our God and make some faith-filled declarations.

1. "In spite of the pain, in spite of the adversity, in spite of the opposition, I'm still in the game! Even bad situations are turning around for my good today!"
2. "The favor of God surrounds me!"
3. "Jesus took the curse so I could be blessed!"
4. "The Father is God for me. The Son is God with me. The Holy Spirit is God in me. I can walk confidently today in His presence!"
5. "The same Spirit that raised Jesus from the dead dwells in me, releasing strength, healing, freedom, and grace into my life in Jesus' Name!" (Romans 8:11)
6. "I am engraved on the palm of God's hands! (Isaiah 49:16) His love for me is perfect and complete causing me to be secure and confident in all I do! Nothing can separate me from His presence and love!"
7. "Even though the horizons in my life may change, my future is already in Father God's hands! God's got this!"
8. "God made me an original with an extraordinary and special purpose. I won't compare, so I won't despair!"
9. "Even when I make a mess, God by His grace can still make a way!"
10. "I am a child of God created in the image of the Lord Jesus Christ filled with endless potential and possibilities!"

DAY 184

Never define your life based on one incident, one mistake, one bad day, or one season. Just because you goofed up doesn't mean you have to give up, don't obsess over failures! Learn to look past the mirror of your own reflection and see the power of who He is in you! Your own image diminishes your tomorrow. His will enlarge it!

There are going to be moments in life where you will feel like you want to turn back, get back under the covers, hideout, and never take another risk or step of faith. It can happen to anybody. Times when you face criticism and rejection or when things didn't turn out like you thought they would. Don't make the choice to go back to where you came from, not internally or externally.

Feelings are fickle! If we don't manage our feelings, our feelings will manage us! We have to train our soul (mind, will, and emotions) to think like a champion. While we can't prevent the enemy from speaking, we can prevent him from keeping our attention!

So today, if you aren't motivated by the words that come out of your own mouth, it's time to change your speech! The atmosphere around you is waiting for your command. It's listening to your words. Speak to it! Declare it today, "I will not be my own opponent. I will not be my own worst enemy! I am the righteousness of God in Christ, unconditionally loved by Him and created in Him for great things! Doors are opening for me today that no one can close, and favor surrounds me like a shield because of what Jesus already did for me!"

DAY 185

Feeling like you're alone in the battle is a lie. I want to remind you today that you never have to face another day alone. Even when it feels like you are alone in the battle, know and declare, "God is always with me."

When people reject us, it's easy to think God does too. There won't always be people who understand who to turn to every day, but no one will ever love you more than Jesus does, and you can always turn to Him.

The weather changes, governments change, people change, circumstances of life change, your body changes, your bank account changes, but have hope! Because Jesus never changes, and His love is eternal. Our needs will never exhaust God's supply!

So, when the world around you seems out of control, God is still good. Whatever circumstances you may find yourself enduring today, know that God's got this, and He's got you!

So, keep your head up, your heart open, your mouth filled with the promises of God and your eyes on JESUS!

"We look away from the natural realm and we fasten our gaze onto Jesus who birthed faith within us and who leads us forward into faith's perfection. His example is this: Because his heart was focused on the joy of knowing that you would be his, he endured the agony of the cross and conquered its humiliation, and now sits exalted at the right hand of the throne of God!"
Hebrews 12:2 TPT

DAY 186

Everyone has been hurt by life. I'm thinking of those today who feel forgotten, displaced, or in the shadows. David was overlooked, Joseph was innocent but imprisoned, Jeremiah was persecuted, Jesus was crucified. The lies can feel true in this place, but it doesn't make them so. Truth has a name and it's Jesus. He sees you. He loves you. He'll never tire of you. God is tender with your weaknesses and fierce in your defense.

Dare to look up and let Him reveal Himself and bring greater clarity. Don't let the emotional wounds of life become tombs where you bury your dreams. Your God-given dreams are worth fighting for.

Fill your mind with God's word. Let God's word comfort, strengthen, fill, soothe, and energize you to keep going. The psalmist prayed,

"Lord, I'm fading away. I'm discouraged and lying in the dust; revive me by your word, just like you promised you would. I've poured out my life before you and you've always been there for me. So now I ask, teach me more of your holy decrees. Open up my understanding to the ways of your wisdom and I will meditate deeply on your splendor and your wonders."
Psalms 119:25-27 TPT

Child of God, don't despair, trust the One who knows your name and keeps His promises.

DAY 187

As we go into a new day, I know we can all gain a fresh perspective. When your heart gets heavy and your hopes seem dim, it's good to step back and take a minute to put everything in perspective. Our destiny is too great, our assignment too important, our time too valuable to let anything or anyone intimidate us or talk us out of God's best. Remember the words God has spoken, the promises He has written, the vision He has planted in you, and the sentiments of His heart He has revealed toward you. He is with you on the mountaintop, in the valley, in the sunshine, and through the storm. Whatever you face, know that you are not facing it alone. Lean on the Lord; He will lead you through. Let's pray today, "Thank you, Father, for always being so faithful to me, especially in the dark times of my life. You are faithful. Jesus, you carried me this far, and when all else fades, and all else disappoints, I'll continue to hold onto this hope in my heart. You carried me when I didn't have the strength to go on. You picked me up when I stumbled and fell. You never left me. With You what is broken can be fixed, what is closed can be opened, what is lost can be recovered, and what was hurt can be healed. The future may be filled with many uncertainties but there is always one certainty, my God will be faithful."

"Now may God, the inspiration and fountain of hope, fill you to overflowing with uncontainable joy and perfect peace as you trust in him. And may the power of the Holy Spirit continually surround your life with his super-abundance until you radiate with hope!"
Romans 15:13 TPT
"The Lord Himself goes before you and will be with you; He will never leave you nor forsake you. Do not be afraid; do not be discouraged."
Deuteronomy 31:8 NLT

DAY 188

It's so important to remember who He is today.

In battle, He's my Warrior King.

In decision, He's my Counselor.

In need, He's my Provider.

In sorrow, He's my Comfort.

In sickness, He's my Healer.

In the storm, He's my Peace.

In the shaking, He's my Solid Rock.

In uncertainty, He's my Sure Word.

In weakness, He's my Strength.

In darkness, He's my Light.

In disappointment, He's my Hope.

In judgement, He's my Righteousness.

In failure, He's my Do Over.

In trials, He's my Song.

He is always faithful and never changing.

He is a loving Father.

*"This forever-song I sing of the gentle love of God! Young and old alike
will hear about your faithful, steadfast love—never failing!"*
Psalms 89:1 TPT

DAY 189

I love the powerful passage from the book of Numbers.

"And the LORD spoke to Moses, saying: "Speak to Aaron and his sons, saying, 'This is the way you shall bless the children of Israel. Say to them: "The LORD bless you and keep you; The LORD make His face shine upon you, And be gracious to you; The LORD lift up His countenance upon you, And give you PEACE.""
Numbers 6:22-26 NKJV

The word "shalom" is most often translated peace, as it is in this passage. But it means so much more. It means safe, well, happy, health, prosperity, favor, rest, be wholly well, reconciliation, being in a state of wholeness with no deficiency. It is a rich word that points to a remarkable quality of life. And here is a powerful application of "shalom" for us today. It was used as both the hello and the goodbye. God gave Moses specific instructions to speak it. It was to be a spoken blessing that was given at hello and goodbye as well, which meant blessing coming and going!

To bless means to empower to walk in grace, peace, and favor in any particular area of your life; to empower to succeed. Today and this year, I release and speak in faith over you the "Shalom" and the "Blessing" of our great God. The Lord bless you coming out and going in and everything in between!

"The LORD shall preserve your going out and your coming in From this time forth, and even forevermore."
Psalms 121:8 NKJV

DAY 190

It's in letting go and letting God that we find our greatest successes. Letting go of our own need to make a place for ourselves, a name for ourselves, a title for ourselves, and allowing God to take us where He wants us to go. Increase is birthed out of the moments of surrender and sowing in faith.

A seed must be released from our hand, from our control, fall to the ground, be covered up, and disappear for a season before new growth can come. Sow your way into the future you desire! Ask God what seed He is asking you to release and trust Him with? Seeds can be more than just material things. Words, acts, and thoughts are seeds. For every dream, there is a seed that will manifest it.

God had given Abraham a dream of fertile land, a blessed place to call his own. In the moment of decision, as he and his nephew Lot looked out into the possibilities, Abraham told Lot, you choose first. Abraham's seed was an *attitu*de. Lot chose what seemed to be the best and most fertile, toward Sodom. Abraham settled in Canaan. It was then that God said to him, "And the LORD said to Abram, after Lot had separated from him: "Lift your eyes now and look from the place where you are — northward, southward, eastward, and westward; "for all the land which you see I give to you and your descendants forever."

Uncertainty is a permanent part of our faith landscape. It never goes away. There will always be what-ifs. The possibility of rejection or failure. The possibility of being taken advantage of. But trusting God and stepping out of our comfort zone in faith creates a zone of supernatural increase. As long as I hold a seed in my hand, in any place of safekeeping and control, that's the most it will ever be. But when I sow it in faith to Him, oh what can it be!

DAY 191

I love holding the door open for someone else. It's a small indicator of service and respect in the natural. To truly be God-called leaders, we need to be willing to serve not just in the natural but in the spiritual realm as well. A Godly leader is someone who sees long-awaited doors of opportunity open up and doesn't just walk through them alone, they hold the door open for others too, even, and especially if no one ever did that for them. To be willing to share opportunities and assignments is so strategic for those who truly desire to be kingdom minded. We grow and others grow in an environment of encouragement and humility. True humility is the open door through which God does great things in our lives. Seeing others in the spotlight doesn't diminish us; it increases us. I don't have to unscrew other people's light bulb in order to shine. God doesn't have to cheat me to bless you!

Watching others achieve is exactly what Jesus gave His life to. And when He left, He said this, "Greater works than these shall you do..." (John 14:12). Our greatest desire shouldn't be to win championships, it should be to help build champions. If you build champions, championships will come. May God help us to see the gifts and anointing He has placed in others and become someone who says, "Let me get the door for you."

"One man's disobedience opened the door for all humanity to become sinners. So also one man's obedience opened the door for many to be made perfectly right with God and acceptable to him."
Romans 5:19 TPT

DAY 192

It's not in vain. Even if you don't see every prayer answered when and in the way you think it should be. God knows what He's doing. It's not in vain, because this life is not all there is. Everything isn't always seen in this earthly realm. Eternal treasures where moth and rust do not corrupt awaits. It's not in vain, even if you didn't get the response you expected for your labor of love, it's never wrong to do right. Keep loving. It's not in vain, the seed had to go beneath the ground to bring forth life. Keep sowing seed, the harvest is in your future. It's not in vain, obedience may not always seem like the fun option, but it is always worth it. As you do what the Word of God says, He is going to be faithful to His promises. His word will not pass away. It's not in vain, trust the process. You always have to believe that things are working out for you no matter what. Being patient and trusting the process means that you believe you'll receive the seed you've sowed. Don't let worry, fear, and anxiety make you dig up or abandon what you've planted just to see if it's growing. It's not in vain, there are things in us that have to die in order for new things to grow. Old ways of thinking have to die, as God unveils new strategies. It's not in vain when God begins to lift you, he begins to separate you from fruitless friends and connections. Worry not about whoever left. They are not part of your vision. Move on! It's not in vain, what appears to be going in circles is about to become walls falling down! It's not in vain, wherever you are right now in this journey called life, remember, this is just one page, one chapter in the book, but it isn't the end.

"So now, beloved ones, stand firm, stable, and enduring. Live your lives with an unshakable confidence. We know that we prosper and excel in every season by serving the Lord, because we are assured that our union with the Lord makes our labor productive with fruit that endures."
1 Corinthians 15:58 TPT

DAY 193

So many voices and opinions want to occupy our hearts and minds. People categorize us and determine our potential based on their labels and their perception. David could have never grown up to become a king if he had spent his life listening to His brothers and comparing himself to them. Men and women of spiritual breakthrough have always been those who have paid the price to listen to Father's voice and heart in order to obey. There aren't enough hurtful things people can say about us to overcome all the good things God says about us in His word! The truth is always more powerful than the facts and will deliver us from their limitations if we believe it.

Our Redeemer lives and His plans for us are way better than any of us could have for ourselves. Our Father knows where we are today. He hasn't forgotten us or lost sight of us. He hasn't turned His back or walked away from us. He is for us, fighting for us, and calling us forward. The purpose He has for us is not an afterthought; it was formed in His heart before the worlds were framed.

We are not the mistakes we've made. We are not the labels that have been put on us. We are not the lies the enemy has tried to sell us. We are not powerless, we are powerful! We are not defined by what surrounds us; we are defined by God's spirit that's in us. We are not defined by our circumstances; we're defined by His covenant. We are not defined by our failures; we're defined by His forgiveness. We are the light of the world! We are who God says we are!

"We have become his poetry, a re-created people that will fulfill the destiny he has given each of us, for we are joined to Jesus, the Anointed One. Even before we were born, God planned in advance our destiny and the good works we would do to fulfill it!"
Ephesians 2:10 TPT

DAY 194

Today I pray,

"May the blessings of the Lord rain down and drown out the spirit of lack in your home. I pray that God will give you houses you didn't build and vineyards you didn't plant! Deuteronomy 6:11

I pray divine closure to every oppressive attack you are facing and fighting you in your purpose, calling, relationships, finances, and health. Victory now!

I pray that God, the source of hope, will fill you completely with joy and peace because you trust in Him.

I pray any soul-tie from your past is broken in the name of Jesus! The blood of Jesus secures you, your family, and your peace!

I pray that you will know that the Lord has called you for such a time as this. He has called you to bring His freedom, breakthrough, and blessings to your family and future generations. He is answering your prayers!

I pray you will grow in your understanding of what Jesus has already given and as do you will abide in a place of untouchable, unshakable security!

I pray for divine favor and uninhibited access to people and places that are connected to the fullness of the will of God for your life! Favor! Favor! Favor! In Jesus' name, Amen!"

"Then prosperity and favor will be their portion, and their descendants will inherit all that is good."
Psalms 25:13 TPT

DAY 195

The church should be a place where the message of victory and hope is preached; but also, a place where people can be authentic in their struggles and pain. I believe in being positive in our confession and outlook, but we should also be able to genuinely work through our times of uncertainty, disappointments, and setbacks without feeling condemned and made to feel small. Many hurting people never achieve breakthroughs because they never feel free to address their issues.

No one should ever be ignored into, humiliated into, shamed into, or mocked into victory. But Jesus, while honest with us, wins us by his undying love, unfailing care, and grace. He lovingly leads us out. While the prodigal son was at his lowest point, his father still ran to him, kissed him, and restored him. This is what we can expect from our heavenly Father. He runs to us. He pours His love on us. When we are at our worst, He restores us.

May He lead you to love. May He lead you to peace. May He lead you to healing. May He lead you to wisdom. May He lead you to freedom. May He lead you to joyfulness. May Father God lead you in His mercies that are new every morning. Today I pray, "That you will remember when trouble comes, God is still there. He's working and He has a plan for you. The Lord's presence is with you today. He loves you, cheers you on, leads you, and walks with you, and carries you when you don't have the strength to go on. With your God, what is broken can be fixed, what is closed can be opened, and what is lost can be recovered! Every day, you are needed! It just wouldn't be the same without you!"

"When they were discouraged, I smiled at them. My look of approval was precious to them."
Job 29:24 NLT

DAY 196

You may have been through some disappointments, but God has not abandoned you. You were on God's mind long before you were formed in your mother's womb. You are not an accident or an afterthought. You are loved on purpose, for a purpose. Don't abort or abandon your purpose; lives depend on it. If Jesus had abandoned His purpose where would we be?

So, whatever you're facing today, keep going, keep moving, keep trusting, keep believing, keep hoping, keep pressing on. God is strengthening you with His grace right now. Your weakness is swallowed up in His strength. You're going to make it!

I declare doors are opening for you that no one can close, and God's favor surrounds you like a shield, in Jesus' name! It's a new season, it's a new day, it's a season of power, blessing, and supernatural intervention from heaven! It's a season of opportunity! Your greatest victories are still in front of you!

"The LORD called me before my birth; from within the womb he called me by name. He made my words of judgment as sharp as a sword. He has hidden me in the shadow of his hand. I am like a sharp arrow in his quiver. He said to me, "You are my servant, you will bring me glory."
Isaiah 49:1-3 NLT

DAY 197

Don't underestimate the power of confession. Let's make a bold declaration of faith today.

"I am the righteousness of God. Therefore, I am entitled to covenant kindness and covenant favor. The favor of God is among the righteous. The favor of God surrounds the righteous. Therefore, it surrounds me everywhere I go and in everything I do. I expect the favor of God to be in full manifestation in my life. Never again will I be without the favor of God. It rests richly upon me. It abundantly abounds in me. I am a part of the generation that is experiencing God's favor immeasurably, limitlessly, and overflowing. Therefore, favor produces supernatural increase, promotion, restoration, honor, increased assets, greater victories, and battles won! The favor of God is on me and goes before. It causes me to be blessed so that I might be a blessing. Therefore, my life will never be the same. This is the time of God's favor in my life. I declare doors are opening for me today that no one can close, and God's favor surrounds me and my family like a shield. In Jesus' name, Amen!"

Stay in faith. A flood of favor is coming your way!

"The righteous shall flourish like a palm tree, He shall grow like a cedar in Lebanon."
Psalm 92:12 NKJV
"Surely, Lord, you bless the righteous; you surround them with your favor as with a shield."
Psalm 5:12 NIV

DAY 198

Today, let's stop wearing other people's labels. You're too this, too that, not enough of this, not enough of that. If someone put a label on you and you believed it, it's time for a divine turnaround! You can let the labels that others give you define you. You can assume an identity of being poor, spoiled, uneducated, inexperienced, young, old, a troublemaker, shy, loser, fat, ugly, hopeless, stupid, ignorant, a criminal, an addict, divorced, a mess-up, weak, pitiful, or worthless and those labels can stick, hurt, and damage you because you start to believe them.

Don't get your value out of how other people treat you or even on your performance, success, or failure. Constantly trying to prove your worth and value is exhausting. How people treat you doesn't affect who you are. And "things" are good, but they don't prove your worth and value. The size of your house may affect your "net worth," but it shouldn't affect your "self-worth!" You are valuable to God!

Determine today to be defined by God's word. Assume the identity of friend, forgiven, a new creation, saint, his workmanship, a royal priest, completely accepted, totally secure, deeply significant, belonging, a child of God, joint heir with Christ, blessed and not cursed, above and not beneath, more than a conqueror, overcomer, loved, and winner!

Allow those labels to take root in your heart and believe them! They are powerful and transforming! God changes the world in us to change the world around us! So, don't let anyone's lack of approval shipwreck your destiny. People may leave you out, but God will never leave you out!!! Amen!

DAY 199

Your Father wants you to know that He has not forgotten you and that another opportunity lies ahead. All of us walk through places of difficulty, uncertainty, waiting, and times when we "don't know" and "don't understand." Times when we're waiting for that turnaround, that breakthrough, that breakout. But even when we don't understand what God is doing, we know He's with us! That's when we keep putting one foot in front of the other, and our eyes focused on Jesus. We are called by God, carried by His strength and covered by His grace! Adversity can push us into our divine destiny! God wants to take what was meant for our harm and use it to our advantage to increase us.

You may have been through a storm, but God will bring you out better off than you were before. Every unfair situation, every hurt you've endured, God is saying, "It's not the end. I have something great in your future. I have called and chosen you. My hand is on you, for you have been commissioned for this very hour and season. Everything the enemy has stolen, I'm going to restore: the joy, the peace, the health, the dreams. I have made you; I will carry you. I will sustain you and I will rescue you!" Thank you, Lord!!!

"I will be your God throughout your lifetime— until your hair is white with age. I made you, and I will care for you. I will carry you along and save you."
Isaiah 46:4 NLT

DAY 200

We rejoice when others are being blessed, but when it comes to ourselves, we can still think deep down inside that we aren't worthy enough or perfect enough to receive blessings. But because of Jesus, we are deserving. So, let's expect it, not just for others but ourselves as well.

So, today, I'm praying your life will be God-filled with many good things. I pray God opens up new doors for you that were not anticipated. New opportunities in the name of Jesus and that your soul will be overflowing with the peace of God. Your greatest days begin today. Your path is getting brighter and brighter until Jesus returns and finds you enjoying abundant life and fulfilling your God-given destiny and purpose! The full provision of the work of the cross is yours, including health. I pray an increase over you- in favor, harvest, success, an abundance of God. In the name of Jesus, let it pour out on you!

What the devil thought would bury you, God will use to bless you. What he thought would eliminate you, God will use to elevate you. God will turn incinerators of adversity into incubators of anointing. He will turn prisons of pain into platforms of power.

"Beloved friend, I pray that you are prospering in every way and that you continually enjoy good health, just as your soul is prospering."
3 John 1:2 TPT

"But the lovers of God walk on the highway of light, and their way shines brighter and brighter until they bring forth the perfect day."
Proverbs 4:18 TPT

DAY 201

It's so important to believe that God wants it to be well with us, that God is glorified when we bear much fruit.

"When you produce much fruit, you are my true disciples. This brings great glory to my Father."
John 15:8 NLT

So I am praying in faith today that you are coming into increase in every area of your lives, that every investment and seed you have sown will produce a harvest that is supernatural and ongoing, that your lives will be marked by the very presence of Him who causes all things to work together for your good and His glory, that you are healed body and soul and that your youth, strength, and hope is renewed. I pray great God things are coming your way and that you live in the assurance that God is working to fulfill and give you the desires of your heart, for you and those you love. I declare it over you in Jesus' name!

Today I pray God's grace strengthens you, His word heals you, His love drives out all fear! Father, I thank You that You love them just as You love Jesus. Therefore, fear leaves, torment ends, and healing comes!

Thank you, Lord, for renewed passion and vision in the hearts of your people today. May they be refreshed, renewed, and re-energized by Your presence. In Jesus Name, Amen!"

"Don't be afraid, for I am with you. Don't be discouraged, for I am your God. I will strengthen you and help you. I will hold you up with my victorious right hand."
Isaiah 41:10 NLT

DAY 202

Your Heavenly Father wants to speak over you and assure you today, "Never let the enemy convince you that there is no hope for your situation, as long as I am on the throne there is always hope! You may have been through the fire, the famine, and the flood, but now it's your time for favor. As though lifted by a wave of the sea, you will experience a sudden surge forward. Yes, there is a time of refreshing, surely just before you. No matter what your circumstances say, expect My favor to be present! It is your *now* season, your *due* season.

I am writing a story for your life and I'm not finished. There are still things for you to do and accomplish in your future. I am the Lord your God, the one you belong to, your defender, strong and mighty, sun and shield. I give grace and glory! No good thing will I withhold from you! So, when your heart feels heavy and your knees feel weak, know that you are still safe. You will not be overcome! You will see my goodness in every part of your life. I love you."

"May the grace and favor of our Lord Jesus be with you."
1 Corinthians 16:23 TPT

DAY 203

Don't let your stress level dictate your day and outlook. God wants us to have a prosperous soul. Prosperity of the soul is tied to health and blessing in our lives. Prosperity of the soul means our mind is not encumbered by fear, worry, anxiety, stress, and all the things that weigh us down in life. As our soul prospers, we are able to think biblically and react biblically, knowing the One who holds the future, the One who holds the stars, and calls them by name, and holds us in the palm of His hand. In every situation, in every circumstance, our God is strong and well able to see us through.

Declare it today, "My God is a good God, a mighty God, a loving God, the great God of the Bible, and He is for me! God is for me! My God can bring peace to my past, purpose to my present, and hope to my future!

I will not despair because I believe I will see the goodness of God no matter how things look. His goodness is following me today and my God will accomplish what concerns me. He will finish what He started, and He will accomplish great things in me and through me and for me!"

"You keep every promise you've ever made to me! Since your love for me is constant and endless, I ask you, Lord, to finish every good thing that you've begun in me!"
Psalms 138:8 TPT

DAY 204

Let's allow our God to inspire us and write some things in our hearts and inscribe them in the fabric of our beings.

"There is so much potential within you. You have no idea how far you can go. Many times, you settle for too little, quit too soon, stop too early. Forget the failures of the past, for yesterday, is over. Forget the things you perceive have disqualified you, for I have qualified you. Forget your shortcomings, for in your limits and weaknesses, I will manifest my strength. Forget about your imperfections, for there is no condemnation upon you. Forget the ways you perceive you have not measured up and embrace the reality of the life you have in me. Do what Ezekiel did and speak to the dry places in your life."

I speak over you today, "God is going to give you fresh creative ideas that will produce great fruitfulness and a whole new level of increase is coming upon your life. New open doors are opening, new provision, new opportunities. God will finish His work in you. You are not hopeless. You are a work in progress. I speak divine progression over you in Jesus' name. I declare you will be full of hope and a fresh vision. The Lord is your Shepherd. He will lead you, feed you, protect you, and guide you into the path of abundance."

"Yes, God is more than ready to overwhelm you with every form of grace, so that you will have more than enough of everything—every moment and in every way. He will make you overflow with abundance in every good thing you do."
2 Corinthians 9:8 TPT

DAY 205

Why matters. Your "why" in life not only keeps you energized; it keeps you prioritized. When people lose their "why," they lose their way.

There is a "why" today that needs to surface for all of us as we face the giants that sometimes try to taunt and intimidate us. God is saying, "Yes, there is a cause." There is something worth keeping on keeping on for in your today that will reap a great harvest in your tomorrow and bring God glory as well! Staying connected to your why takes you beyond yourself into an arena marked by the supernatural intervention of God. My "why" will lead me to places of fulfillment I could never experience on my own a dimension of life that is achieved only through the God birthed "why" in me.

The scripture tells us that Jesus focused on His why when He went through the time of His most intense battles.

"Therefore we also, since we are surrounded by so great a cloud of witnesses, let us lay aside every weight, and the sin which so easily ensnares us, and let us run with endurance the race that is set before us, looking unto Jesus, the author and finisher of our faith, who for the joy that was set before Him endured the cross, despising the shame, and has sat down at the right hand of the throne of God."
Hebrews 12:1-2 NKJV

We were His "why." We were the joy that was set before Him that caused Him to go through everything He went through. What an example to all of us. May we all stay focused on our "why" so that we can be energized and prioritized in our daily routines and never give in to the roaring taunts of our enemies. There is a why in you that's calling out, keep going, keep standing, keep pressing in.

DAY 206

King David knew what it was like to face opposition and jealousy. He lived it for much of his life. Much of what he writes in Psalms was written during periods of duress and attacks. In Psalms 18:1-2, as he is facing Saul's brutality, he writes, "Lord, I passionately love you and I'm bonded to you, for now you've become my power! You're as real to me as bedrock beneath my feet, like a castle on a cliff, my forever firm fortress, my mountain of hiding, my pathway of escape, my tower of rescue where none can reach me. My secret strength and shield around me, you are salvation's ray of brightness shining on the hillside, always the champion of my cause."

David wasn't speaking to a huge audience when he wrote this; he was speaking to himself of a very important truth as he dealt with Saul trying to destroy him. He said to himself, "The Lord is with me." That has to be the greatest reality in our hearts and lives. God is with me and it's as real as the ground beneath my feet, more real than anything I'm facing. Our victories are won as we do what David did and remind ourselves of the greatness of our God! I hear the Father saying today, "I haven't forgotten about you or the plans I have for you. My hand is on you and I am working in your life to take you from "here" to "there." Nothing you are going through can nullify my Spirit's vow to never leave your side. My supernatural strength is available for every weak place and struggle. Whatever is overwhelming you right now, your God and King is stronger, greater, bigger, more powerful, and victorious!"

"What a God you are! Your path for me has been perfect! All your promises have proven true. What a secure shelter for all those who turn to hide themselves in you! You are the wrap-around God giving grace to me. Could there be any other god like you? You are the only God to be worshiped, for there is not a more secure foundation to build my life upon than you."
Psalms 18:30-31 TPT

DAY 207

Somebody is thinking they're powerless because life is hard and over-whelming. Yes, it can be hard. I know what it feels like to look ahead and think, "what are we going to do?" But we serve a God who spoke the worlds into existence. Speak the change that you need. Even if it feels like you're drowning right now, find a promise in scripture and allow God to speak from His heart into your life. Let that be your lifeline!

What is the enemy's greatest fear? Fear of the word getting inside of us and changing us where we truly believe in the resurrecting power working inside us. That's why he tries to steal it, destroy it, and make us question everything about it because if we truly believed it, our outlook would change.

So, what am I saying to myself? What am I saying to change the at-mosphere in my life, my family's life, my job, and about other people too? Am I just accepting everything as, "It is what it is?" No way! It can be what we speak from the word and heart of God!

God created us and then spoke the blessing over us and instructed us to be a blessing! (Genesis 1:28)

"Father, thank You that something very big and blessed is about to happen to us and through us. We declare in faith that the rest of this year will be filled with our God's amazing goodness! May we never un-derestimate Your power. The resurrecting power that is working in us as it worked to raise Jesus from the dead. Let us tap into it today to change the way we think, act, speak, and live! This is our season to pursue, over-take, and recover all! Thank you, Jesus!"

DAY 208

You are who God says you are. You are a person of destiny hand-picked by the Creator. You're never too old, or too young, or too any-thing to do something amazing with God! Today is your day to bounce back from every failure. Every stigma from your life is released. I speak life over you, your family, your health, your hopes, and your dreams. You will walk in restoration!

Moving forward creates friction and can be uncomfortable. Friend-ship circles shift in your life. Not because your caring has changed but because some people are not able or willing to move past the memory of who you used to be. Move forward anyway. You are redeemed from shame and the curse of being a slave to unworthiness.

It's time to rise above those negative circumstances and say what God says about you. I decree over your life the favor of God and the em-powerment of His Spirit will defeat every enemy of your success. You will progress and succeed supernaturally. Any and every weapon formed to hinder your upward elevation is destroyed by the fire of God! You shall prevail and prosper in all things!

"Now, if anyone is enfolded into Christ, he has become an entirely new person. All that is related to the old order has vanished. Behold, everything is fresh and new. And God has made all things new, and rec-onciled us to himself, and given us the ministry of reconciling others to God. In other words, it was through the Anointed One that God was shep-herding the world, not even keeping records of their transgressions, and he has entrusted to us the ministry of opening the door of reconciliation to God."
2 Corinthians 5:17-19 TPT

DAY 209

God gave specific instructions concerning the power of the blessing. He says, "This is the way you shall bless the children of Israel. *Say* to them." (Numbers 6)

Today I declare over you that peace and wisdom reign over every decision you make, that you will experience a blessed assurance in your heart and life that you're never facing this (whatever this is) alone. Your faithful God is your constant companion and that God will turn your disappointments into an appointment for blessing.

Today I proclaim over you that your reality is that every provision of the finished work of Jesus is fully yours, including provision, protection, peace, healing, health, and guidance.

Today I say that you will know you are a mighty weapon in the hands of your God, fully fulfilling His divine purpose, plan, and destiny for your life!

Today I declare and speak over you the provision of our good, good Father to meet every need that you have, that it's His heart to take care of you, that the blessing of the Lord overtakes you in every area of your life today, tomorrow, and always. In faith, I speak this promise over you.

"Your favor will fall like rain upon our surrendered lives, like showers reviving the earth. In the days of his reign the righteous will spring forth with the abundance of peace and prosperity forevermore."
Psalm 72:6-7 TPT

DAY 210

Today is a new day. Every day is a new beginning, so take a deep breath and start again.

Remember, God still uses people who have failed! If you have failed, it is because you are trying! We all have setbacks in our yesterdays. But your past doesn't define your future. Let go of your history and reach for your destiny!

No matter what happens, no matter how far you seem to be away from where you want to be, never stop believing that through God's faithfulness, you will somehow make it! God is always working behind the scenes. So just because you don't see anything happening doesn't mean God is not working. God is going before you and preparing a way for everything that is ahead of you. God has you in the palm of His hand.

He knows your every need, every struggle, and every desire. He has it all figured out! Your hardest times often lead to the greatest moments of your life. Today's mighty oak is just yesterday's seed that held its ground! Never give up! God is for you! Keep the faith. It will all be worth it in the end!

"Through the Lord's mercies we are not consumed, because His compassions fail not. They are new every morning; Great is Your faithfulness."
Lamentations 3:22-23 NKJV

DAY 211

They said, "This problem will never end,"
But God said, "I'm bringing you out!"
They said, "You might as well give up the fight,"
But God said, "The battle is already won."
They said, "It is over for you,"
But God said, "It has just started."
They said, "You couldn't have it,"
But God said, "It's yours."
They said, "You might as well throw in the towel,"
But God said, "This storm will pass."
They said, "You will never be enough,"
But God says, "I'm raising you up for my glory."

God says It's a new day, new mercies. Pharaoh is no longer your master. Egypt is no longer your home. You are not making bricks anymore! You are delivered to be a deliverer; you've been forgiven to be a forgiver. Your story will lead many to an encounter with God. It's time to live your liberty in Christ Jesus!

So, no matter what *they* say, you have precious promises from God. You are valuable. You are worthy. You are loved. Yes, you are!

"Let me be clear, the Anointed One has set us free—not partially, but completely and wonderfully free! We must always cherish this truth and stubbornly refuse to go back into the bondage of our past."
Galatians 5:1 TPT

DAY 212

God is making a way for you with that impossible situation. He will be glorified!

In the name of Jesus! I declare doors are opening for you today that no one can close, and God's favor surrounds you like a shield! You will not be left alone in the wilderness or humiliated. God has seen your struggle when others didn't. He is fulfilling every promise! You will see the fruit and the fulfillment of the promises you've been holding onto through fierce winds and waves of warfare. God is the promise maker, not a promise breaker!

So, do not align yourself with what the lying spirit of fear and dread is saying. Don't fret or give into the spirit of intimidation. You will no longer allow lies and misunderstandings to lead you to believe you are defeated, incompetent, unloved, undesirable, or incapable. Nothing can stop what God is releasing into your life. The future belongs to those who belong to the one who holds the future. He is holding you up and making a way for you to come out in complete victory!

"Lord, how wonderfully you bless the righteous. Your favor wraps around each one and covers them under your canopy of kindness and joy."
Psalm 5:12 TPT

DAY 213

Mistakes, regrets, missed opportunities, or blown chances all of us at some time in our lives have been there. Whatever the reason, when things don't go our way, it's tempting to think, "Too bad for me. I'll never have that chance again. I've missed my season." The good news is that God always has another season, a "Kairos" season, an appointed time. I speak over you that for every opportunity you've missed, every chance you've blown, God can restore and bring bigger and better things across your path in this season of your life! You may have been through heartache and pain. You may have had disappointments and unfairness in your life, but the pain of your past is nothing compared to the joy of your future! Don't settle for less than God's best.

Declare it, "God has been preparing me. This is my season, my "Kairos" moment. This thing will not defeat me. I may have lost some years, but God will restore those years! God will bring me out better than I was before!" He said in Joel 2 that He will restore the years that have been stolen from me. "Thank you, Lord for restoration! Only my God can restore years! I may not be able to go back but God can make the rest of my life so rewarding and so fulfilling that it makes up for lost opportunities in my past! God has new opportunities in front of me. God will bless me with opportunities I missed because I was in the wrong place at the wrong time! Even when I've failed, God is so good. He's so full of mercy and His grace is so powerful that He will give me another chance because He wants the rest of my life to be better than the first part!"

"For his anger lasts only a moment, but his favor lasts a lifetime!
Weeping may last through the night, but joy comes with the morning."
Psalms 30:5 NLT

DAY 214

The battlefield on which many of us fight is not out in the world; it's between our ears. The enemy's lie is, "You're finished, burned out, used up, replaced, forgotten, and left out." When you dwell on negative thoughts, you're using your faith, but you're using it in reverse!

Never look at yourself as insignificant or tossed to the side. God has a powerful way of using those that feel passed over and called nobodies. Never think what you have to offer doesn't matter. God designed you on purpose for a purpose. Just be who you are in Christ. You are unique and your gift will be distinctive. God uses people of every personality type to achieve His will.

Remember, we don't have to let the enemy walk all over us! We are in "right standing" with God, through Christ, a child of the most high God, created in His image and likeness, God's workmanship in Christ Jesus!

God is faithful to lift you up when people and life have let you down. Take the limits off of God. Like Ruth, instead of working in the field, you are going to own the field! Believe it! You cannot be defeated with God's favor going before you and working on your behalf! What an awesome God we serve!

DAY 215

Our God is not like any idol, philosophy, or any other great man. Our God is the only living God and He is faithful and true. We do not worship a dead leader or an empty philosophy; we worship the living God who gives life and breath to all things.

He's alive and He's moving in the hearts and lives of people all over the world. I believe in the resurrection of Jesus Christ because I have seen it in the lives of others, and I have experienced it myself!

The women who went to the tomb that Easter morning came crying in sorrow, but they went back weeping with joy. This is where He was but it's not where He is! The stone has been rolled away! If you feel trapped today, God is saying, "The stone has been rolled away! Weeping may endure for the night, but joy comes in the morning. It's your morning! You are free!" He's alive!

DAY 216

Everything in our lives may not have turned out as we wanted, but we still have much to be grateful for. I'm thankful for each of you. If you have a family that loves you, a few good friends, food on your table, breath in your body, and a roof over your head, you are richer than you think. In everything you do, everywhere you go, celebrate the goodness of God revealed in the small and everyday things.

Jesus said, "I have come that you might have life and have it more abundantly." He did not die just so we can have new misery with a Christian label on it. He died that we might enjoy life! So even if everything isn't "perfect," this day is a priceless gift from God enjoy it and thank Him for it for those you love and those who love you.

"You're kind and tenderhearted to those who don't deserve it and very patient with people who fail you. Your love is like a flooding river overflowing its banks with kindness. God, everyone sees your goodness, for your tender love is blended into everything you do."
Psalms 145:8-9 TPT

DAY 217

The most beautiful people we know are those who have known ups and downs, defeat and victory, known struggle and breakthrough, and have found their way out of the depths. People who don't claim to have it all figured out, just that they know "the One" who does. They have an understanding of life that fills them with perspective and compassion. These kinds of people don't just happen. They work from the reality that the gospel is more than a past invitation and a future hope, but that it also provides what you need right here and right now to be what you've been chosen by God to be, so you can do what He has called you to do in the midst of it all. People who know that if we are faithful in the mundane places of everyday living, we position ourselves to be enlarged to places of greater responsibility.

While it can be difficult at times to trust in what the Lord has for us, those are the moments in which we can find hope in knowing God has our back. God's plans for each of us is beautiful. Knowing this, we can find the assurance we need and stand in awe before Him in all that He is and all He has for us!

Always remember that you're in God's hand and especially close to His heart. No matter what kind of season you're in, know this, Jesus is with you and invites you to experience more of who He is. We can learn to flourish when we cooperate with Him, move with Him, and trust Him. Thank you, Father!

"Well done, good and faithful servant; you have been faithful over a
few things, I will make you ruler over many things..."
Matthew 25:23 NKJV

DAY 218

I believe our Father wants to send a note to you today from His heart to yours.

"I want to remind you today, on the cross, a beautiful, powerful, glorious, redemptive exchange took place. My son was the sacrifice. He bore your scars. He took your pain. He took your sin and failure. He took your labels, mistakes, and wounds upon Himself and they died with Him! You are new. Never let the enemy convince you that there is no hope for your situation, as long as I am on the throne, there is always hope! You may have been through the fire, the famine, and the flood, but now it's your time for favor. As though lifted by a wave of the sea, you will experience a sudden surge forward. No matter what your circumstances say, expect My favor to be present! It is your new season!

I am writing a story for your life, and I'm not finished. There are still things for you to do and accomplish in your future. I am the Lord your God, the one you belong to, your defender, strong and mighty, sun and shield. I give grace and glory! No good thing will I withhold from you! So, when your heart feels heavy and your knees feel weak, know that you are still safe. You will not be overcome! You will see my goodness in every part of your life. I love you."

"Every promise from the faithful God is pure and proves to be true. He is a wrap-around shield of protection for all his lovers who run to hide in him."

Proverbs 30:5 TPT

DAY 219

We are the workmanship of Almighty God. No one can define us, arbitrarily determine our potential, limit us, or defeat our purpose. What God started in us, He will finish! Lord, help us to remember that our destiny and fulfillment is not just at the end of the journey, but it is in the journey. We must never accept the thought that we won't make it or that it's too late for us.

"Thank You, Lord, that our future is filled with bright hope as the Holy Spirit leads and guides us! Thank you that Your word is a lamp to us, a light to guide our way, a solid place on which we stand secure every day in You! Lord, bless us indeed, enlarge our borders, expand our impact beyond our own limitations, and the limitations life and others have tried to place on us. Be glorified in our lives. May our lives and the lives of those coming behind us declare the glory and greatness of our God! In Jesus' mighty name! Amen!

"So that his name may be honored forever! May the fame of his name spring forth! May it shine on, like the sunshine! In him all will be blessed to bless others, and may all the people bless the One who blessed them."
Psalms 72:17 TPT

"Jabez cried out to the God of Israel, saying, "Oh that You would indeed bless me and enlarge my border [property], and that Your hand would be with me, and You would keep me from evil so that it does not hurt me!" And God granted his request."
1 Chronicles 4:10 AMP

DAY 220

The necessity for continued vision in our lives is so important and powerful. No matter what season of life you're in, keep dreaming, sowing, and believing for a "God Blessed," "God Ordained" future. When we have a sense of purpose and destiny, our world looks and feels different. We are motivated to keep going forward. Problems become speed bumps and obstacles are viewed as challenges we can overcome. Proverbs 29:18 says, "Where there is no vision, the people perish."

I remind you today, you are here for a God-given purpose. The enemy isn't just fighting what you're doing; he's fighting who you are becoming in the process of fulfilling your God-given dreams and visions. God's definition of winning is when you fight the battle and come out even more established in your God-given identity and calling than you were before, just like Jesus on the mount of temptation.

Let's make a declaration over our lives, "I will keep my heart open to the work of the Holy Spirit and I will live the adventure. I will walk in my God-given purpose and passion and I will see the provision for the vision. I will keep dreaming, praying, worshiping, believing, standing, praising and I will see the goodness of the Lord in the land of the living!"

"The lovers of God who chase after righteousness will find all their dreams come true: an abundant life drenched with favor and a fountain that overflows with satisfaction."
Proverbs 21:21 TPT

DAY 221

Thoughts of the future can cause us to be filled with anxiety. Questions of what if? how will? who can? can cause uncertainty and insecurity. Each day has its own obstacles. But fear and dread of tomorrow can threaten our focus and peace of mind for today. Taking one step at a time is so important to maintain a life of victory.

There was a creek close to Abraham Lincoln's home that he had to cross by walking on a narrow log. He never once fell off the log into the water. When they asked him how he did this so successfully, he said, "I never cross it until I get to it." That is great advice for us.

When we get "there," our God will be "there" with us to carry us across. I don't know everything you're facing, but I do know that for everything your tomorrow holds, His grace is sufficient. He will be the steady hand on your shoulder that keeps you on the path no matter how treacherous or uncertain the journey may be.

There is nothing in our tomorrow that will take our God by surprise. There is nothing that can invade our future that He hasn't already made provision for through our Savior, Jesus. Even if the streams we may have to cross are overflowing their banks, He can cause us to walk on water. There is nothing in our future that is greater than our God. He is the same yesterday, today, and forever. If He brought you through yesterday, He's going to do the same today and tomorrow. The grace that got you started is the grace that will carry you through. Our hearts can rest secure as we journey through our today, knowing our God will make a way.

"Refuse to worry about tomorrow, but deal with each challenge that comes your way, one day at a time. Tomorrow will take care of itself."
Matthew 6:34 TPT

DAY 222

Who we connect with in life is so important, especially those we allow to speak into our lives and look to as leaders. Value the God-birthed relationships in your life. They are the currency of the kingdom and we all have a part to play. Who you relate to and who you partner with in life has a great influence on your quality of life and future. It has nothing to do with titles or positions and everything to do with genuine, real respect and being respected. Those you run into on the road of life can be a path or a detour to your destiny. Pray for the discernment and confidence to choose correctly, allowing the people in our lives who will love us through it all and help us access everything God has for us, both valuing and being valued. Join those that facilitate growth, maturity, and fulfillment, not decreasing, stagnation, and unhealthy dependence. Don't give people a place in your heart and life for which they don't qualify. Jesus treated everybody right, but He didn't treat everybody the same. Our hearts and lives should be *gated*, not *walled*.

Our heartfelt desire for each other should be for each of us to become the best us we can be. Seeing others rise from the ashes to become successful in any area of life should be one of the most rewarding things we can experience in life. Pray prayers for others that you are believing for yourself. Believe for others to experience things you are believing for even before you do. Sow into others' lives what you're believing for yourself. Love is the essence of life and I believe that what we pray and help facilitate in the lives of others God will abundantly bless us with. To live life loving and being loved. How rich is that?

"Give generously and generous gifts will be given back to you, shaken down to make room for more. Abundant gifts will pour out upon you with such an overflowing measure that it will run over the top! Your measurement of generosity becomes the measurement of your return."
Luke 6:38 TPT

DAY 223

To live in a "forward" mindset is to live in expectation of God's goodness and blessing in our lives, not hopelessness and depression. Don't spend decades obsessing over who rejected you, spend your years rejoicing in God accepting you in Christ and all that means. Be careful what you think about because you'll eventually conform to what you focus on. "As a man thinks in his heart so is he." (Proverbs 23:7) Thoughts and words have energy. Do not feed on or continually entertain negativity. Never allow what others say about you to cancel out what God says about you. Sometimes it's the people that are closest to us that fail to see what God wants to do in our lives, but our value doesn't decrease based on someone's inability to see our worth.

We don't need to win every argument and we don't need to engage in every battle. Pick your battles and choose what you give your emotional focus to carefully. Not every opinion is worth your energy. Some battles are supposed to be ignored because they're just a distraction. Sometimes the boldest, confident, and spirit-led thing you can say is nothing. Knowing who you are and being confident in who God is in you gives you the freedom to confront what needs to be confronted but also the freedom to know when to walk away. You're too valuable to allow all your validation to come from other people. Jesus validated your worth on the cross. So today, stop putting your happiness in other people's words and opinions. You might not feel important to anybody else, but you are important to God. Tear down every negative thought and word that has held your mind captive. If it doesn't line up with the word of God, it has to go! Keep moving forward and living in expectation of the goodness of God!

"The Lord is my revelation-light to guide me along the way; he's the source of my salvation to defend me every day. I fear no one! I'll never turn back and run from you, Lord; surround and protect me."
Psalms 27:1 TPT

DAY 224

We hear the words "God bless you" regularly. God bless you is more than a cliché. After God created Adam and Eve, the first thing He did was, "He *blessed* them and said, "Be fruitful and multiply. Fill the earth and rule it." Being blessed is not being selfish; it's God's idea. To "bless" means to empower to succeed. It's necessary to fulfill God's purpose for your life. The blessing of our Father empowers us and equips us to do what He calls us to do. It's a life of empowerment, a life of victory, a life of increase, a life of impact, and being able to make a difference. Living in the blessing is when your body is getting better because the same Spirit that raised Jesus from the dead lives in you. Living in the blessing is when you get stronger and have a vision for the future even when you get older and things don't always look promising in the natural. Living in the blessing is not just having enough to get by but more than enough to help someone else. Living in the blessing is having the right thing to say at the right time because the Holy Spirit is your guide, giving you supernatural insight. Living in the blessing is having God's favor surrounding you like a shield and having God's strength to deal with whatever life throws at you.

Do as Jabez. He is a great example for us of someone who made a choice to live in the blessing! His name means "pain!" His family had named and sentenced him to a life of pain. But the Bible tells us that he didn't allow his pain to define him; he let the blessing of God define him.

"Now Jabez was more honorable than his brothers, and his mother called his name Jabez, saying, "Because I bore him in pain." And Jabez called on the God of Israel saying, "Oh, that You would bless me indeed, and enlarge my territory, that Your hand would be with me, and that You would keep me from evil, that I may not cause pain!" So God granted him what he requested."
1 Chronicles 4:9-10 NKJV

DAY 225

Power points for today

1. Success is faithful stewardship of our own God-given assignment, not comparing ourselves to others.

2. The devil doesn't throw rocks at dead birds; you must be a threat to his agenda.

3. Your faith-filled prayers and words have power, presence, prophetic implications, and no geographical limitations.

4. Faith doesn't have to know how God will work it out, only that He will work it out.

5. The greatest form of wealth is love.

6. It's way more effective to influence others by loving them rather than nagging them. The Holy Spirit leads, guides, and prompts us, but He leaves the choices up to us.

7. Trust must be rebuilt over a period of time. If people hurt you over and over again, the Bible says you are obligated to forgive them, but you are not obligated to trust them instantly.

8. If you are not willing to fail, you will never succeed. Get out there, God is with you.

9. A question we need to ask ourselves from time to time to make sure we haven't lost our way, "What's it all for?"

10. Humility is the fertile soil for growth. If we already know everything, learning is impossible.

DAY 226

God speaks to our potential, to who He created us to be. He sees what is possible in our lives when we begin to discover what He has made possible for us. God speaks to who He sees us as, calling us up higher, not calling us out on what we lack. In Numbers 6, God relentlessly speaks only to who Gideon really is: a mighty man of valor, a man who the Lord is with, a victorious man sent by God to save Israel from their enemy, not a fearful, defeated man hiding out in the winepress.

Most of us are really good at calling people out, including ourselves, for shortcomings instead of calling them up to their potential. Of all the people on earth today, I believe that Christians should be the most imaginative, creative, confident, and secure. Out of that, creative confidence should flow abundant life, not arrogance but a confident humility.

Ephesians 1 reminds us of how God sees us and what Jesus has made possible for us. We have been blessed with every spiritual blessing, we have been chosen, adopted, redeemed, forgiven, grace-lavished, and unconditionally loved and accepted. We are pure, blameless, forgiven, and seated with Him in higher realms. We are meant to be masterpieces that fully reflect who God really is, while uniquely expressing who He created us to be.

"I'm writing this letter to all the devoted believers who have been made holy by being one with Jesus, the Anointed One. May God himself, the heavenly Father of our Lord Jesus Christ, release grace over you and impart total well-being into your lives. Every spiritual blessing in the heavenly realm has already been lavished upon us as a love gift from our wonderful heavenly Father, the Father of our Lord Jesus—all because he sees us wrapped into Christ. This is why we celebrate him with all our hearts!"
Ephesians 1:2-3 TPT

DAY 227

Don't waste precious time trying to impress people who only want the worst for you. Appreciate those who love you. Help those who need you. Forgive those who hurt you. Release those who leave you.

Your time is precious. So, don't waste it on anyone who doesn't realize that you are too! Spend your time looking and moving forward. Brush off the dust from others' negative opinions and start moving towards your destiny. We don't have to know the future to have faith in God. We have to have faith in God to be secure in our future!

Remember, people will hate you, rate you, shake you, and try to break you, but how strong you stand in God is what makes you!

"Now my beloved ones, I have saved these most important truths for last: Be supernaturally infused with strength through your life-union with the Lord Jesus. Stand victorious with the force of his explosive power flowing in and through you."
Ephesians 6:10 TPT

DAY 228

Moments, sweet moments. Life tends to just march along moment by moment with little notice of the things that really matter getting our attention. We get so caught up in making a living and we forget to live. But it doesn't have to be that way. It takes intentionality. We can make the minutes count instead of counting the minutes.

Listen, love, look, feel, notice, care, share, and above all, invest yourself in the hearts and lives of others, especially those closest to you. Never take the precious people and time you have with them for granted. The greatest joy in life isn't in material possessions or fame. It's in the laughter, smiles, tears, hugs, struggles, and the growing. The simple things that can drift by us unnoticed every day.

For those who have the love and acceptance of family, both natural and spiritual, thank God for a community to love and be loved. Take a minute and really listen, really hear, and really take it all in. Enjoy the blessings of each other. Seasons change. Time goes by, and some things we thought were so important fade away. But love is a constant. It never fails, it never goes out of style. It's the greatest of all. Take a minute and take in the love. Take a minute and give out love. Love can last a lifetime.

"For now we see but a faint reflection of riddles and mysteries as though reflected in a mirror, but one day we will see face-to-face. My understanding is incomplete now, but one day I will understand everything, just as everything about me has been fully understood. Until then, there are three things that remain: faith, hope, and love—yet love surpasses them all. So above all else, let love be the beautiful prize for which you run."
1 Corinthians 13:12-13 TPT

DAY 229

Precious ones, Let's jump-start our day with prayer.

"Father, I am grateful for every day to serve You. I am greatly blessed, highly favored, and deeply loved by You. Lord, You are my shield and the very source of my strength and my life. Jesus took my sin, curse, and shame on the cross. Therefore, I am forgiven, free, healed, protected, blessed, favored, and loved today! You are the burden bearer. Therefore, I cast all my anxiety and stress on you. Thank You for peace!

From Genesis to Revelation, You are good and You are a giver. Doors are opening for me no man can close. Therefore, I receive Your provision and supply for every need of my life. I have Your word, Your presence, Your promises, and Your protection in Jesus' name!

I am made in Your image and likeness with victory in my DNA. I have comebacks in my DNA. Even bad situations are turning around for my good! The same spirit that raised Jesus from the dead lives in me and is bringing freedom to every part of my life!

Father, thank You for enabling me to live each moment to the fullest, totally involved in Your will and grand plan for my life! Even when things don't look good, I worship You because You are good, and You can make all things work out for my good! Thank you, Lord!!!

DAY 230

Today, no matter what you feel like or what it looks like, let's say it, "I decide to stop condemning myself and beating myself up for my short-comings. I believe God is working in me every day! I am created by the Master's hand. There is an awesome purpose within me, and what God calls me to be and to do, He enables me to become and accomplish! God is calling me forward today. I set the course of my life and future with my thoughts, words, prayers, and decisions. I will not be defeated, discouraged, or depressed. I will not let anyone take away my joy today!

I choose to remember that...

- God is not mad at me.

- God is not against me.

- God is not ignoring me.

- God is not punishing me.

- And most of all, God is not finished with me!

I choose to build my life on this truth. I have the only true and living God leading me and guiding me! People can't stop me! Tough times can't stop me! Other people's negative thoughts and words won't stop me from accomplishing what God has put in my heart! I will dare to dream it and dare to live it! There's nothing that I can't overcome with God on my side!"

"But thanks be to God, who gives us the victory
through our Lord Jesus Christ."
1 Corinthians 15:57 ESV

DAY 231

As we begin a new day, may we all begin to see our setbacks as temporary, our delays as detours, and our heartbreaks as opportunities to experience God's precious, powerful healing. In the meantime, may God give us glimpses of glory and insights into His good plans for us.

I declare over you today that your wilderness will not take you out, but it will take you to your next level in God. What the enemy meant for evil, God will turn it for your good. By faith, get ready to be an eyewitness to a supernatural turnaround. Hear your Father say, "I am the God of your past, present, and future! I am redeeming your past. In the present, I am working all things together for your good. I have a future and a hope for you to journey into.

May you be assured that God has never left your side and He'll never let you go. May God help you see with supernatural insight so that you won't be discouraged by the enemy of your soul, by any past pain, lies, or fears of the future. I pray this week you will defy the odds, defeat giants, and dominate the enemy and bask in the presence of God in every area of your life!

"For the Lord God is brighter than the brilliance of a sunrise! Wrapping himself around me like a shield, he is so generous with his gifts of grace and glory. Those who walk along his paths with integrity will never lack one thing they need, for he provides it all! O Lord of Heaven's Armies, what euphoria fills those who forever trust in you!"
Psalms 84:11-12 TPT

DAY 232

Do not allow the fire in your soul to go out. Stir it up in us today, Holy Spirit! Thank you, Lord.

"Goodness and mercy are following me and God's plans are to bless me and prosper me, not harm me! I speak victory and increase in not only my life, but my family's as well. I declare that we have redemption over the lies of the enemy. We are overcomers and more than a conqueror, the head and not the tail, above and not beneath, blessed and not cursed! I declare our freedom in Christ from anything that has bound or limited us. I declare today His mercy is unlimited, His grace unhindered, His forgiveness unmatched, His love unconditional, His faithfulness unending. We are ready for divine possibilities, awesome God moments, life-changing turnarounds, obstacles overcome, and favor coming our way! We will keep standing, keep believing, and keep trusting because our God is a good God and He knows how to take care of us! And He will take care of us, always!"

"Give thanks to the LORD of Heaven's Armies, for the LORD is good. His faithful love endures forever!' For I will restore the prosperity of this land to what it was in the past, says the LORD."
Jeremiah 33:11 NLT

DAY 233

Sometimes the greatest things we do are pondered in our hearts long before they are birthed into reality. But never forget the importance of daily faith and faithfulness. It is possible to dream so far ahead for what is coming that we don't structure today to reach it. Success is not only achieved by vision, but by planning and daily discipline. Start building today to house your dreams for tomorrow. Paddle your rowboat while you're waiting for your ship to come in! Faith operates in the present to create in the future. Stay in faith and stay faithful; God is a rewarder! One of the greatest pleasures in life is doing what man said was impossible and then giving God all the glory.

Say it today, "I affirm that I am full of life. I am conscious of the supernatural life of God that is in my spirit. I will not stand here in unbelief when the God of this universe who created me in His image is speaking to my heart. I am going to get up, and I am going to move forward in faith, believing in God for the miraculous to happen in my life! No problem is too great; no dream is too big with God's favor I can and will do amazing things!

"The confidence of my calling enables me to overcome every difficulty without shame, for I have an intimate revelation of this God. And my faith in him convinces me that He is more than able to keep all that I've placed in his hands safe and secure until the fullness of his appearing."
2 Timothy 1:12 TPT

DAY 234

God wants us to live with a sense of value. He wants us to know today that He loves us more than we can imagine. We have so many things that fight to rule in our lives; guilt, regret, rejection, fear, depression, failures, and shortcomings, hurts, and heartaches.

The things the enemy tries to use against us have held us back long enough. Nothing that has happened because of us or to us is too great for the redemption of our God. Our ability to live in freedom and approach God today has nothing to do with us living a perfect life; it has everything to do with Jesus being a perfect sacrifice! It was a perfect sacrifice by a perfect person to perfect some very imperfect people who needed a perfect savior.

We do not have to live discouraged and defeated lives. We are not victims of our failures. We are victors because of our victorious Savior. Jesus' redemptive work was perfect and complete lacking nothing. It is eternal. When Jesus cried out, "It is finished," everything the enemy uses to try to dominate our lives was finished!

Remember, today is a new day! New favor! New divine appointments! New hope! New possibilities! Build your future today by resisting looking back to what should've or could've been. God is calling you forward! I decree breakthrough to what has caused your secret hurts and tears! Because of Jesus' great redemption, it is your turn, and it is your time.

"God is not man, that he should lie, or a son of man, that he should change his mind. Has he said, and will he not do it? Or has he spoken, and will he not fulfill it?"
Numbers 23:19 ESV

DAY 235

Even when setbacks happen in our lives, God has a way of turning them around and bringing an even greater increase to us. God can turn a furnace of persecution into a factory of anointing. Shadrach, Meshach, and Abed-Nego were thrown into the fire, but the only thing that burned were the ropes that had them bound. He is with you in the fire!

The people of Israel suffered under the rule of Egypt, but Exodus 1:12 says the more they were afflicted, the more they multiplied!

God is a God of the turnaround. He can use your adversity to cause a greater increase. Your setbacks will not cause you to diminish but have positioned you for increase and greater. Our God is amazing at taking the places of pain that you have borne silently and turning them into a public demonstration of His goodness and faithfulness. Your private battle is about to be turned into a public breakthrough. The people and places that created the pain and loss of the past have no power over the blessings of your today and tomorrow.

I stand in agreement with you today. For every door the enemy closed, God will open doors that are filled with even greater opportunities. Shift and change are in the atmosphere of your life. There is a fresh stirring in your heart that is birthed by the Spirit of God. Your greatest days are before you, and as you lean in closer to God, you will see His mighty hand like never before!

"Yes, God is more than ready to overwhelm you with every form of grace, so that you will have more than enough of everything—every moment and in every way. He will make you overflow with abundance in every good thing you do."
2 Corinthians 9:8 TPT

DAY 236

We are created for movement, growth, increase, interaction, and challenge. Motion is the seed for emotion. Grace is not passive; we are graced for something. Great grace always follows great faith. Favor is not passive; it's energetic and alive, flowing, and moving.

"The steps of a good man are ordered by the Lord: and He delighteth in His WAY."
Psalms 37:23 NKJV

The passion translation says it this way, "The steps of the God-pursuing ones follow firmly in the footsteps of the Lord, and God delights in every step they take to follow him."

God wants us to increase, prosper, and live a blessed life. The more blessed I am, the more of a blessing I can be! But God wants us to become prosperous, not just be prosperous. God is not just interested in working for me; He's working in me. God prospers us by enlarging us personally until we naturally produce greater results. He wants our accomplishments to be the "fruit" of the person we have become, for our prosperity to be first and foremost an inside job. He wants us to grow into our places of increase, to increase our character as He increases our blessings. So today, join with me in declaring in faith, "Father, thank you for the awareness in my heart and imagination of Your plan for me. I will hold to faith in You to see beyond the immediate into the eternal. I will hold an advancing spirit rejecting attitudes of retreat and intimidation. This is my time for going forward and in Jesus' name, I will walk in Your plan, Your purpose, Your potential, Your power, and Your provision. Blessed that I might be a blessing! Thank you, Lord Jesus!"

DAY 237

Forward! It's not always easy to keep moving in the right direction, especially when things don't happen like you thought they would and people or circumstances disappointment you. Family put Joseph in a pit, a leader tried to kill David, and church people conspired against Jesus, but God turned it for their good and He can for you too! Jesus was lied on, kicked, spit on, and abandoned by his friends but guess what he did next. He got up and kept going forward.

Remember to press towards the mark and not towards the drama! The enemy will throw you a pity party every day that your feelings and focus are willing to attend. He wants you to rehearse losing in your mind, so that's all you see when life doesn't go your way.

But even when our circumstances don't make us happy, we can choose thoughts that will. Keep your heart God-focused and not circumstance focused and you can be in joy, even in adverse circumstances.

Stress makes you believe it has to happen now; faith says to trust God's timing. You can have confidence in what God will do because of what God has done! So, never lose hope. When the sun goes down, the stars come out. There has never been a night, no matter how dark, that has been able to stop the sunrise! It's not over! His love is as sure as the sunrise! Hope reigns eternal!

"Against all hope, Abraham in hope believed and so became the father of many nations... He did not waver at the promise of God through unbelief, but was strengthened in faith, giving glory to God, and being fully convinced that what He had promised He was also able to perform."
Romans 4:18; 20-21 NIV

DAY 238

Paul encouraged Timothy, "Stir up the gift that is within you." 2 Timothy 1:6. Be you. Never lose the uniqueness of your individuality. Refuse to dumb down to fit in. Refuse to live as an echo of someone else's opinion and as a poor copy of someone else's life. Stop living in comparison. Never judge your weakness compared to someone else's strength. You are unique and have greatness within you. There never has been and never will be anyone like you.

But that isn't a testament to you; it's a testament to the God who created you! It means God has made you with unique gifts and talents. He loves to see you use those gifts to bring love and hope to the world around you.

May we all start praying and searching for ways to use our gifts for His glory. Lord help us to understand that every breath, every heartbeat, the ability to see, speak, walk, and reason are all blessings, You bestowed on us every day of our lives. Lord, let us always remember to be thankful for the opportunities we have to move in our uniqueness.

So, remember today, long before you were born and became a part of history, you existed in the heart of God. You are His special, unique, and precious child. You are loved, a light, a city on a hill, the salt of the earth, a special possession, and He delights in you. He created you to live and shine, not just exist. Jesus came, suffered, and died to give us abundant life. So today, speak life because your unique you is listening!

"For you are a holy people to the LORD your God, and the LORD has chosen you to be a people for Himself, a special treasure above all the peoples who are on the face of the earth."
Deuteronomy 14:2 NKJV

DAY 239

Today I pray favor over you, favor that will take you to divine appointments and open doors of opportunity! Praying that you will enter a season when God will exceed all you expect. He will increase all you invest in every area, spirit, soul, and body. I pray against every spirit of oppression against you, any heaviness, or weariness on you. Let it be removed. Let every burden be lifted, every sorrow comforted, and every sickness healed!

I am praying that He will cause you to live life at the speed of grace and favor! Supernatural timing! He will accelerate time to accomplish His purpose in you and for you! Every spirit of failure over your life and family is broken in the name of Jesus! You have victory by the Blood of Jesus! I am praying that God will promote you like Joseph, intervene for you like Esther, protect you like Daniel, and use you like Paul! In Jesus' name, this is your time of breakthrough, restoration, and recovery!

Amen, Lord!

DAY 240

Every day is filled with many uncertainties and there are times in life you feel overwhelmed, but remember, God has never been overwhelmed by anything, ever! We can always be certain that God still reigns, and this is a day He has made!

So, as you go through your day, speak blessings over your life. Something supernatural happens when we speak out the promises of God! You may not feel capable in your own strength, but God says He will always cause you to triumph! In your weakness, His strength rises up and sustains and energizes you to face whatever is happening. Now, give yourself and your worries to God and begin enjoying the abundant life He has planned for you!

Say it, "The God that I serve is a God of might and miracles, hope and healing, comfort and grace, life and liberty! I am equipped, empowered, fully loaded, and lacking nothing! I declare that my steps are ordered, my pace is quickened, my path is secure, and my hands are strengthened. It's forward into the good and perfect will of God for me! Hallelujah!"

"The steps of a [good and righteous] man are directed and established by the Lord, And He delights in his way [and blesses his path]."
Psalm 37:23 AMP

DAY 241

Declare today, "God will make a way for me!"

If some of the things God has put in your heart seem overwhelming and impossible outside of God's divine intervention, take heart today. Faith is a force that resides on the inside of our spirit, and when it is released, tremendous things can happen in our lives. Weeping may endure for the night, but joy comes in the morning.

Declare it, "my story doesn't end at night!" Never let the "experts" talk you out of the things God has put in your heart. God has demonstrated that He can and will overcome the "odds" to accomplish His promises and purposes in our lives. He can still the storms, part the sea, heal the sick, restore the broken, put money in a fish's mouth, bring promotion from prison, rain manna from the heavens, bring water from a rock, and bring life from death! With the Lord, nothing is ever hopeless!

Your current battle isn't too big for God. Whatever you're going through, you can conquer with Him! Never give up hope! You have not been forgotten. You may have weaknesses, but God has strength. You may have stumbled, but God has grace. You may have failed, but God remains faithful!

Declare it again, "God will make a way for me!"

DAY 242

Because we all know our own imperfections and shortcomings, we can begin to think that God shouldn't bless us or answer our prayers because we haven't done everything right, we've failed, messed up, and come up short. But, whenever you encounter a promise unfulfilled in your life, remember, Jesus paid for that! He deserves it! He's worthy of its fulfillment in you!

"Worthy are you to take the scroll and to open its seals, for you were slain, and by your blood you ransomed people for God from every tribe and language and people and nation, and you have made them a kingdom and priests to our God, and they shall reign on the earth."
Revelation 5:9-10 ESV

That breakthrough you're waiting for, Jesus already paid the price for it. He sacrificed Himself so that you can reign in life (Romans 5:17). After giving up His perfect life on your behalf, isn't Jesus worthy to see His promises and vision for you fulfilled?

Refuse to give up hope. Don't even consider that an option! Have faith in God's faithfulness. If you knew what was coming, you'd rejoice no matter how distant it seems!

If you find yourself ready to quit, I encourage you to change the way you perceive God's promises. May Jesus see the full reward of all He has done for us! Worthy are You, Lord!

DAY 243

Keep Believing!

Sometimes when the going gets tough you just have to believe by faith that no matter what you may be facing, no matter what trial you may be going through, God has a plan to turn things around in your favor. You have to keep believing that right now, He is working out a plan for your good, orchestrating the right people to come across your path, and the right opportunities to open up to you. You have to keep believing God is working on your behalf behind the scenes and keep believing Romans 8:28 over your life, your children, your spouse, and all your loved ones.

"May God cause everything to work together for the good of those who love God and are called according to his purpose for them." You have to keep believing God to give you a new solution, a new strategy, and a new perspective on an old problem. To keep believing old things are passed away; behold, all things have become new. (2 Cor 5:17) To keep believing that it is God's will for you to overcome every obstacle and prosper in spite of the setbacks. To keep believing that God has prepared something awesome for you in your future and has scheduled a head-on collision for you with favor, success, prosperity, health, and fulfillment!

"And we know that God causes everything to work together for the good of those who love God and are called according to his purpose for them."
Romans 8:28 NLT

DAY 244

I want to encourage you to not throw in the towel. God has not abandoned you, and He's there to help you persevere through the tough times. Keep your eyes fixed on Jesus and rejoice in your great salvation because Jesus is better and superior to anything else you could run to. When problems come, we can cope or conquer, give up or get up, back up or step up, speak up or shut up, breakdown, or breakthrough. Failure should be our teacher, not our undertaker. Failure is a delay, not a defeat. It is a temporary detour, not a dead end.

For believers, even if we lose a battle, the war isn't lost. Wherever you are right now in this journey called life, remember this is just one page, one chapter in the book, but it isn't the end.

Sometimes all it takes besides believing in God is to believe in God in you! Stir it up in your life today, rise up on the inside and declare, "The greater one lives in me. He has brought me this far; He's not going to leave me now. I am blessed coming in and blessed going out. No weapon formed against me or my family will prosper! His promises will not fail in my life, they are yes to me, and amen in Christ. He is watching over His word to perform it. Let God arise, and His enemies be scattered!"

"You are the Lord who reigns over your never-ending kingdom through all the ages of time and eternity! You are faithful to fulfill every promise you've made..."
Psalms 145:13 TPT

DAY 245

Today I pray you would have a renewed passion for your relationship with God and your God-breathed purpose. You are here on purpose and with a purpose. One look at the cross of Calvary reveals the true value God puts on every person. Heaven's greatest gift was given for mankind's worst sin. I love you was written in red across the fabric of our hearts and lives.

"Before I formed you in the womb I knew you, and before you were born I consecrated you; I appointed you a prophet to the nations."
Jeremiah 1:5 ESV

God is saying, "You are loved, and you are wonderfully made."

So, start your journey today toward finishing the rest of this year, push off, set your sails to the glorious purpose that God has called you to and believe for a great adventure! If you fall, get back up! If you stumble, regain your balance! Never give up! Keep your focus on the positive promises God has given you. Father God is saying to you today, "You don't have all of the answers, but I do. That is why I need you to place your trust in Me. I am your answer. I am your healer. I am your provider. I am Your restorer. I am your comforter. I am your protector. I am your strength. I am your assurance in times of uncertainty. I am your deliverer. I am the provider of everything that you need."

"So now I live with the confidence that there is nothing in the universe with the power to separate us from God's love. I'm convinced that his love will triumph over death, life's troubles, fallen angels, or dark rulers in the heavens. There is nothing in our present or future circumstances that can weaken his love."
Romans 8:38 TPT

DAY 246

Our days can be a tomb or a womb depending on our attitude and focus. Our attitude is affected by our perspective. Go up for a higher view and we may see that our momentary discomfort is more about our purpose than about being uncomfortable. When something happens, we don't understand we have three choices. We can either let it define us, let it destroy us, or we can let it grow and strengthen us. It's actually when life gets rough and rugged that the sweetness of God's faithfulness makes itself even more real in our heart and the victory is even more beautiful. As we walk through those storms in complete reliance on His strength, our trust in His character becomes part of who we are and strengthens us inside. I don't have to try to stay in faith if I stay in fellowship.

So, let's focus on the promise giver, not the need. Magnify the goodness of God, not the size of the mountain. Choose deliberate praise, over dark doubts. So today, when there are things I don't know, I fall back on what I do know! And who I know! I keep my eyes on Him! I rely on the Holy Spirit, the Parakletos, the advocate, the one called to walk along the path with me always! And when I don't know, He does know! He can get me through it all; from beginning to end and everything in between! He is saying, "Trust me, I've got this!" Trust in the God you know when there are things you don't know!

"For we have no power against this great multitude that is coming against us; nor do we know what to do, but our eyes are upon You."
2 Chronicles 20:12 NKJV
"But those who trust in the Lord will find new strength. They will soar high on wings like eagles. They will run and not grow weary. They will walk and not faint."
Isaiah 40:31 NLT

DAY 247

Child of God keep on keeping on. Even if you feel unappreciated for what you have done, God wants you to know that He sees you, the hours you have put in, the sacrifices you have made, the giving you have done, the kindness you have shown, it's all making a difference in the hearts of the people around you, and God is working through you in more ways than you realize.

I hear Father saying over us today, "Even though there has been hardship, disappointment, and discouragement, surely my grace, love, and forgiveness are greater than these. As you come to know me and experience me, I will be your great reward. I am calling you close to my side, to rest in my shade, and restore your soul in my presence. For surely, I have seen your tears and felt your heartache, even in times of secret, in times when no one was around, I saw the disappointments, offenses, and hurts. Still, even in these times, I am with you. I never left you and never will. I've noticed even the smallest of details.

But also know I am birthing compassion that will surpass your offenses. My compassion will flow into you and your hurts will rule no more. So, come close to me. Look to your future. Celebrate today as you walk in total freedom and embrace your destiny."

We receive it, Lord!

"Yet when holy lovers of God cry out to him with all their hearts, the Lord will hear them and come to rescue them from all their troubles. The Lord is close to all whose hearts are crushed by pain, and he is always ready to restore the repentant one. Even when bad things happen to the good and godly ones, the Lord will save them and not let them be defeated by what they face."
Psalms 34:17-19 TPT

DAY 248

The Mighty God we serve is interested in our life, every aspect of our life, and is available to work in us and through us at all times. Because we serve a mighty God, we live possibility!

This is the attitude of all things are possible, anything can happen, living life with expectancy, anticipating something good can and will happen. This is living life with a forward-looking mentality, not a looking back one, believing that God's favor on my life means there are possibilities and expanded boundaries for me! It's a yes attitude that propels me through hardship and difficulties, knowing God doesn't have to wait for the conditions to be favorable to bless my life. He can make rivers in the desert. He can bless me in any season!

So, be confident in God's power in your life today. There is nothing in the world that can come close to matching Him. No problem is too great. No dream is too big. When you are touched by God's favor, you can and will do amazing things.

Today I pray you see the tangible goodness and favor of God in and on your life today, and instead of all hell breaking against you, I prophesy all heaven is breaking toward you and for you!

"Be alert, be present. I'm about to do something brand-new. It's bursting out! Don't you see it? There it is! I'm making a road through the desert, rivers in the badlands."
Isaiah 43:19 MSG

DAY 249

Today let's pray, "That the Spirit of the living God that called you from your mother's womb rises up in you and creates assurance and confidence in you that you are still on the way, that it's not over and there are still things for you to do and experience this year. That you will know that God is still painting a picture of His will for your life, looking it over, and just loving it! He's calling it good!

Pray you will hear Him saying, "I chose you, I called you, I am shaping you, and I am sending you!"

Declare it today, "God has purpose and intention for me. And I won't be distracted by the noise of the world or the opinions of man! Whatever God has designed and spoken over me will come to pass as I cooperate with the Holy Spirit! I will bring God glory! That is, I will bring forth the splendor and majesty of God in the earth through my life by manifesting the evidence of who He is! Lord, let my life demonstrate who You are, knowing that You can even turn around the messed-up stuff in my life and get the glory!

Thank you for making my life a living epistle that carries the message of who You are, great, glorious, powerful, mighty, all-knowing, redeeming, loving God. Amen!"

"God, keep us near your mercy-fountain and bless us! And when you look down on us, may your face beam with joy! Pause in his presence Send us out all over the world so that everyone everywhere will discover your ways and know who you are and see your power to save."
Psalms 67:1-2 TPT

DAY 250

Remember that winter is not the cancellation of autumn, it's the preparation for spring. During this time, may God's goodness surround you and your family. God is saying, "You will be okay. Yes, you will be okay. I am with you. Greater things are coming. I will repay you for the years the locusts have eaten."

Believe your God is with you, the life-giver, the one who brings all things to pass, the performer of all promises, the absolute unchangeable one. He will be all that is necessary as the need arises. Your desert will bloom again. There's a promise coming down your road and it will not pass you by. We can have joy even on days when everything about "life" isn't "good" because God is always good. He is amazing and He is the God of the turnaround! Your disappointment is turning to a divine appointment. You will be victorious over the challenges coming your way. I pray you walk in the future you've always believed to have, that you never stop dreaming God dreams and you never stop living in expectation of the goodness of God. This is a time when a divine reversal begins when all that has been stolen from the generations is given back, and the set time of God's favor is released!

"Yet even in the midst of all these things, we triumph over them all, for God has made us to be more than conquerors, and his demonstrated love is our glorious victory over everything!"
Romans 8:37 TPT

DAY 251

One of my favorite prayers is found in 2 Chronicles 20. Jehoshaphat was facing a situation that was overwhelming and seemingly hopeless, one with no answers. He prayed, "Lord, I don't know what to do, but my eyes are on You."

When we face times like these, we have to stay focused on Him. It is better to be focused on God with tears in our eyes than react carnally with weapons in our hands. What I have come to know and believe is that at all times, in all situations, and under all circumstances, my only job and often the most difficult task I face is to trust in the goodness of God and to make myself available to God's love and voice.

In spite of how we may feel and what we're going through, our God is greater. He is all-powerful and faithful to perfect that which concerns us. He is the author and finisher of our faith.

As believers, we have the most powerful person in the universe guiding us as we keep our eyes on Him. People can't stop us, tough times can't stop us, and people's negative opinions can't stop us. There's nothing that we can't overcome with God on our side and our eyes fixed on Him!

"Therefore, since we are surrounded by so great a cloud of witnesses, let us also lay aside every weight, and sin which clings so closely, and let us run with endurance the race that is set before us, looking to Jesus, the founder and perfecter of our faith, who for the joy that was set before him endured the cross, despising the shame, and is seated at the right hand of the throne of God."
Hebrews 12:1-2 ESV

DAY 252

Being content doesn't mean I have no desire to increase or go to another level. It just means I'm not going to be miserable while I'm on the way and, in fact, I'm going to make sure I make every effort to enjoy the journey. We're going to have rainy days, but we also have the power to turn those days into watering days. Plants grow when the sun is shining and when it is dark and rainy. Overcomers have learned to water their journey with the word, abundant love, and worship. As we do, we become more aware of His Spirit, which is in us and surrounding us, always! There's no substitute for the presence and power of God.

Overcomers press forward in sunshine and storms. They learn to treasure the precious moments in life, to appreciate the journey, to spend some time celebrating others along the way and enjoying God's goodness.

They press on when they have every reason not to: rejection, age, frustration, fatigue, feelings, criticism, you name it, through it all, they press on. Success is a journey, not a destination. The process is often more important than the outcome. Keep showing up. The God of resurrection is at work. So, where we are might not be where we want to be in some areas but let's do the same thing Abraham did. Lift up our eyes and look out from the place where we are and press on in faith and expectation of the goodness of God. It is impossible to live abundantly without loving abundantly. Our God is good, and He is faithful.

"The confidence of my calling enables me to overcome every difficulty
without shame, for I have an intimate revelation of this God. And my
faith in him convinces me that he is more than able to keep all that I've
placed in his hands safe and secure until the fullness of his appearing."
2 Timothy 1:12 TPT

DAY 253

We serve an amazing, holy, supernatural, loving, forgiving, merciful, always present, mighty, powerful, creative God. We should think of God as being so huge that it takes a lifetime to get to know everything about Him and there is still more beyond that!

We have an image on the inside that is so important for our lives and future. As a believer, God has placed a deposit in you, a wealth of purpose and power to harvest. The Bible says it's a treasure.

"I pray that the light of God will illuminate the eyes of your imagination, flooding you with light, until you experience the full revelation of the hope of his calling—that is, the wealth of God's glorious inheritances that he finds IN US, his holy ones!"

Ephesians 1:18

So, don't just think outside of the box, think like there is no box. Never ever stop growing, learning, discovering, and proclaiming, "I am alive to God's greatness and majesty. I am in Christ. I am loved and valued by the creator of the universe. He has made a deposit in me. There are gifts in me waiting to be developed and released. I affirm that I am a special treasure unto God; I have a purpose and destiny in life, a destiny of blessing and fulfillment. I will live the glorious and supernatural life, fulfilling God's purpose, in my expression of His virtues, gifts, excellence, and wisdom. The wisdom is working in me to guide and lead me on the right path to fulfill the dreams and visions that the Spirit of God has given me.

The treasure that is in me is so much greater than the trouble around me! Thank you, Lord, for the journey of discovery that is ahead of me. It's on to the good, acceptable, and perfect will of God for me! It's harvest time! Thank you, Lord!"

DAY 254

God is a God of increase. Don't allow what you've been through to reduce you or to limit you. Allow God to increase greatness and wholeness from what you've been through. Never allow bad "moments" to develop into bad "mindsets." Listen to God and let His Word take you into the blessing prepared for you. He is the God of divine turnarounds.

I'm praying today that, your pain will be turned to purpose, your hurt will be turned to healing, your wounds will be turned to wisdom, your stagnation will be turned to supernatural success, your disappointments will be turned into divine appointments, and your battle will be turned into a blessed future that is bigger and better than you think!

Whatever negative things have happened to you doesn't have to create negative expectations. Set your mind and expectations on the unlimited possibilities that exist in Him. Believe that God is leading you and propelling you forward into victory.

"Now thanks be to God who always leads us in triumph in Christ, and through us diffuses the fragrance of His knowledge in every place."
2 Corinthians 2:14 NKJV

DAY 255

We live in a broken and hurting world. Sometimes we hurt. Sometimes our hearts ache. Sometimes we cry out in pain, and sometimes we have to encourage ourselves because no one else does. But all the time we have His presence and His Word to encourage and comfort us. All the time, we need to speak victory no matter how we feel. We need to daily speak the Word of God over ourselves and encourage ourselves in the presence of our Lord. Through it all, God is creating a new story with our life.

This week stir up what God put in you. Make the most of this day. Don't let the fear of failure, fear of what people are going to think, or fear of being criticized hold you back.

"Now David was greatly distressed, for the people spoke of stoning him, because the soul of all the people was grieved, every man for his sons and his daughters. But David strengthened himself in the Lord his God."
1 Samuel 30:6 NKJV

Worrying does not take away tomorrow's troubles, but it does take away today's peace. We have to learn to turn up our hope. We serve a God that loves to speak victory in the face of defeat, life to dry bones, and hope to dead dreams! Meditate on His promises until the picture is so clear on the inside of you that nothing can shake it out of you. That's what hope is all about. It's a divine dream. It's an inner image that's bigger than you are because it's built on the love and promises of God. All His promises to you are yes and Amen!

"May the God of your hope so fill you with all joy and peace in believing - through the experience of your faith - that by the power of the Holy Spirit you may abound and be overflowing (bubbling over) with hope."
Romans 15:13 AMP

DAY 256

God didn't put us on earth to continually struggle, settle, and give up. He wants us to be humble, but also to prosper. Don't feel guilty for wanting more out of life! We can be content without being complacent.

Your current situation is not the end unless you choose to settle and let it be! Get up, get moving, and start believing again! Life changes when we become more committed to our faith, dreams, and purpose than we are to our comfort zone!

So, keep honoring God with your life. Trust in his timing and He will open doors no man can close! When we leave everything in God's hands, we will eventually see God's hands in everything!

"Trust in the LORD forever, For in YAH, the LORD, is everlasting strength."

Isaiah 26:4 NKJV

DAY 257

No matter what has happened to you, God still has a plan for your life. God always wants to give you a fresh beginning. We need to give Him time. He makes everything beautiful in its time. What do we do in the meantime while we're waiting? Worship and trust Him.

Worship happens when you realize how small you are compared to how big God is. Worship happens when you realize He is greater than your yesterdays, todays, and tomorrows because He is not limited by time and distance. Even work becomes worship when we dedicate it to God and do it with an awareness of His presence. Worship knowing there will come a day you will look back and marvel at how good He was and is and that time and time again He knew better than you. For ages to come, He has so much more in store for you than you can see right now.

"Father, we worship You today while we're waiting. Lord, renew our hearts. Restore our souls. Refresh our spirits today. We're coming to You Lord. As we worship, we know You're coming to us. We're coming to You, only You. You alone have the words of life we need. You alone can satisfy the longing of our hearts."

"He has made everything beautiful and appropriate in its time. He has also planted eternity [a sense of divine purpose] in the human heart [a mysterious longing which nothing under the sun can satisfy, except God]—yet man cannot find out (comprehend, grasp) what God has done (His overall plan) from the beginning to the end."
Ecclesiastes 3:11 AMP

DAY 258

What we say yes to in life is so important, but so is no!

The "no" position empowers the believer to take a stand and say "no" to any and all things the enemy seeks to do in and around your life. The enemy seeks to crowd you and take an unlawful opportunity in your life. He seeks to take from you and bring into your life things that destroy.

We are to have an attitude that says no. "No, it stops here! No way, not even one more inch!" No is a way of taking a stand. It is a spiritual stubbornness, a resolve, an attitude that shouts out, "Enough! That's it! Enough is enough!" So, let's do it!

Today, in Jesus' name, I take my position of faith and stand my ground. I make my choice to resist the enemy with a definite "no" to his invasions into my spirit, soul, and body. I draw a line and give him no more opportunity to take advantage. I command the enemy this day to take his hands off my God-given inheritance in Christ! No more! No further! In Jesus' name, I take my stand and I will not be intimidated! My best is yet to come and I will fulfill my God-given destiny through Jesus Christ, my Lord! Amen!

DAY 259

I want to release some God affirmations over you today.

God carefully planned and designed you before you were born. You were no accident. Long before you showed up on the earth, God was thinking about you. You're not the product of a moment. You are a child of eternity. You're the result of the counsel of heaven and your worth to God is beyond measure. You are chosen, you are on the way, you are needed, you are loved, and you will make it. You are a person of destiny, handpicked by the Creator, you have His DNA and come from a long line of champions.

Jobs come and go. Bank accounts rise and fall. Economies go up and down. Politicians succeed and fail. People come and go. Seasons change. But your security is in a living and faithful God. He will take care of you.

Know this, even on your worst days when you don't feel great, there is greatness within you. You will not be shaken.

"What delight comes to the one who follows God's ways! He won't walk in step with the wicked, nor share the sinner's way, nor be found sitting in the scorner's seat. His pleasure and passion is remaining true to the Word of "I Am," meditating day and night in the true revelation of light. He will be standing firm like a flourishing tree planted by God's design, deeply rooted by the brooks of bliss, bearing fruit in every season of his life. He is never dry, never fainting, ever blessed, ever prosperous."
Psalms 1:1-3 TPT

DAY 260

Vision is accomplished in life by the things you faithfully do, not about how you feel all the time. Don't get caught up in your own emotional trap with not disciplining yourself for greatness because of how you feel. Get up and go out there and do what is necessary. Most beautiful things in our lives aren't created instantly or overnight; they take time. They're not just the results of what we do in the spotlight when it's fun, but what we do when no one else is around to pat us on the back.

Consistency is so important. To continually, rain or shine, day or night, in every season, no matter how we feel or what it looks like, show up every day simply doing what we're called to do can create powerful and amazing things.

It's not just the big things but the small things done consistently over time that can make a huge impact. Great blessings are a result of perseverance! Great distances can be covered by small steps! Remember that one of the greatest keys to success is to stay steady and keep your peace knowing and trusting that God is continually working on your behalf, even when it doesn't look like it.

So, if you're feeling tired and weary from the hurt, disappointment, and confusion, I pray for a renewed energy and focus from the Lord to be released in your life that will empower you in the daily things, that no matter what knocks you down in life, you are going to get back up and keep going, one step at a time, one day at a time. Never give up! Get up and go get it!

"His lord said to him, 'Well done, good and faithful servant; you were faithful over a few things, I will make you ruler over many things. Enter into the joy of your lord."
Matthew 25:21 NKJV

DAY 261

God does some of His best work when your back is up against the wall. He can use the crisis you are in to show you His power, His presence, and His ability to turn your situation around. God has countless ways to turn your situation around that you've never even thought of. Just because you don't see a way doesn't mean God doesn't have a way.

God is not finished with you. He has not given up on you. He has not turned His back on you. His purpose for your life has not been abandoned. Everything that has come against you and endeavored to limit you is being shattered off of you! There are days ahead of you that are going to be filled with satisfaction and fulfillment. Goodness and mercy are following you, and His plans are to bless you and prosper you, not harm you. I speak favor over you now, divine possibilities, awesome God- moments, life-changing turnarounds, and obstacles overcome. You will overcome this battle. He's a supernatural God. He gives beauty for ashes. I hear a sound echoing over you today, "A sound of hope, a sound of forgiveness, restoration, new beginnings, healing of broken hearts, rescuing you from your dark valleys, and lifting you up on eagles' wings! God is for you. Do not allow the fire in your soul to go out. Stir it up today!

"Faithful is he that calleth you...who also will do it."
1 Thessalonians 5:24 KJV
"Do not be anxious about anything, but in every situation, by prayer and petition, with thanksgiving, present your requests to God."
Philippians 4:6 NIV

DAY 262

Grace is the power of the Holy Spirit to enable you to go through things that seem impossible. We should be continually thankful for the gift of past grace but also filled with expectation for the hope that future grace brings us and in the midst of it all, we must always be aware of our need for the right here, right now grace that keeps us day by day. We should always remember, we will never be so spiritual or mature to the point where we've outgrown our need for God's amazing grace.

The gospel is the persistent God never giving up on me, always loving me, always welcoming me with open arms, through all my faults seeing my needs. God knows me completely; He understands me completely, and still loves me completely.

"Father, today, I pray for an outpouring of your goodness, an overflow of your blessing, and an abundance of your grace to all your children. I pray they will be free from depression, anxiety, debts, toxic relationships, sickness, guilt, and shame. I pray for divine connections and prosperity in all things, spirit, soul, and body. Today I pray God's grace strengthens you, His word heals you, His love drives out all fear. Thank you, Lord."

"Your love is so extravagant, It reaches to the heavens! Your faithfulness so astonishing, It stretches to the sky!"
Psalms 57:10 TPT

DAY 263

I want to pray over you today. Your Father wants you to know that He personally cares and is there for you, always! You matter. Your daily battles matter. Your life matters!

"I pray in agreement with you today that God will restore all that's been broken, stolen, or destroyed in your life. I pray that it's turning around for you and it won't take years, months, or even weeks. I am believing you will pursue, overtake, and recover all. Your life will flourish like a watered garden!"

Pray it with me, "...*and the LORD will guide me continually, and satisfy my soul in dry places, and make strong my bones; and I shall be like a watered garden, and like a spring of water, whose waters don't fail.*" *Isaiah 58:11 NKJV*

I pray the Lord will release a sudden upshift and a wave of favor like never before, that your days of unfulfillment and unhappiness will come to an end. That God is giving you a new mentality, a new path, and a new direction in Jesus name.

Say it with me, "Father, by faith I will rise up., start fresh and see the bright opportunity today! Things I've struggled with for years, you can turn around in a day! Today my steps will be directed by God and it's going to be a great day, a great week, and a great year filled with divine possibilities!"

I pray that your life is filled with nothing but bigger blessings, new doors opening, big opportunities, total provision, and health. Your new season of victory has already been provided for! I speak financial increase, unrestricted breakthroughs, and overwhelming peace over your life today!

DAY 264

When my natural eyes can't see what's on the road ahead, what's around the next turn, when fear and uncertainty try to take over, that's when my heart says I will not fear, my God will lead me in the right direction.

The greatest assurance in our life comes from the absolute certainty that we are loved by God and while there may be times when waves of discouragement try to crash over us, God is faithful and greater than it is! His Spirit is in you!

During these times, the Lord will remind us, "Never forget that My Spirit is in you and with you. Ready to strengthen, sustain, love, and guide you. When you're slipping, lean on me. Not just I've got this, I've got you!"

I declare He will rescue you, carry you, and hold you up. Even more than that, He is getting ready to amaze you! Keep trusting in Him and watch what He can do. Believe it and receive it today.

"Fear not, for I have redeemed you; I have called you by your name; YOU ARE MINE!" When you pass through the waters, I will be with you; And through the rivers, they shall not overflow you. When you walk through the fire, you shall not be burned, Nor shall the flame scorch you. For I am the LORD your God, The Holy One of Israel, your Savior..."
Isaiah 43:1-3 NKJV

DAY 265

In the midst of life, words and opinions can echo through our minds and hearts and influence us in so many ways. They said this, they think this, he said, or she said, even the voices in our own heads and hearts condemning us.

Naomi, in the book of Ruth, went through a season like this. Naomi means pleasant, joyful. But after her season of loss, she said, don't call me Naomi anymore, call me Mara, or bitter.

Don't let the hard times in life make you change your name! God doesn't call you by your shame or by your pain. He calls you by your name. He calls you beloved, redeemed, precious, son, daughter, king, family, overcomer, creative, anointed, talented, made in God's image, and graced to succeed!

So, you may be experiencing difficulties or just going through a lot right now, but whatever you are going through has an ending, your desert will bloom again! Stay true to the God birthed you! Believe that no matter what has come against you, and no matter how unfair it was, things can and will shift in your favor. Keep dreaming bigger than anything you are qualified to do. God-sized dreams require faith and total trust in Him. So, today is a great day to remember; your future is as bright as the promises of God!

"For we are God's masterpiece. He has created us anew in Christ Jesus, so we can do the good things he planned for us long ago."
Ephesians 2:10 NLT

DAY 266

Life-Giving Power Points

1. There can be a big difference in what people say to you and what they say about you- discern.

2. People that are highly critical of others to you will also be highly critical of you to others.

3. Great opportunities can be hidden in very common tasks. Never despise the seasons of "small things."

4. There is only one person you spend your whole life with, and that is you. If you aren't ok with you, there is going to be a problem with everybody else.

5. Our destiny is not just a place but a new way of seeing things.

6. The cure for every frustration is found at the feet of Jesus.

7. Always be more impressed with your God than you are your problems.

8. Happiness is not a state of being; it's a state of thanking! Gratitude is the seed for increase.

9. Your most effective ministry will come out of your deepest hurts. If you're hurting, hold on! You're about to have an awesome message when you get through this mess.

10. You can grow up in the church but not grow up in Him. Revelation is not powerful until it becomes personal.

DAY 267

Many times, in life, the attacks become greater because the blessing is getting closer. The anointing that's on your life attracts attacks! Don't look at it as trouble; look at it as confirmation! You're getting closer, so close, don't you dare give up and quit when things get ugly. There is beauty at the end of the struggle! Many times, your ministry will be where your misery has been!

The chapters of your life are still being written by the hand of God and in spite of the trials, the transition is powerful because it announces the fact that a new season of fruitfulness is on its way. Through it all, God is there to pull you out, carry you through, lift you up, lead the way, and get you through the attacks and storms! The greater the battle, the greater the triumph!

So, when you feel like giving up, remember, the greatest man ever to live is continually interceding for you before God's throne. He loves you!

"Therefore He is also able to save to the uttermost those who come to God through Him, since He always lives to make intercession for them."
Hebrews 7:25 NKJV

DAY 268

Here are some life journey affirmations!

I affirm today that the joy of the Lord is my strength. I've been blessed and fortified in Christ Jesus with everything I need for life and godliness. I walk in God's glory, pleasing Him in all things, and prospering in every good work. The Spirit of God is making my life pleasant; therefore, in every season, I am a fruitful land, a tree of righteousness, producing fruits of righteousness! Freedom belongs to me! Wholeness belongs to me!

I have God's DNA; therefore, success is my birthright, excellence is my calling, and winning is my lifestyle. No weapon formed against me will prosper!

I am a new creation in Christ Jesus, the seed of Abraham, and an heir according to the promise. I live perpetually in the peace and rest of God because "In Christ Jesus" is my address! I have been ordained to excel, win, and make progress without continual stress and anxiety!

My life is in sync and aligned with God's will, purpose, and direction for me. I am fulfilling His perfect will and bringing Him glory in all things. I am energized and empowered for victory, restoration, and increase by the Spirit of God who lives in me!

The Spirit of love, power, and of a sound mind indwells me; therefore, my mind is sound, filled with divine insight, and I am excellent in all things! The eyes of my understanding are enlightened. I see the invisible and I am empowered to do the impossible!

DAY 269

There is no cure for past pain like present desire. So, whether we're exhausted by our victories or discouraged by our losses, we must always allow God to draw us back to Himself, to allow Him to rekindle within us a desire to be all He wants us to be. In God, our next can be better than our now.

Faithfulness is not a feeling; it is a choice we can make even in the midst of great frustration. The strength of our faith is directly related to our willingness to apply it in places we do not fully understand yet. Sometimes, today's events may not be fully understood until tomorrow. It can feel discouraging when we look around and it seems like others aren't going through things like we are, but it feels that way because we compare our behind-the-scenes with everyone else's highlight reel!

So, remember, the storms of life are continually changing, but your great God remains the same. He is consistent and reliable. While storms are inevitable, your anchor is immovable! God is with you in all things and He has already created a solution to every problem you will ever face. There's never any moment God is not with you. There's never a moment He doesn't love you or His grace and favor aren't extended towards you.

"So we are convinced that every detail of our lives is continually woven together to fit into God's perfect plan of bringing good into our lives, for we are his lovers who have been called to fulfill his designed purpose."
Romans 8:28 TPT

DAY 270

Everything doesn't have to be perfect in our life for life to be good. What happens along the way turns out to be more meaningful and fulfilling than the end result because of who we become and what we experience along the way. The triumph of genuine faith is not that we have run the race perfectly or never made a mistake. Our faith is proven genuine when we have learned through all of life's ups and downs to depend on Jesus. Great faith is fixing our eyes on Jesus and continuing on in spite of what we don't understand.

How you perform when you're "feeling it" is not as important as how you perform when you're not feeling it. Faith and discipline will carry you when you're not "feeling it." Whether it's in business, marriage, ministry, or any part of life, if you wait for feeling, you might be waiting a long time. If you want to manifest your destiny, you will have to move forward without knowing all the details. By trusting God with each step forward, there will be provision, there will be favor, and there will be opportunities.

I'm convinced we don't give up because it's hard, we give up because we get discouraged and disillusioned. That's why it's so important to encourage ourselves and others. So, join me today, let's all keep our eyes on Him, our head up, our hearts filled with love, our hands reaching out in compassion, and our mouth filled with the promises of God!

"Fixing our eyes on Jesus, the pioneer and perfecter of faith."
Hebrews 12:2 NIV

DAY 271

The daily grind of life can take its toll. We can feel overwhelmed. Feelings are only indicators they do not have to be dictators! They can remind us that there are things that need to be addressed in our lives, but they can also deceive us into quitting. When we are tired, weary, and facing the prospect of just totally backing off, we need to remember why. When we lose our why, we lose our way. We don't get burned out because of what we do. We get burned out because we forget why we do it. Our why connects with our purpose and keeps us fresh and energized.

Remember you why? Because you are needed. You are needed in your church. You are needed in your community. You are needed in your family. You are needed in your ministry. You are needed in that place of prayer. You are needed in that place of caring. You are needed in that place of giving and loving. You are needed in this world. You are needed in so many ways. If you weren't needed, God would not have created you. You are here to make a contribution with your life.

You are chosen and placed for such a time as this. Your life matters, and you are making a difference. Today needs you, tomorrow needs you, and there are things that are yet to happen and people you are yet to meet that need you!

"I thank my God upon every remembrance of you, always in every
prayer of mine making request for you all with joy,"
Philippians 1:3-4 NKJV

DAY 272

Life is a journey and change is a natural part of the process. As we age and mature, our perspectives change. The longer we walk with Him, the more we begin to discover what really matters and why it matters. It's all based on how honest we are willing to be with ourselves and how open we are to being a continual learner. The most impactful and fulfilled people are those who recognize they have much to do, a lot to learn, and at the same time, nothing to prove. Real-life is always accomplished 'inside out'! While it is not always comfortable to come face to face with truth in any area of our lives, it's so worth it because God's desire in all of it is that we are truly free. Jesus said, "You'll know the truth and the truth shall make you free." Walking in truth is seeing everything we face through His eyes and perspective. This is how old cycles are broken and new hope rises up. Cycles of hopelessness, despair, and depression will no longer reign in your life as truth triumphs.

So, if you want to keep advancing into the promises of God, you must constantly choose to make what Jesus said about you and what He did for you, greater than what people said to you, said about you, thought about you, think about you, did to you, and did not do for you. Every wall that's been holding you back will come tumbling down in the face of the reality of God's love and truth. I'm praying over you in faith today that God is about to disappoint your haters, confuse your attackers, reward your supporters, and shower you with favor for your future!

"Jesus said to those Jews who believed in him, "When you continue to embrace all that I teach, you prove that you are my true followers. For if you embrace the truth, it will release true freedom into your lives."
John 8:31-32 TPT

DAY 273

"You will find true success when you find me, for I have insight into wise plans that are designed JUST FOR YOU. I hold in my hands living-understanding, courage, and strength."
Proverbs 8:14 TPT

God never intended success to be an end, a satisfier, or the ultimate aim in life. Success was meant to give us credibility and provide a platform to influence others to reach forward, to be part of an abundant life, to be a witness to the faithfulness of God. Our elevation is about God's agenda for our lives and purpose. Godly success is good and brings no sorrow with it. (Proverbs 10:22) Along the way, we get to enjoy the blessings that come with following the journey as He leads us forward.

But you will experience some rainy days on this journey. It rains on everybody, the just and unjust. Sometimes we have to realize that life is not about trying to "stay dry" in the rainy days of our life., it's learning how to dance in the rain, to rejoice as we remind our problems who our great God is.

So today, I pray you will know that you are God's chosen vessel, captured by His grace for such a time as this. You matter. You are needed. Your Godly influence is needed. Continue to move forward by faith into a new system in your life. Your strength is found as you move forward. Your destiny is found as you move forward. Your purpose is found as you move forward. Your passion is found as you move forward. You're not an accident. You are not a mistake. You are loved and God has a purpose for your success! Forward in faith!

DAY 274

There is only so much of us to go around, only so many hours in the day, and only so much we can give ourselves to at any given time and moment. What we devote our time, energy, emotions, and focus to are so important. Wrong focus leads to wrong attitudes, wrong emotions, wrong words, wrong thinking, wrong habits, and diminished opportunities. Thoughts and words have energy. Don't entertain continual negativity. If the enemy can't stop us, he'll distract us. Let's use our faith and energy to increase our Godly dominion and influence, not trying to diminish and put others down. What someone else is doing or not doing isn't worthy of forfeiting our lives or delaying our destiny. Don't spend decades obsessing over who rejected you. Spend your years rejoicing in God's acceptance of you in Christ.

If we want to live a life that is energized and renewed on a daily basis, we should focus on who your God is and who you are in Him, not what you aren't, and not on what other people are or aren't. Focus on what you can do through Him, not what you can't, not on what other people are doing or not doing. Focus on what you do have, not what you don't, not on what others have or don't have or whether or not you think they deserve it. God doesn't have to cheat me to bless you. What you do with what you have is more important than what you have. So, don't let the position of others determine who you are. You are an original, one of a kind, special in ways no one else is, graced with special gifts. In Christ, you are smart, creative, anointed, talented, filled with powerful potential, made in God's image, and graced to succeed.

"So keep your thoughts continually fixed on all that is authentic and real, honorable and admirable, beautiful and respectful, pure and holy, merciful and kind. And fasten your thoughts on every glorious work of God, praising him always."
Philippians 4:8 TPT

DAY 275

"Father, I declare Your blessings over my life. Thank You for the transformation in my thoughts, in my ways, and in my actions, that I may see an explosion of Your goodness. I will experience the surpassing greatness of Your favor. I will experience Your faithfulness. I won't worry or doubt. I will keep my trust in You, knowing that You will never fail. May I give birth to every promise you have placed in my heart and become everything You've designed me to be. I pray that my life will be marked by the very presence of Him who causes all things to work together for my good and His glory, that my body is healed and my youth is renewed, that great things are coming my way and God is working to fulfill and give me the desires of my heart.

I pray for the right doors to open, wrong doors to close, new opportunities, increased vision, divine connections, the right people that will make a positive impact on my life for my future.

Father, I will use the breath you have blessed me with to bless and honor You and anyone else I encounter. Thank You for awesome god moments, life-changing turnarounds, overcoming obstacles, and supernatural favor coming my way. By faith, I declare, my greatest days begin today. Your word is a lamp to my feet and a light to my path! Thank you, Jesus!

"But we thank God for giving us the victory as conquerors through our Lord Jesus, the Anointed One. So now, beloved ones, stand firm, stable, and enduring. Live your lives with an unshakable confidence. We know that we prosper and excel in every season by serving the Lord, because we are assured that our union with the Lord makes our labor productive with fruit that endures."
1 Corinthians 15:57-58 TPT

DAY 276

It's so important and vital to respond correctly when we are wounded or hurt or feel let down by others. Expecting people to always do what we would do is a set up for disappointment and frustration. We must never allow our hurts and disappointments to establish our thoughts, our futures, or our focus.

Our minds are like magnifying glasses, whatever we focus our attention on becomes bigger and more dominant in our lives. Holding on to hurt and disappointment is costly because it takes us on a course change internally that leaves God's path for our lives.

There will always be people who are against you, don't believe in you, or who will be here for you one day but not the next. We must keep our eyes and focus on God and not people. If you stay focused on the people that left you, you'll never appreciate the ones who stayed.

Genesis tells the story of Joseph, who lived a God-dependent life. He lived it in the midst of great adversity and hatred from his own family, but he knew the Lord held his future.

We have to learn how to give people to God because if we don't, it's going to poison us and our futures. You can't get fresh water from a bitter well. While forgiving may not change the past, it opens up an extraordinary future! In the frustrating seasons of life, hold on to this revelation, "God is good, and He is for me."

"Brethren, I do not count myself to have apprehended; but one thing I do, forgetting those things which are behind and reaching forward to those things which are ahead, I press toward the goal for the prize of the upward call of God in Christ Jesus."
Philippians 3:13-14 NKJV

DAY 277

"For I know the thoughts that I think toward you, says the LORD,
thoughts of peace and not of evil, to give you a future and a HOPE."
Jeremiah 29:11 NKJV

Jesus came into the world to deliver us from desperate, meaningless lives. He came to give us hope and a sense of well-being. When your heart gets heavy and your hopes seem dim, it's good to step back and take a minute to put everything in perspective.

Jesus, you carried me this far, and when all else fades and disappoints, I'll continue to hold onto this hope in my heart because You remain my faithful God. You carried me when I didn't have the strength to go on; You picked me up when I stumbled and fell, you never gave up on me, you never quit on me when others did.

"Thank You, Lord, for this new day. Touch every person reading this today and give them hope for their future! Renew their vision. Strengthen and refresh them with your unfailing love. Stir their imagination with a vision of possibilities. With You, what is broken can be fixed, what is closed can be opened, and what is lost can be recovered! The day may be filled with many uncertainties, but there is always one certainty, my God loves me, and He still reigns!"

"Now may God, the inspiration and fountain of hope, fill you to over-
flowing with uncontainable joy and perfect peace as you trust in him.
And may the power of the Holy Spirit continually surround your life
with his super-abundance until you radiate with hope!"
Romans 15:13 TPT

DAY 278

Our God is not outdated and boring. He is not dreary and drab. He is not harsh and mean. Our God is love. Our God is breath-taking! He is majestic, powerful, and engaging! There should be a sense of awe about Him. He is awesome and glorious. He loves to bring possibilities to places of impossibility. It is His pleasure and delight to step into all that we are not with all that He is! Proclaiming God's ability shifts our viewpoint. We stop seeing through the lens of our inadequacy and start looking through the lens of what our great God is capable of and what He can do through us.

Joshua and Caleb saw giants in the promised land just like the other ten did but said: "We are well able." They were willing to step out and go exploring with God in their future. Saying 'Yes' to God's prophetic promise for us is a powerful first step to seeing that promise fulfilled.

After the death of Moses in the time of great transition as Joshua stood on the verge of the Promised Land, God spoke to him and let him know that He was with Him and for him.

"Have I not commanded you? Be strong and courageous. Do not be afraid; do not be discouraged, for the Lord your God will be with you wherever you go."

Joshua 1:9

Our great God is with us and for us, just like He was with Joshua. God is not finished with us and He has not given up on us. He has not turned His back on us and His purpose for our life has not been abandoned. There are days ahead of us that are going to be filled with satisfaction and fulfillment. Goodness and mercy are following us and His plans are to bless us, prosper us, and not harm us. Here we go, step by step into God's best!

DAY 279

There's a revelation of God and an understanding of yourself that you will receive in times of stretching that you could not receive any other way. Who is God to you right now? Are you being extended to your limits? Hear your Father say, "Know that you are not going to break. You will see the miracle of enlargement."

Every challenge is an invitation to prepare for the fullness of our inheritance in Him. We grow into what we're called into. In order to grow into your calling, you will face times of stretching again and again. These are points of decision, orchestrated by the Holy Spirit, in which you have the opportunity to follow and obey God's direction and call on your life.

Circumstances stretch us beyond our current limitations and expand our capacity to perceive and think more like Jesus. I pray we say yes to the greatness that is calling us to stretch beyond the comfort of our familiar. It should be the intention of every generation to live full and die empty, to stop living our life in reserve for a day that may never come. We have circled this mountain long enough. It's time to take new territory. Let's step out, step forward, and stretch out our life and future to Him today.

"Sing, O barren, thou that didst not bear; break forth into singing, and cry aloud, thou that didst not travail with child: for more are the children of the desolate than the children of the married wife, saith the Lord. Enlarge the place of thy tent, and let them stretch forth the curtains of thine habitations: spare not, lengthen thy cords, and strengthen thy stakes; For thou shalt break forth on the right hand and on the left; and thy seed shall inherit the Gentiles, and make the desolate cities to be inhabited."
Isaiah 54:1-3 NKJV

DAY 280

Relationships are so important. They have the potential to bring so much real value to our lives. You will never have a truly significant life without deep spiritual relationships. Material possessions will ultimately not give us the satisfaction we are looking for. The only things of real value in this life are our relationships with our Heavenly Father and each other. The truth is, most people want to have great relationships but have been disappointed and wounded early in life and can miss the blessings Godly relationships bring.

The love that God has called us to is to consider people as precious, hold them in high regard, and allow our lives to "sharpen" one another. It means we have the opportunity and need to grow and change. Real spiritual growth doesn't just happen in the prayer closet. Praying is a vital step of growth, but real growth only happens in the application. Faith without works is dead. It's one thing to pray for others and pray for yourself to grow, but it's another level of true spirituality to walk alongside others through life. If we can truly believe for others to benefit from our lives and take great joy in them being blessed and becoming the best they can be our lives are so much richer. Find some people that you genuinely celebrate and who will genuinely celebrate your blessings, not take pleasure in you languishing in your pain. Your relationships will prosper and be blessed, and you will taste and see the goodness of God in the land of the living.

"So, our dear brothers and sisters, in the midst of all our distress and difficulties, your steadfastness of faith has greatly encouraged our hearts. We feel alive again as long as we know that you are standing firm in the Lord. How could we ever thank God enough for all the wonderful joy that we feel before our God because of you?"
1 Thessalonians 3:7-9 TPT

DAY 281

The main theme in the book of Exodus is God delivering His people out of Egypt. The word "to go out" in Hebrew is "yatsa" which means to come out, to go forth, to go forward, to lead out, and to deliver.

We can feel trapped sometimes. The "Pharaohs" in our life don't like letting us go. They fear our freedom. But we have promises from God. In Exodus, it was the blood of the Passover Lamb that protected the Israelites from the destroying angel. God also told them that they would not leave the land empty-handed. As they left, God caused Israel's enemies to hand over silver and gold for their journey as they set them free. When Pharaoh changed his mind again later and wanted his slaves back, God saved them again, splitting the Red Sea and making a path for them to walk through on dry land.

Today, it is the blood of Jesus, the lamb of God that covers us, keeps us, redeems us, and births our future. Jesus exchanged our death for His eternal and abundant life. This is a new day full of new mercies for us. Pharaoh no longer has authority in our life. Yesterday may have worn you out or brought you down, but God will lift your spirit today as you look to Him. You will leave that challenge and you're not leaving empty-handed! For every step of faith you have taken, in the face of tremendous pressure, God is going to pour out a blessing that you don't have room enough to receive! May He lead you out and take you in! Thank you, Father, for your faithful vision and provision in our lives!

"You will be the inner strength of all your people, the mighty protector of all, the saving strength for all your anointed ones. Keep protecting and cherishing your chosen ones; in you they will never fall. Like a shepherd going before us, keep leading us forward, forever carrying us in your arms!"
Psalms 28:8-9 TPT

DAY 282

Today, I pray that any negative words you or others have spoken over your life are broken in the name of Jesus. I pray for strength, guidance, energy, love, and comfort. That through the good and the bad, you will continue to move forward! I pray our Father will rescue you, carry you, and sustain you and that He is getting ready to amaze you!

I pray as you go through the day, you will intentionally forget what lies behind and commit to press forward into the future God planned for you. I pray that you are blessed with God's divine purpose and perfect plan for your life and that you are blessed with the strength of character, favor, and fulfillment! May His favor open and escort you through open doors!

Your deliverance is coming. Delay is not denial! Your breakthrough is on the way! Yes, Lord!

"For the mountains may move and the hills disappear, but even then my faithful love for you will remain. My covenant of blessing will never be broken," says the LORD, who has mercy on you."
Isaiah 54:10 NLT

DAY 283

I want to remind you today that you never have to face another day alone. Even when it feels like you are alone in the battle, know and declare, "God is always with me!" Feeling like you're alone in the battle is a lie!

When people reject us, it's easy to think God does too. There won't always be people who understand, to turn to every day, but no one will ever love you more than Jesus does, and you can always turn to Him. The weather changes, governments change, people change, circumstances of life change, relationships change, your body changes, but have hope because Jesus never changes!

So when the world around you seems out of control, God is still in control. Whatever circumstances you may find yourself enduring today, know that God's got this, and He's got you! Keep your head up, your heart open, your mouth filled with the promises of God, and your eyes on JESUS!

"Looking unto Jesus, the author and finisher of our faith, who for the joy that was set before Him endured the cross, despising the shame, and has sat down at the right hand of the throne of God."
Hebrews 12:2 NKJV

DAY 284

Don't let your troubles convince you things will never get any better. You are made for more and you have seeds of greatness on the inside. It doesn't matter if you are moving inch by inch or foot by foot; the key is to keep moving in the right direction. Ask Father God to order your steps and stay in faith.

Remember, something good is happening in your life even when you can't see it yet. God has lined up solutions for you. That very thing the enemy has stolen from you is what God is going to use as a powerful weapon. He is the God of the turn-around. The Lord of breakthrough is your Father and your harvest is being released! Let God do the revealing in His timing. Through it all He is always there for us. In every season, He is our forever faithful Father!

"All God accomplishes is flawless, faithful, and fair, and his every
word proves trustworthy and true. They are steadfast forever and ever,
formed from truth and righteousness. His forever-love paid a full ransom
for his people so that now we're free to come before Jehovah to worship his
holy and awesome name!"
Psalms 111:7-9 TPT

DAY 285

We overcome when we love more than others think is wise, risk more than others think is safe, and dream more than others think is practical. We should always expect more than others think is possible because God is a God of the impossible!

I proclaim over you today, "There's favor in your future. There's healing in your future. There's provision in your future. Something good is in your future because God is in your future!"

I pray that as you look toward your future, you are filled with hope and expectation because You know the plans God has for you and you rest in that promise! I pray you are filled with great thoughts for your future that your heart beats with deep feelings of hope and great anticipation of what God is doing and will do! I pray you won't let your vision die just because time has passed, that God's presence will keep it alive and fresh, believing that this could be the day, the week, the season where those things and even greater things begin to happen! I pray that your future is full of supernatural help, supernatural provision, miracles, and God birthed surprises.

Thank you, Lord, for a future filled with breakthroughs, divine intervention, God birthed suddenlies, and supernatural turnarounds. Through Christ Jesus our Lord, Amen!

"Not one promise from God is empty of power, for nothing is impossible with God!"
Luke 1:37 TPT

DAY 286

I want to make some bold and faith-filled prayers and declarations over you today.

God is shifting things in your favor. He will cause opportunity to find you. He has unexpected blessings waiting for you. Nothing can stop the blessing of God in your life. What God has blessed, no one or nothing can curse. I'm believing and expecting His blessing for you today. Expect the best today!

"Bring quickly the best robe, and put it on him."
Luke 15:22 ESV

You are God's child. He wants the best for you!

No weapon formed against your life shall prosper! Declare over yourself today that your life will be a walking billboard of testimonies and possibilities. The wind sent to stop you is actually pushing you into your assignment. You shall refuse to sit down and give up. The enemy has engaged an all-out war against you to bring discouragement and defeat, but God is sending angelic reinforcements to your defense.

The Lord's presence is with you today. He loves you, cheers you on, walks with you, and carries you when you don't have the strength to go on. With your God, what is broken will be fixed. What is closed will be opened. What is lost will be recovered.

"God is not a man, that He should lie, Nor a son of man, that He should repent. Has He said, and will He not do? Or has He spoken, and will He not make it good? Behold, I have received a command to bless; He has blessed, and I cannot reverse it."
Numbers 23:19-20 NKJV

DAY 287

When God speaks to you about your future, He is speaking to the manifestation of what He put in you that sometimes you don't even know is there. He is calling things that be not as though they were, calling the greatness that is in you out of you, so it manifests in your life.

"God called Abraham what he wasn't, but he became what God called him. Because "Abraham believed in the God who brings the dead back to life and who creates new things out of nothing."

Romans 4:17 NLT

The angel of the Lord called Gideon a mighty man of valor. Gideon said, "No way, you got the wrong guy. I am the least in my family, and my family is the least family in our tribe, and our tribe is the least." But he didn't know how God saw him. God speaks to who we are created to be. We grow into our calling.

God chose you in Christ long before the earth came into existence. He has a plan and you are part of it. In Christ, you are a carrier of greatness, the temple of the most high God, fearfully and wonderfully made! You will never rise higher than the picture you have on the inside. Revelation brings exaltation!

The DNA of your destiny is embedded in your identity. Know who you are in Christ, and your destiny will discover you! Though I don't know what your future holds, I do know who holds your future. As you see, hear, and feel God's spirit, you will abandon the lies of the enemy and embrace the revelation of who He has created you to be! God can take our ordinary and make it something extraordinary!

DAY 288

We all have had setbacks and unfair things happen in our lives. But God is working to turn it around!

God is making things happen for you! Even if you don't see it, can't feel it, or it is not evident. He's answering prayers now that you prayed last year! It may not have happened in the past, but God has favored for your future. Disappointments are only for a season, but God's favor is for a lifetime. You may have been overlooked, disrespected, lied about, and abandoned, but God says you're coming back stronger, wiser, and with authority.

So, get up! Get out! Get stirred up! And get going! Your life story is still being written and God's hand is guiding you! While you're believing for your miracle, take advantage of your opportunities! Long distances are covered one step at a time and big miracles sometimes take place one small miracle at a time! Remember, your God is amazing. You are amazing. This year is going to be amazing because of God's amazing grace and faithfulness! And to everything that rises against you to try to limit you and intimidate you, make this powerful declaration, "But God!"

Remember this promise.

"Instead of shame and dishonor, you will enjoy a double share of honor. You will possess a double portion of prosperity in your land, and everlasting joy will be yours."
Isaiah 61:7 NLT

DAY 289

Power Points for abundant living

1. Integrity and self-respect are about doing your best when no one notices, cares, or does likewise.
2. Sometimes God gives answers directly. But most times, He initiates a process, leading us on a journey, not just a destination.
3. The gospel is not only your promise of forgiveness and your guarantee of a future, but also a lens to look through at everything in life.
4. Do not fight battles with small-minded people. Your dreams and destiny are too great to be distracted. Please understand that everybody can't go where God is sending you.
5. Our past doesn't define us. God and His Word does.
6. Your mind believes your mouth. It conforms to verbal authority. What you speak, the heart and mind embraces.
7. Expecting others to always do right because you do right is like expecting a lion not to eat us because we didn't eat him.
8. Most of the meaningful things in our lives aren't created instantly or overnight, they take time. They're not just the results of what we do in the spotlight but what we do when no one else is around to pat us on the back.
9. Sometimes, nobody really understands what you are going through except God. He is always available to listen to you, help you get through, heal your heart, and make you whole.
10. Never measure life by your possessions. Measure it by the hearts you touched, the smiles you created, and the love you shared.

DAY 290

After God created Adam and Eve, the first thing He did was "He blessed them and said, "Be fruitful and multiply. Fill the earth and rule it." Genesis 1:28. Being blessed is not being selfish; it's God's idea! It's God's will for your life! To "bless" means to empower to succeed. It's necessary to fulfill God's purpose for your life. It empowers us and equips us to do what God calls us to do. We are blessed to be a blessing. It's a life of empowerment, a life of victory, a life of increase, and a life of impact and being a blessing.

Living in the blessing is when your body is getting better because the same Spirit that raised Jesus from the dead lives in you. Living in the blessing is when you get stronger and have vision for the future even when you get older. Living in the blessing is having the right thing to say at the right time because the Holy Spirit is your guide. Living in the blessing is making an impact in the lives of those around you, having God's favor surrounding you like a shield and having God's power to deal with whatever life throws at you.

So today, do what Jabez did, ask and receive! He is a great example for us of someone who made a choice to live in the blessing. His name means "pain!" (1 Chronicles 4:9). His family had named and sentenced him to a life of pain. But he didn't let his pain define him. He made a choice. He refused to accept a life of cursing and pain. So, he prayed boldly, "Oh that you would bless me indeed!" Jesus paid for it. Now let's receive it. God Bless you!

"So that his name may be honored forever! May the fame of his name spring forth! May it shine on, like the sunshine! In him all will be blessed to bless others, and may all the people bless the One who blessed them."
Psalms 72:17 TPT

DAY 291

Father, today I pray for an outpouring of your goodness, an overflow of your blessing, and an overdose of your grace to all your children. I pray they will be free from depression, anxiety, debts, toxic relationships, sickness, guilt, and shame. I pray for divine connections, abundance, and prosperity in all things, spirit, soul, and body. I speak to every mountain of fear, discouragement, stress, depression, and lack, "Be removed and cast into the sea in Jesus' name!"

Today I pray God's grace strengthens you. His word heals you. His love drives out all fear! I pray that God opens a door of supernatural favor for you in the name of Jesus; it's time! May every step you take be guided by the Spirit of the Lord. I pray the LORD's peace and protection over you and your family. Thank you, Lord, for renewed passion and vision in the hearts of your people today. May they be refreshed, renewed, and re-energized by Your presence!

I pray you will put your trust in God and in the great future He has already put in motion for you, that you will have an assurance that things are happening behind the scenes that you can't always see. I pray you will keep dreaming, keep believing, and keep celebrating each step of victory, knowing that God is faithful! In Jesus' name, Amen!

"Trust in the Lord with all your heart, and do not lean on your own understanding. In all your ways acknowledge him, and he will make straight your paths."
Proverbs 3:5-6 ESV

DAY 292

As we go through the day, let's try to keep our eyes on Jesus, surrender to the Spirit more than to our fears, be quicker to forgive than criticize, give more encouragement than advice, and kingdom dream more than we daydream. Let's use our tongue to bring joy, peace, and happiness into the lives of others, thank others for their friendship, encourage those who are struggling, and tell others of your love for them. Every word we speak can be a brick to build with or a bulldozer to destroy.

May we remember that great relationships aren't built in a day; they are built daily. Most of all, use our words and attitude to honor God.

Decree over yourself, "I take courage today because Jesus has overcome the world; therefore, I also have overcome the world. I will no longer be a victim of life, but rather a victor over life. What happens to me will be transformed by what happens in me, in Jesus' name!"

"Stop imitating the ideals and opinions of the culture around you, but be inwardly transformed by the Holy Spirit through a total reformation of how you think. This will empower you to discern God's will as you live a beautiful life, satisfying and perfect in his eyes."
Romans 12:2 TPT

DAY 293

Everyone deals with personal pain on some level. But just as pain is personal, so is Jesus. He was and still is touchable.

"For we have not a high priest which cannot be touched with the feeling of our infirmities..."
Hebrews 4:15 KJV

I've learned and am still learning whatever the depths of our personal pain; it is possible to be raised up. It is possible to heal. It is possible to forgive. It is possible to love and live again. Even when it's my own mess I've made, the Lord still makes a way! Therefore, no matter who or what tries to knock you down, it is important for you to know that God will always embrace you, hold you, and help you get back up again. He is the God who restores emotionally, mentally, physically, financially, and relationally.

"Thank you, Lord, for touching, raising up, and restoring every person reading this and filling them with love, hope, peace, and strength and turning any disappointment into fulfillment. We look to you Lord; our eyes are on you."

"Arise, shine, for your light has come, and the glory of the Lord rises upon you."
Isaiah 60:1 NIV

DAY 294

Just because the past has been painful doesn't mean the future has to be. There is more ahead of you than anything behind you! Let God's grace rewrite the story of your life. Trust God to restore and bring you out better. Even in the midst of difficulty, abundant supply of Kingdom possibilities are unlocking and breaking open as you say *yes* to the future from a faith perspective.

I am praying for a divine shift to begin in your life, a future marked by blessing, prosperity, favor, and filled with divine opportunities! Dream big, but don't be afraid to start small! Let doors open for you that no one can shut. Whatever held up blessings that belong to you, I command the unconditional release in Jesus' name! Every battle you have to fight is an opportunity for the glory of God to be revealed. The greater the obstacles, the greater the victory!

So, I believe that your season will shift! Stand in faith today and know weeping endures for the night, but joy comes in the morning. You are who God says you are, and you will do what God says you will do. You are loved. You are wonderfully made. You are precious. You have purpose. You are a masterpiece. God has a great plan for you. He said so!

"The Lord will fulfill his purpose for me; your steadfast love, O Lord, endures forever."

Psalm 138:8 ESV

DAY 295

Every day's obstacles can feel so overwhelming. What we see tries to demand our emotional and mental energy and focus. To know and believe that God is working in unseen realms at times seems so foolish. But for the believer, there is an unseen world that can only be accessed through the eyes of faith. Our destinies and God's promises to us are tied to our willingness to hear and see the things others can't, to believe that more is happening supernaturally than is happening in our circumstances, and then step out in faith on nothing more than a word and vision from God.

In Genesis 13, Lot had just turned his back on Abraham and walked away. Abraham had treated him like a son and had given him everything, and Lot had washed his hands of their relationship and walked out. Abraham could have given up; he could have cried out to God. What did God tell Abraham during this time? The Lord said to Abram, after Lot had separated from him: "Lift up your eyes now and look from the place where you are; northward, southward, eastward, and westward; for all the land which you see I give to you and your descendants forever." Genesis 13: 14-15

Just like Abraham, God has things prepared for you. Stop focusing on what "wasn't," on what is, and by faith, start focusing on what will be. Even if you lost the last battle, it doesn't mean you've lost the war. There are still mountains to climb and things worth fighting the fight of faith in your life. Your future days can be greater than your former as you lift up your eyes of faith today. God is expanding you past the things you once believed to be your limits into a broader land. There are God-ordained suddenlies awaiting you. Suddenly, opportunities that were not available are available, doors that had been closed and locked tight open wide, and increase is released on an unprecedented level! Father let your suddenlies be released into your people's lives today!

DAY 296

The battlefield on which many of us fight our fiercest wars is not out in the world, it's between our ears. Our thoughts and imagination make us or break us. When we dwell on negative thoughts, we're using our faith, but we're using it in reverse.

The devil is not just a liar, he is the father of lies. He wants us to believe lies about the truth by telling half-truths, which makes it sound true. The enemy's lie is, "You're finished, burned out, used up, replaced, forgotten, left out, too much this or too little that." Never look at yourself as insignificant or tossed to the side. God has a powerful way of using those that feel passed over and called nobodies. Never think what you have to offer doesn't matter. God designed you on purpose for a purpose. Just be who you are in Christ. You are unique and your gift will be distinctive. God uses people of every personality type to achieve His will.

The TRUTH is, "I don't have to stay where I am. I refuse to be a victim of my circumstances because I am a victor over my circumstances. I am not my past, I am not my failures, I am not what happened to me. I am not who they say I am. I am not the label they put on me. I am loved and valued by the creator of the universe. I am in for an abundant supply of grace that is headed my way. The enemy that has tried to intimidate me is losing the battle. The Prince of Peace lives in me! Therefore, I will not stress out, burn out, or freak out! The battle is already won."

"We can demolish every deceptive fantasy that opposes God and break through every arrogant attitude that is raised up in defiance of the true knowledge of God. We capture, like prisoners of war, every thought and insist that it bow in obedience to the Anointed One."
2 Corinthians 10:5 TPT

DAY 297

Who do men say that I am, who do you say that I am? That's the question Jesus asked his disciples and it birthed a moment of profound revelation on Peter's part. It still echoes to us today. Who does He want to be to us now? How does He want to be known in our lives today? What amazing and life-changing part of himself does He want to become a reality for us as we face our day and future?

What if we stopped being so self-conscious and became more God-conscious, aware that there is still so much more of who He is that we need to embrace.

Who God is and what He has given us in Christ is more than enough to face what life has not given us or throws at us and He wants us to see it. Don't think you have discovered everything about Him yet. He can reveal himself in personal ways to you that are beyond your imagination. He can and I believe He will!

The truth is, there is always more, more joy, more hope, more comfort, more goodness, more Jesus, more of who He is that we need to know Him today. Our question to Him should be, Father, who do you want to be to me today? He is love, comfort, grace, strength, healing, provision, abundance, hope, insight, peace, assurance, understanding, favor, creator, wisdom, power, security, protection, defender, guidance, increase, sustainer, rest, deliverer, and so much more.

"Holy Spirit reveal every aspect of who you want us to know you as today. As You do, we thank you that we will grow in the knowledge of who You are, grow in the knowledge of your plans for us, and our identity and security will become unshakable. We shall taste and see and experience the goodness of our God. Thank you, Jesus."

DAY 298

God is a visionary God. As God's sons and daughters, we have been given the profound ability and responsibility to grow, dream, increase, and expect. There is so much more for us. Don't accept limitations and restrictions God never intended. We are created to grow, expand, and make progress in every season of our life. We don't have to live small, restricted, and shut down. We can live with a full expectation of God's leading, guiding, and broadening our boundaries.

This is not just a pep talk. We need to continually engage emotionally in life, to build ourselves up on every level, spiritually, emotionally, mentally, and physically. Love your story enough to take good care of yourself, to make healthy choices, to rest well, to honor the house you live in, and to trust that God makes a difference in your physical, emotional, and spiritual life.

It's not about just being busy; it's about embracing the things that will cause you to grow. You don't grow physically by looking at the weights, you take hold and you press through the resistance to grow.

I love how the psalmist sees himself in Psalms 1:3. This guy is moving on. He sees himself as growing, flourishing, thriving, and prospering.

"He will be standing firm like a flourishing tree planted by God's design, deeply rooted by the brooks of bliss, bearing fruit in every season of his life. He is never dry, never fainting, ever blessed, ever prosperous."
Psalms 1:3 TPT

So, look in the mirror of God's word today and declare, "You beautiful and sharp; vibrant and anointed; and full of life!"

DAY 299

Don't mistake God's patience for His absence. His timing is perfect, and His presence is constant. God's timing isn't always our timing. He may not work things out the way we planned, but He is working things out for our good.

I know there are promises that God has given you just like He did Abraham and I agree that there is an Isaac in your future. But I want to encourage you today to trust God's timing, not just His promises.

"For the vision is yet for an appointed time; But at the end it will speak, and it will not lie. Though it tarries, wait for it; Because it will surely come, It will not tarry."

Habakkuk 2:3 NKJV

The promise is yet for an appointed time. The appointed time is the best time. When we refuse to use manipulation and our own schemes to get what we want and trust God's timing, He gives us a supernatural grace and peace to sustain us while we are waiting and we get an Isaac, not an Ishmael! The blessing brings no sorrow with it!

Remember, God sees the big picture. He sees what we can't, knows what's best, and when it will be best. Timing belongs to God; preparation belongs to us. Trust God for direction as well as pace. He has a great understanding of where we're going as well as when we need to arrive. The promises of God will outlast your problems.

I remind you today, heaven is having conversations about you. God is making a way for you right now. Heaven has heard your prayers. God is working on your behalf. The promise is on the way! Trust in His timing. Rely on His promises. Wait for His answers. Believe in His miracles. Rejoice in His goodness. Relax in His Presence.

DAY 300

"For as he thinks in his heart, so is he."
Proverbs 23:7 NKJV

Most people don't see that there is a direct connection between the way they view themselves and their destiny. It's so important to see ourselves the way heaven sees us because when we see how we're known in heaven, it changes how we walk on earth, in relationship to God, the people around us, and the circumstances we face. God knows us and speaks to us from a prophetic dimension to our prophetic potential. We need people around us to remind us of our true identity, to speak into our future destiny, someone who sees the treasure and not just the earthen vessel. Don't be surprised when your faith and optimism is met with opposition. Your perception of yourself is far more powerful than the circumstances of your life. Every challenge in our life has within it the potential to discover a new aspect of God's greatness. We have to repeat what God says about us and who we are instead of what the enemy says.

The way the majority of the Israelites saw themselves certainly wasn't the way God saw them. It wasn't the way Joshua and Caleb saw themselves or their fellow Israelites. They saw themselves as failures, like grasshoppers, and they failed. Joshua and Caleb saw themselves as successful, and they eventually succeeded. What you're doing in this season is preparing you for the next season, but you won't know it until you get there. Your today is always connected to your destiny. In God's kingdom, the journey is always part of the destination.

"But we all, with unveiled face, beholding as in a mirror the glory of the Lord, are being transformed into the same image from glory to glory, just as by the Spirit of the Lord."
2 Corinthians 3:18

DAY 301

What God is, He is abundantly. He is abundantly love, grace, and life. He is extravagant in who He is and what He does. He never wants us to live under a poverty spirit. Poverty is about more than economics; it's living with the mindset that we are hopeless in any area of our lives.

He is not moody. We never have to wonder if He's good or not. He is good all the time and He loves us all the time. He believes the best about us even though we aren't there yet and are constantly in transition. We're incomplete, but He loves us completely. We're not perfect, but He loves us perfectly. When we fail, His love never does. His love is based on His character, not ours. His love is unchanging, but it changes us! He loves the opportunity to get close to us, the opportunity to work with us, the opportunity to bring us joy and peace, and help us grow.

You were conceived in God's heart from a place of love and purpose. God's design and plans for you are always to love and bless you. Where else can we find a love that is perfect, unfailing, pure, and eternal? You are loved today and every day! Jesus loved you enough to die for you. His love triumphed over the grave and He rose again to offer you His grace. Celebrate the fact that God loves you forever! He's brought you this far; He's not going to leave you now!

"So now I live with the confidence that there is nothing in the universe with the power to separate us from God's love. I'm convinced that his love will triumph over death, life's troubles, fallen angels, or dark rulers in the heavens. There is nothing in our present or future circumstances that can weaken his love. There is no power above us or beneath us—no power that could ever be found in the universe that can distance us from God's passionate love, which is lavished upon us through our Lord Jesus, the Anointed One!"
Romans 8:38-39 TPT

DAY 302

God's heart for us and His desire to make it known is amazing. When God shows up in our lives, He brings revelation with Him; and as He gives us a revelation of His love, it becomes prophetic in our lives as He enables us to see from heaven's perspective. Our primary focus should be to receive His love and then live our lives in response. He tells us our true identity and reveals His true identity. We can never know who we really are without first knowing who He really is and the great love He has for us.

The enemy trembles at the love of God and revelation of the goodness of God because perfect love casts out his number one weapon, fear. May we all avoid the Judas tragedy. You hang around Jesus for years and never fall in love with Him or never get a revelation of His great love for you.

God is passionately in love with you today. Forge a partnership with the Holy Spirit and embark on an adventure of discovery: the discovery of who God has really created you to be, breaking through every internal barrier of insecurity. Your situation may take time to catch up with your revelation but be patient, focused, and persistent.

I pray today that our Father will flood your being with more than you can contain, more than you can imagine, taking you deeper, taking your further, moving you into realms of greater experience, knowledge, revelation, possession, expression, and manifestation!

"May your tender love overwhelm me, O Lord, for you are my Savior
and you keep your promises."
Psalms 119:41; 119:92-94 TPT

DAY 303

We have to learn to focus on the plan, the purpose, and the promises: not the people, the problems, the pain, or the past. Paul said, "I forget!" To forget means to not focus on it anymore, to stop letting it affect us. To press forward, we must stop looking back. Our lives move in the direction of our most dominant thoughts. What we focus on, we magnify. When we magnify something, we don't change the size of the object; we only change our perception of it.

Negative focus is draining and doesn't give back to us; it takes away without replenishing; it robs us of joy. Joy is our strength, our defense, a force, a rock, a hedge, a wonderful gift from God that will protect our peace.

If we want to live a life that is energized and renewed on a daily basis, we have to focus on who we are, not who we aren't, and not on who we are compared to others. Never allow Satan and his minions to magnify the memories of your failures. Focus on what we can do, not what we can't, not on what other people are doing or not doing. Focus on what we do have, not what we don't, and not on what others have or don't have.

Gratitude is recognizing what is right and celebrating it. People who have gratitude move towards abundance because they're magnifying the blessings of God they already possess. If we remain focused on our God and His goodness, He has a way of turning the very thing we once thought was going to be our ending into a platform for a new beginning. When we magnify the Lord, we are not making Him bigger; we are seeing Him bigger.

"Oh, MAGNIFY the LORD with me, And let us exalt His name together."
Psalms 34:3 NKJV

DAY 304

There is something about a song in the night seasons of life. Singing many times announces new seasons of joy, peace, and prosperity and breaks old seasons of sorrow and struggles.

"Rejoice with singing, you barren one! You who have never given birth, burst into a song of joy and shout, you who have never been in labor! For the deserted wife will have more children than the married one," says Yahweh. *Increase is coming, so enlarge your tent and add extensions to your dwelling. Hold nothing back! Make the tent ropes longer and the pegs stronger. You will increase and spread out in every direction. Your sons and daughters will conquer nations and revitalize desolate cities."*

Isaiah 54:1-3 TPT

As we lift our lives in worship before Him, He announces to us, even in the midst of barrenness, breakthroughs in all areas, extravagant increase, wonderful surprises, answered prayers, abundant health, and happiness for you and your loved ones. No matter where we are in our spiritual, financial, emotional, and physical journey, we aren't restricted to natural solutions alone. The spiritual always precedes the natural.

I decree Isaiah 54:1-3 over your life. Your barren places are about to become abundant. May your path to success be marked with His continual favor. May your family enjoy health and blessed relationships. May you be overwhelmed by favor and increase. May the next seasons of your life be the best ever. May the good that comes to you in every area be like the heralding of angels at the birth of our Messiah. May even your enemies have to join in singing His praises too! May every storm you are weathering lose its strength, and when you come out on the other side, you will not be the same person you were when you started into the storm. Your God is giving you beauty for ashes, the oil of joy for mourning, and He is making all things new!

DAY 305

Today, I pray an increase over you, an abundant harvest, success, an overflow of God's presence, and God's favor immeasurably and limitlessly overflowing. Favor that produces supernatural increase, promotion, restoration, honor, increased assets, greater victories, battles won, divine possibilities, awesome God-moments, and life-changing turnarounds, in the name of Jesus. Let it pour out on you and through you.

I pray a peace to you that only God can provide. May the presence of the Holy Spirit comfort you and the peace of the Lord overtake you. I pray your heart and emotions be strengthened and protected in Jesus name. I pray for breakthrough for you, something is going to get better. Something's going to break your way in Jesus' name!

"Rejoice with singing, you barren one You who have never given birth, burst into a song of joy and shout, you who have never been in labor! For the deserted wife will have more children than the married one," says Yahweh. "Increase is coming, so enlarge your tent and add extensions to your dwelling. Hold nothing back! Make the tent ropes longer and the pegs stronger. You will increase and spread out in every direction. Your sons and daughters will conquer nations and revitalize desolate cities."
Isaiah 54:1-3 TPT

DAY 306

Jesus is the way to eternal life but also abundant life. Let's not settle for part of the gospel.

It is God's will that we live in the fullness of the blessed life that God intended. It's a life of empowerment, a life of the victory, a life of increase, and a life of impact and success. Living in our God-given rights and privileges is made possible through the finished work of Jesus. Ephesians 3:20 says, "God is able to do exceedingly abundantly above and beyond all that you can ask or think according to the power that works within us."

I pray for a holy boldness to rise up within us today, to be daring, to expect more in our lives, to believe for more than we ever believed for before.

"Let us then approach God's throne of grace with confidence, so that we may receive mercy and find grace to help us in our time of need."
Hebrews 4:16 NIV

Like Jabez, in 1 Chronicles 4:10, we have to refuse to accept a life of curses and pain. We must choose the blessed life, by boldly asking for it, without guilt or shame. God loves to bless His children! It is time to get beyond our pain and step into the power of the blessing!

Jesus shed His blood so we could boldly go before the throne of God (Hebrews 10:19) and receive all that He promised! No matter what has defined our past, we refuse to let it define our future! Declare it, "Father, I am grateful for every day to serve You. I am greatly blessed, highly favored, and deeply loved by You. Lord, You are my shield and the very source of my strength and life. Jesus took my sin, curse, and shame on the cross; therefore, I am forgiven, free, healed, protected, blessed, favored, and loved today!"

DAY 307

Never let a day pass without looking for the good, praising God, appreciating, blessing, and being grateful. Put a smile on your face; keep a song in your heart; keep the passion in your spirit. Don't start the day focusing on the disappointments. This is the day the Lord has made. He's on the throne.

Ask God to show you what the enemy does not want you to see about your situation. Sometimes your difficulties will do more to promote you than your times of ease. The enemy thought he was going to stop you, discourage you, or intimidate you, but God used it to light a fire on the inside. He meant it for harm, but God used it to your advantage.

Whatever God has put on the inside, no matter how long it's been, no matter how impossible it looks, stir it up. No matter where you are in your life, no matter what age you are, it is never too late to believe for your God-given dreams. Get in agreement with God. He's the giver of dreams; He's the one that put that desire in you.

You have to walk by faith and not by sight. Keep expecting it. Keep talking like it's going to happen, acting like it's going to happen, thinking like it's going to happen. Release your faith. Your faith is going to take you where you couldn't go on your own. Your God is bigger than what you're facing. He's more powerful than any enemy. He's your provider, your healer, your way maker, and your deliverer. How great is our God! He's the God who chose us when we were nothing! His tender love for us continues on forever! He has rescued us from the power of our enemies!

"Give thanks to the great God of the heavens! His tender love for us
continues on forever!"
Psalms 136:23-24, 26 TPT

DAY 308

I sense a powerful prophetic word today for those who need it. God wants to accelerate His presence and power in your life and in the life of your family. Get ready for open doors of favor. Position your heart and spirit for it. Your time in the secret place will prepare you for your next level. As you spend time with God and let your heart be saturated with His word, you are going to a higher level of God's anointing and power on your life. You are coming fully awake and alive in the Spirit. You will walk with Him in the secret place and know the beauty and presence of His glory. In Jesus' name, freshness, a divine flow of His spirit in you and through you.

There is a fresh wind of God that is blowing over you. He is forming a new wineskin that will be able to hold and facilitate what is being poured out. God is aligning you for your next season. You are positioned for increase. He is too faithful to fail you and even when others fail you; He will not. He is good when people are bad. He is strong when you feel weak. He is all-powerful, ever faithful, always with you, and always knows best!

Today His hands hold you. His wisdom leads you. His Spirit comforts and protects you. Continue to walk in courage, knowing God is initiating His plans according to His timing, ushering you into a new land and season of your life. Even when it looks like you are losing, you are still winning! There is power in the blood of Jesus!

"Your anointing has made me strong and mighty. You've empowered
my life for triumph by pouring fresh oil over me."
Psalms 92:10 TPT

DAY 309

I want to encourage all the faithful ones who do so much and sometimes feel unnoticed and taken for granted. I'm sure Jesus felt this way when He was rejected by the very ones He sacrificed, suffered, and died for. It takes eyes of faith to sow seed in times of lack, to use your gifting even when it seems unappreciated. But never forget that the things you do, the love you show, the prayers you pray, are making a difference and you will reap an abundant harvest. God is faithful even when people aren't.

There are more good things ahead of you than bad things behind you. So even when others don't always express their gratitude, keep on loving fearlessly, giving generously, speaking truthfully, and forgiving quickly. God knows your every act of obedience. Those who are faithful with their giftings even in times of famine will have great opportunities in their future.

In your life and situations today, I declare an abundant harvest in the name of Jesus. God is accelerating your life with grace and favor. Your latter days will be greater than your former because grace and favor are waiting on you. I'm believing with you today for provision and that God will pour out blessings to you in every way, including financially. You will not lack any good thing! His presence will overflow in every part of your life. You will walk in fearless faith! He is the God of the turn-around. The Lord of breakthrough is your Father and your harvest is being released!

"You have been faithful over a few things I will make you ruler over much- enter in to the joy of your Lord"
Matthew 25:21 NKJV

DAY 310

God is never surprised by our circumstances or situations. He knows all things and is working in the midst of all things. Whatever you are dealing with, trust Him. That thing that's been stressing you out, God is turning it and working it out for your good. He is good. He is faithful.

No one can love you like Jesus. No one can help you like Jesus. No one can redeem you like Jesus. When you know Jesus, you can know joy, peace, and love in the midst of what you don't know.

When you're being stretched, remember you can't have growth without change and you can't have change without some discomfort. Keep speaking what you know to be true. Keep doing what you know to be right. Keep sowing what you desire to reap. When it's tough, you get tougher. Tough times don't last but tough people do. Even in your wilderness, God is making a way. You will come out. Even in your struggle, God is turning your trial into triumph. You will overcome. Whatever *it* is, God is already on *it*. No problem stands a chance against God's plan.

You will prevail. You will go from ruins to restoration. You will go from problems to provision. You will go from depression to deliverance. Walls that have prevented you from moving forward are now destroyed. You will overcome. You will break past previous boundaries. You will breakthrough to abundant living.

"Though the mountains be shaken and the hills be removed, yet My unfailing love for YOU will not be shaken nor My covenant of peace be removed, says the Lord who has compassion on YOU."
Isaiah 54:10 NIV

DAY 311

I'm praying over you today.

1. May you always have more than enough so that not only you are blessed, but that you may also bless others.
2. Because the Lord is your Shepherd, may not only your steps be ordered by God, but also your stops as well, causing you to avoid frustration, pain, and wasted time!
3. May there be doors of opportunity open for you and your family. Favor instead of rejection!
4. In Jesus' name, I believe every need is met with heaven's best. I pray that you will prosper and be in health as your soul prospers. (3 John 2)
5. May you experience the maximum return on your giving because you give in faith and obedience to the Lord. Increase to all you put your hand to, good measure, pressed down, shaken together, and running over!
6. Anything the enemy has stolen from you will be brought back with great abundance.
7. I declare every seed of bitterness planted by the painful past no longer productive in your life today, in Jesus' name. Your life is a fruitful field, spirit, soul, and body!
8. I pray you to see and experience the tangible goodness of God in places you have been believing for. The goodness of the Lord in the land you're living in now!
9. I pray you experience an overflowing harvest full of opportunities, favor, and blessings that will take you to new levels of fulfillment and satisfaction!
10. That Father God causes you and your family to increase more and more in every area of life, spirit, soul, and body. That abundant life rules and reigns in you, around you, for you, and through you!

DAY 312

Before you were even born or formed, God knew that the world was going to need one of you, that you would have a unique and special purpose. He made you in His image and likeness with a purpose that only you can do. You are an original!

No matter the twists and turns your life has taken, He hasn't changed His mind about you. No matter what you do, say, or think, God never changes His mind about you. He's relentlessly, unfathomably, irresistibly in love with you. Nothing in this universe can change that; His mercies are made new every morning. It's a new day!

In case you didn't know this already, God's not finished with you yet. His strong hand is on your life and future. I'm sensing there are some who need assurance and reminding today that God is leading you, guiding you, and working on your behalf. When you wait on the Lord, it will be worth what He sends into your life. You might not be able to see where you're headed, but He does, and He's holding your hand, walking with you, and breathing life into every aspect of your present and future. Your deepest struggles can lead to your greatest victories. Your place of greatest pain can lead to your greatest mission. What is in you is greater than anything outside of you! The Author and Finisher of your faith is on it. He will finish what He started in your life, no matter how it looks right now!

"No, in all these things we are more than conquerors through him who loved us. For I am sure that neither death nor life, nor angels nor rulers, nor things present nor things to come, nor powers, nor height nor depth, nor anything else in all creation, will be able to separate us from the love of God in Christ Jesus our Lord."
Romans 8:37-39 ESV

DAY 313

Let's begin our day with some declarations of faith and confidence in our God.

My God will show himself strong not only in my heart and mind, but in my circumstances too, for He knows what I need before I even ask. Therefore, I won't be defeated by problems, overcome by circumstances, or intimidated by the enemy. To those things that come against me, I boldly declare, "But God!"

I will run the race with my eyes on the goal, press toward the mark, and by faith cross the finish line with my head held high. When times get tough, I won't back up, back off, back down, back out, or backslide. I will not waste my time or energy on shallow living, petty small thinking, negative talking, worthless doing, useless regretting, hurtful resenting, or faithless worrying. Instead, I will glorify God, grow to maturity, fulfill my calling, and be a responsible member of the family of God. I will walk in love and compassion, full of thankfulness for every day, and every blessing that God has given me. I will walk in the confident assurance that comes from knowing I am a child of the King.

This day His hands hold me. His peace fills me. His Spirit comforts and protects me. He is omnipotent, omniscient, omnipresent, and He is too faithful to fail me. I will rest in the blessed assurance of His great love and presence.

"So now I live with the confidence that there is nothing in the universe with the power to separate us from God's love. I'm convinced that his love will triumph over death, life's troubles, fallen angels, or dark rulers in the heavens. There is nothing in our present or future circumstances that can weaken his love."

Romans 8:38 TPT

DAY 314

King David faced discouraging times. David and his men lost everything in Ziklag. People were so upset they even spoke of stoning David. But just like David, remember God never intends to leave us in the valley. We pass through the valley.

Don't surrender to your circumstances. Surrender to God and trust Him. Never allow the enemy to bury your destiny in the ashes of your adversity. Never let the tears blind you to your dreams and vision. Don't get consumed with bitterness and miss out on the blessing. It's time to rise above those negative circumstances and believe what God says about you. You are blessed, favored, and loved.

Just like God spoke to David, He speaks to us today.

"So David inquired of the LORD, saying, "Shall I pursue this troop? Shall I overtake them?" And He answered him, "Pursue, for you shall surely overtake them and without fail recover all."

I Samuel 30:8 NKJV

Pursue and recover all. Continue to reclaim everything the enemy has stolen! This is not the final chapter! I declare over us today that just as David did, we shall see the goodness of the Lord in the land of the living!

Father, I ask you to restore every lost opportunity, stolen blessing, and good thing that belongs to your children. I declare restoration. Walls that have prevented you from moving forward are now being demolished. You will pass through. You will go to another level. You will smash glass ceilings. You will breakthrough and breakout and recover all! In Jesus' name, Amen!

DAY 315

Believers always keep learning and growing. We are created for continual growth and expansion. The biggest enemies of our future success are indifference, arrogance, the unwillingness to learn, unlearn, relearn, renew our minds, change, and grow. Next-level living is preceded by next level believing and thinking. Stay hungry for more. The greatest investment you make every day is what you do with your time, don't waste it, use it wisely and expectantly.

In order to become everything God wants us to become, we must continue to develop our gifting, our character, our perspective, our vision, our heart for God, and our dependence on Him. God wants more for His people than just a promised land; He wants our hearts. God is continually inviting us to know Him closely and intimately as He reveals all He is, all we are together in Him, and His vision for us. Vision is a mental picture that God puts on the inside of us that is powerful enough to shape our present and mold our future. So, let's continue to launch out into the deep, explore new levels of abundant living, and never let the desire to become all He wants us to be die. There is a fire, a fresh determination being released, and it is pouring through your spirit. This isn't an end; it's the start of a new beginning!

"I admit that I haven't yet acquired the absolute fullness that I'm pursuing, but I run with passion into his abundance so that I may reach the purpose that Jesus Christ has called me to fulfill and wants me to discover. I don't depend on my own strength to accomplish this; however I do have one compelling focus: I forget all of the past as I fasten my heart to the future instead. I run straight for the divine invitation of reaching the heavenly goal and gaining the victory-prize through the anointing of Jesus."
Philippians 3:12-14 TPT

DAY 316

I'm sensing there are some who need assurance and reminding today that God is leading you, guiding you, and is working on your behalf. No matter what you are going through right now, it doesn't overwhelm God or stop His plans for you. He knows your end from your beginning. Let's agree that every bad situation is turning around for your good! What is in you is greater than anything outside of you.

When you wait on the Lord, it will be worth what He sends into your life. You might not be able to see where you're headed, but He does, and He's holding your hand, walking with you and breathing life into every aspect of your present and future. Your deepest struggles can lead to your greatest victories. Your place of pain can lead to your greatest mission.

I declare God is your unfailing and immediate supply of all that's good. You will not lack in any good thing. His presence will overflow in every part of your life. You will walk in fearless faith. I declare the favor of God to open supernatural doors. You will taste and see the goodness of the Lord in the land of the living. You will know you are loved and led by Him. The author and finisher of your faith is on it; He will finish what He started in your life, no matter how it looks right now! Thank you, Lord!"

"The faithful lovers of God will inherit the earth and enjoy every promise of God's care, dwelling in peace forever." So don't be impatient for the Lord to act; keep moving forward steadily in his ways, and he will exalt you at the right time. And when he does, you will possess every promise, including your full inheritance...."
Psalms 37:29, 34 TPT

DAY 317

"Father, help us to make the most of today and not sweat the small stuff. May we take time to pause, breathe, take a break, go for a walk, and realign with what matters most. May we center our life around the things of God, enjoy what we have, and what we have to do. May we love our family and be there for them, may we be a friend, and smile and enjoy life while we have it. Remind us that every difficulty in our life has within it the potential to discover a new aspect of the greatness of God. May we stop trying to perform and start enjoying the experience of Your presence and out of that become better at fulfilling our calling and giftings. May we never stop growing, learning, and reaching.

May this day be a day of discovery. May we never lose our sense of amazement and wonder at what You've done in our lives and all that's around us that You've given us to enjoy. May we dream big and believe big because You are too big, and life is too big to be intimidated by small minds and opinions. May we dream with You about who we are becoming and what is possible. May we simply listen for Your voice in everything we do and everywhere we go."

"When you live a life of abandoned love, surrendered before the awe of God, here's what you'll experience: Abundant life. Continual protection. And complete satisfaction!"
Proverbs 19:23 TPT

DAY 318

There is something in your future that is worth fighting for in your today, "Every place that the sole of your foot will tread upon I have given you." It's great to know that we've been delivered from Egypt, but it shouldn't stop there. I've been brought out to go in. I've got Canaan potential! Stop praying to become a better slave in a place you're not supposed to be a citizen of. Guard your freedom. Stop praying for a better Pharaoh. The enemy will try to yoke you to things that are not of God, that are designed to crush you, bind you, limit you, but Jesus came to set you free!

God allowed Israel to see with their eyes the defeat of their enemies so they could know that they no longer had power over them. Our enemy has been defeated; we no longer have to fear a drowned army. But Israel still faced an enemy within- the way they perceived themselves. Many died in the wilderness because of what they believed. The way Israel perceived themselves is ultimately why they died in the wilderness. They had come out of Egypt, but Egypt had not come out of them. They had left physical slavery, but not mental slavery. God says, "Pharaoh is no longer your master; Egypt is no longer your home. You are redeemed and restored, and your story will bring God glory!"

"May God give you every desire of your heart and carry out your every plan as you go to battle. When you succeed, we will celebrate and shout for joy. Flags will fly when victory is yours! Yes, God will answer your prayers and we will praise him! I know God gives me all that I ask for and brings victory to his anointed king. My deliverance cry will be heard in his holy heaven. By his mighty hand miracles will manifest through his saving strength. Some find their strength in their weapons and wisdom, but my miracle deliverance can never be won by men. Our boast is in the Lord our God, who makes us strong and gives us victory!"
Psalms 20:4-7 TPT

DAY 319

When Paul prayed for us in Ephesians 1, he prayed that the eyes of our understanding would be enlightened.

Today I pray that the Spirit of the living God who called you from your mother's womb rises up in you and creates assurance and confidence in you that you are still on the way, that it's not over and there are still things for you to do and experience. I pray that you will know God is still painting a picture of His will for your life, looking it over and loving it. He's calling it good! I pray for supernatural insight, revelation, and wisdom for you today. May God give you divine strategies to advance His purposes and bring great victories to your life in the name of Jesus. May you focus your attention on faith in God and His promises and not fixate on problems and obstacles. I pray you will walk in the confidence that God has purpose and intention for you. Whatever God has designed and spoken over you, will come to pass as you cooperate with the Holy Spirit. You will experience the goodness of God and your life will bring God glory. I pray that your life will become a living epistle that carries the message of who your God is, the great, glorious, all-powerful, mighty, all-knowing, redeeming, gracious, loving God.

"I pray that the light of God will illuminate the eyes of your imagination, flooding you with light, until you experience the full revelation of the hope of his calling, that is, the wealth of God's glorious inheritances that he finds in us, his holy ones! I pray that you will continually experience the immeasurable greatness of God's power made available to you through faith. Then your lives will be an advertisement of this immense power as it works through you! This is the mighty power that was released when God raised Christ from the dead and exalted him to the place of highest honor and supreme authority in the heavenly realm!"
Ephesians 1:18-20 TPT

DAY 320

Today, and this weekend I pray for you to have a new glory story to tell, one of healing, success, wholeness, abundance, love, breakthrough and great joy. I declare that every lack shall be turned to overflow, and you will be stronger, wiser, and full of life. May nothing stop your promises from being fulfilled and it be a time for the supernatural power of God in your life, a time for increase and great blessing, a time for favor, and the blessing of Abraham to be experienced. I am praying that your lives will be marked by the very presence of Him who causes all things to work together for your good and His glory, and that anything burdening you and weighing you down be lifted in Jesus' name!

I am praying that your bodies are healed, and your youth is renewed! I pray you are strengthened, and any spirit of weariness is removed, and in the name of Jesus, supernatural strength and energy are rising up inside you!

I declare in faith that great things are coming your way and that God is working to fulfill and give you the desires of your heart, and the days ahead of you are going to be filled with satisfaction and fulfillment! And not just for you, but your family and all those you are believing for! Thank you, Lord!

"And I pray that he would unveil within you the unlimited riches of his glory and favor until supernatural strength floods your innermost being with his divine might and explosive power."
Ephesians 3:16 TPT

DAY 321

What God knows and says about us is more important than what others think and say about us, always!

I AM... secure in knowing my life is written out in Your book, oh, Lord! You had plans for me before I was born.

I AM... loved and valued by the creator of the universe!

I AM... in His heart always!

I AM... bought with His blood, rescued from the dark power of Satan's rule and filled with hope and expectation!

I AM... forgiven of all my past and He has removed my sins as far as the east is from the west!

I AM... destined to be a blessed person, to live an abundant life, and to receive great things from HIM!

I AM... set apart and placed for such a time as this. I matter, my life matters!

I AM... making a difference!

I AM... chosen!

I AM... on the way!

I AM... needed!

I AM... loved and I will make it!

I AM... in for an abundant supply of grace that is headed my way!

I AM... entering the greatest season of my life! My best days begin today!

I AM... Yours and You are mine, forever mine.

"Fight the good fight of the faith. Take hold of the eternal life to which you were called when you made your good confession in the presence of many witnesses."
1 Timothy 6:12 NIV

DAY 322

In this life, there will be times when things don't make sense and you have questions without answers. You will have times of disappointment and deliverance, hurt and celebration, setbacks, and breakthroughs. But through it all, don't believe the lies of the enemy. You have not missed out; your time has not passed, and God has not forgotten about you! Even on days when your life is filled with unstable, unreliable, undependable people and circumstances, you have one source in your life that is constant, your God!

Jesus is with you and whatever you're believing for in this season of your life. I declare success is yours. Whatever battles you are fighting, I declare victory is yours. Whatever challenges you are facing, I decree you will overcome them. May your life be fruitful, your obstacles overcome, and your life lived to the fullest. I pray the atmosphere of your life continues to be filled with expectation. May the environment your faith creates become the breeding ground where miracles are birthed, and in spite of everything coming against you, never forget who you are and who you belong to! You are a change-maker and chain breaker, and it's impossible to exaggerate the goodness and greatness of your God! No matter what darkness tries to surround you or wilderness you're going through, expect the goodness and greatness of God to outshine and overtake it all!

"The wilderness and the wasteland shall be glad for them, And the desert shall rejoice and blossom as the rose; It shall blossom abundantly and rejoice, Even with joy and singing. The glory of Lebanon shall be given to it, The excellence of Carmel and Sharon. They shall see the glory of the LORD, The excellency of our God."
Isaiah 35:1-2 NKJV

DAY 323

Sometimes it feels like there's a Red Sea in front of you and Pharaoh's army behind you but stand back and see the salvation of the Lord! The enemy's strategy is to paralyze you with fear and discouragement, but God! You will overcome it because God is your strength.

I pray that God enlarges your territory and shows you great favor!!! This day I declare breakthrough in every area of your life, the enemy is defeated, and you will walk in the victory that is already yours! You are seated with Christ far above all the power of the enemy. As Jesus is, so are you in this world!

You will walk in everything Jesus paid for you to have and rule and reign with Him in life! You will never again submit to the rule and reign of the enemy! Your chains are broken, and you are free: spirit, soul, and body!

Jesus has already won the battle for you, there are more that are for you than against you. Jesus is interceding on your behalf right now. No matter what things look like, you will overcome!

"Be strong and take heart, all you who hope in the LORD."
Psalm 31:24 NIV

DAY 324

You're going to make it! I break every spirit of weariness over you in the name of Jesus and pray for supernatural joy and strength! You will run and not be weary!

I declare the enemy will gain no advantage over you, no trap will prevail, no snare will hold! In the name of Jesus, every bondage be broken!!! Lord, let every spirit of stress, anxiety, and heaviness be removed in the name of Jesus! Let them be destroyed!!

I declare peace! I pray against every spirit of oppression against you in the name of Jesus! Any heaviness or weariness on you, let it be removed!! I pray for rest for you, that peace takes over, and you are refreshed and replenished spiritually, emotionally, and physically, in Jesus' name! No chaos!!! You will not be shaken!

"Cast your burden upon the Lord and He will sustain you; He will never allow the righteous to be shaken"
Psalm 55:22 NASB

DAY 325

Kingdom principles will propel you, promote you, prosper you, and protect you, but they will also process you. Motives are revealed, heart desires are tested, and character-building takes place. Processes take time. Joseph waited 13 years, Abraham waited 25 years, Moses waited 40 years, Jesus waited 30 years.

In the book of Genesis, Esau exchanged his birthright with his younger brother Jacob for a bowl of stew. A birthright was a special honor given to the firstborn son. It included a double portion of the family inheritance, along with the honor of one day becoming the family's leader. The oldest son could sell his birthright or give it away if he chose to, but in doing so, he would lose both material goods and his leadership position. Therefore, by trading his birthright for a bowl of stew, Esau showed complete disregard for the spiritual and material blessings that would have come his way if he had kept his birthright. This is why the scripture says that Esau "despised" his birthright. Esau despised the process. (Genesis 25:34)

Sometimes it takes a while for the roots to go down deep to support the magnificent fruit that will be on the tree. God has a bright future planned for you and those connected to your purpose and dreams. Growing is a process. You have to feed it good thoughts. Surround it with a good environment: value and nurture the process itself and not just the promise. Never abandon hope in your life. God has perfect timing for everything. Some of the things fighting you are simply preparing you for where you are going, God has a plan!

"I pray with great faith for you, because I'm fully convinced that the One who began this glorious work in you will faithfully continue the process of maturing you and will put his finishing touches to it until the unveiling of our Lord Jesus Christ!"
Philippians 1:6 TPT

DAY 326

We live life out of our convictions. Don't base your convictions on the facts, base them on the truth- what He says about you! Have a conviction that you are His son/daughter, born of His seed, empowered by His Spirit to live a life beyond your human capacity. If you are a born again, Spirit-filled believer, the Holy Spirit dwells in you; you have a built-in divine corrector and connector that will help you be able to dream big, pray honestly, and ask for what you desire, without fear of going wrong. Live life with unreasonable, illogical anticipation of God's miraculous provision.

Jesus did. He expected a fig tree to give Him figs completely out of season. (Mark 11) Our Father's intention is greater than the seasons. You can live life safe and under the rule of survival, or you can break out and live life in the freedom of daring faith and conquest. We can settle for too little. If our motivation is for the extension of His kingdom and helping and loving others, then we must increase. Abraham heard from God, obeyed boldly, sacrificed willingly, believed God for his future provision, and prospered! Say it today, "Every challenge is a doorway to a new opportunity. The eyes of my understanding are enlightened every day to the perfect will of God in my life. God's purpose shall prevail!"

"I'm writing this letter to all the devoted believers who have been made holy by being one with Jesus, the Anointed One. May God himself, the heavenly Father of our Lord Jesus Christ, release grace over you and impart total well-being into your lives. Every spiritual blessing in the heavenly realm has already been lavished upon us as a love gift from our wonderful heavenly Father, the Father of our Lord Jesus—all because he sees us wrapped into Christ. This is why we celebrate him with all our hearts!"
Ephesians 1:2-3 TPT

DAY 327

Our circumstances are never just about what's happening to us; they're about who God wants to reveal Himself to us as and what's happening in us. He is deeply and personally concerned about our life. He wants to walk with us through all of life, through the fire, through the rain, through the storms, and reveal more of His nature to us in everything we face. It's in our need that we discover something about Him we've never known before, we go deeper.

When we come to these troubling situations we need to look to Him and start confessing that He is so great that He can make the universe; He can say a word and light up the sky; He can touch our heart and heal the hurt; and as we do, our view lifts as we focus on the God who is so much greater than the circumstances and the situation. As we go deeper into who He is, we develop a new and different perspective of our God that will carry us through our life circumstances. Our soul is enriched for the rest of our lives. We build our lives on who He is!

Though difficulties will be part of our story, this is who God has promised to be for us, and who He has promised we can become in Him! We learn that He will always be faithful. He is with us in our present, showing us who we can be in our future, who we can be in our now, and in our next! "Faith enables the believing soul to treat the future as present and the invisible as seen." – J. Oswald Sanders

"Father, thank you today for your precious promises to us that are yes and amen but also Your empowering presence that allows us to live in expectation of your goodness and promises fulfilled as joint-heirs with Jesus, our Lord. Thank you, Jesus. Amen"

"He satisfies all who love and trust him, and he keeps every promise he makes."
Psalms 111:5 TPT

DAY 328

I feel the Lord's heart of compassion and desire to encourage those who are growing battle-weary and on the verge of losing their hope. Today, God is confirming His plans for you, reviving hope, affirming your desire to follow, love, serve, and walk in all He has promised. I'm praying today that God gives you peace, hope, and love in every place you need it and that God's love for you overflows in your heart and becomes so powerful and real that it comforts your heart like never before. I hear our Father saying, "I have chosen you; you are mine. I want you. I will never reject you. You are forever mine." As we begin this day, I want to release one of my favorite verses over us,

"Return to your fortress, you prisoners of hope; even now I announce that I will restore twice as much to you."
Zechariah 9:12 NIV

Lord, let us be prisoners of hope; captured, taken, filled by a hope that will never let us go no matter what happens! May we be people who hold on to Your promises in the midst of everything. People who refuse to be intimidated. People who refuse to allow someone or something small to keep us from Your best. People who know there's going to be a payback, a harvest, a season where what has been stolen will be repaid double. People who refuse to take no for an answer when You have said, "yes!" People who have a life story that brings God glory; where people will say one day I have never seen or heard anything like that! I bless you today in the name of Jesus! I declare and decree you are "drenched" with favor!

"The lovers of God who chase after righteousness will find all their dreams come true: an abundant life drenched with favor and a fountain that overflows with satisfaction."
Proverbs 21:21 TPT

DAY 329

The Bible is filled with stories of people going through hard seasons and God using them in the middle of their difficult times. Jesus moves in the mess and births a message from our lives. So, take heart today and join with me in proclaiming, "I stand on the promises of God this day and declare, my life matters and I will shout the message. that God is Good!" I am chosen and placed for such a time as this. My life matters and I am making a difference. Today needs me; tomorrow needs me; there are things that are yet to happen that need me!

I will step forward and stretch out my life to God, embracing faith as my attitude to face all things. I will step up and do exploits with God and for God. I will step beyond my current limitations and reach out to grasp a blessed future. I will step above into a higher place, a new position, and a new future filled with God-hope! I stand against the darkness and let my light shine in my place in this world, in my place of influence and authority. I will keep my heart open to the work of the Holy Spirit and I will live the adventure. I will walk in my God-given purpose and passion, and I will see the provision of the Lord! I attach myself to the love of God today and every day, clinging to Him. I expect to taste God's goodness and I believe what God has done and what He says. I am the righteousness of God through the blood of Jesus.

My heart awakens each day to the love, grace, and righteousness of God. I am walking in God's grace and glory, I am on the way, I am chosen, I am needed, I am loved, I will make it, God is for me. God is with me. I am a finisher.

"You keep every promise you've ever made to me! Since your love for me is constant and endless, I ask you, Lord, to finish every good thing that you've begun in me!"
Psalms 138:8 TPT

DAY 330

Life is God's gift to us; how we live it is our gift to Him. Let's make it epic! Live it passionately, on purpose, intentionally, loving out loud, a difference-maker, and a world changer!

There's an overwhelming amount of peace you receive when you choose to just simply love the people around you that need love the most. You never know what someone's going through and how your love can impact them. Be caring. Speak sincerely. Love always.

When you think something good about someone, tell them. Never rob someone of the blessings of an unspoken treasure. No one can smell the flowers on their own coffin, give them their verbal bouquets now! Remember, life and death are in the power of your tongue. Just one word spoken at the right time can be the difference in life and death. It sounds so small, but it's so big. The smallest act of disobedience can destroy so much, but the smallest act of obedience can achieve so much!

So, this year, let's be the reason someone smiles.; be the reason someone feels loved; be the reason someone pursues a dream and doesn't give up; be the reason someone believes there are still good people who care; be the reason someone shares their heart. The more we value, the more we listen. The restraint of our own opinion allows us to hear the heartbeat of those we love. Be the reason someone knows God loves them and wants to have a relationship with them. You have so much to give.

"But sanctify the Lord God in your hearts: and be ready always to give an answer to every man that asketh you a reason of the hope that is in you with meekness and fear:"
1 Peter 3:15 KJV

DAY 331

I declare victory, grace, and great favor over you, your projects, and your future. Let the enemies who are gathered against you, turn on each other in Jesus' name! Everything contending against your destiny has lost its power to stop you! You shall overcome, progress, prosper, and succeed in spite of obstacles and opposition! The Lord Almighty has made room for you in the realm of His greatness and He will crown this year with an abundant harvest!

I pray any lying spirit of fear and dread is powerless against you. Expect the fulfillment of His promises! Absolutely nothing that the enemy unleashed will be able to stop the powerful move of God that you are walking into, in Jesus' name. There is no scenario, situation, or circumstance in which you will find yourself without hope because you are a child of God! There was hope yesterday, there is hope for you today, and there will be hope tomorrow. I speak peace over every fearful heart. In the darkest hour, God's glory is going to breakthrough! When that wave of worry that seems so big you can't even see what's on the other side tries to sweep over you, know that your future is covered in God's faithfulness! God will restore you. He will turn it around. He will vindicate you!

Today I pray that you hear the Father say, "Right here, right now, in this seeming delay, I am with you. I am guarding you and guiding you. The moment has come for you to perceive Me. Look deeper into My word. See Me afresh and new. Be transformed as you look into My face and see the radiance of My love for you."

"These things I have spoken to you, that in Me you may have peace. In the world you will have tribulation; but be of good cheer, I have overcome the world."
John 16:33 NKJV

DAY 332

You have probably heard a lot of negative talk over the years, we all have. But we must stop coming into agreement with those negative words spoken towards us and agree with God's promises instead! It's never wrong to remind yourself of all that God has done for you in Christ! King David encouraged himself; we need to as well! Never expect another person to say to you what you aren't saying to yourself.

Your favorite motivational speaker should be you! A reminder today, your destiny is too great, your future is too bright to allow anything or anyone to pollute it. What we're called to do will require us to stay in faith no matter what anybody else says or does! If the enemy knows you'll listen to what "they say," he'll place so much "they say" in your life that you'll never do what God says!

Stop hanging out with people who reinforce your brokenness and develop relationships and friendships that take you to a higher level! "When the lies speak louder than the truth, remind me I belong to You, Lord. When I can't see past the dark of night, remind me You're always by my side. May I never forget I am a son/daughter of God!" Keep your faith focus today. It's easy to quit; it takes faith to go through. You are going through! Yes, you are!

"Death and life are in the power of the tongue, and those who love it will eat its fruits."
Proverbs 18:21 ESV

DAY 333

"Father, it is so easy to become anxious and fearful about the everyday issues of life we are facing, but instead, we choose today to thank You for Your promises. We pull down the stronghold of anxiety in the name of Jesus, and we bring every thought captive to your lordship.

When feelings of anxiety rise up, thank you that the precious Holy Spirit will replace those feelings with assurance. Assurance because You are at the center of our life. Help us to stand strong on Your word and to not be swayed like a reed in the wind when problems seem to be blowing out of control. Psalm 56:3 says, "When I am afraid, I put my trust in You." Thank You, Lord, for being there for us and for giving us the assurance that everything will work out in your perfect time!

So, therefore, we will not be anxious about anything. Thank you that you have empowered us to be at peace in every circumstance we face. Help us to give You thanks in the times we don't understand. We rely on Your supernatural strength to overcome every attack of the enemy! We declare that the God that we serve is a God of might and miracles, hope and healing, life and liberty, showing yourself strong in the middle of trouble. Where others see our failures, you see our future. Thank you, Lord!"

"Give all your worries and cares to God, for he cares about you."
1 Peter 5:7 NLT

DAY 334

I pray you have a renewed passion for life and your purpose today and that the weariness from the attacks and delays draining you comes to an end in the name of Jesus! I pray you have the courage to press forward, the strength to go through it, and faith that everything will turn out for the best as you trust Him.

There are days that life is about dreams, goals, brightness, shining, and fulfillment. And there are days that life is just about putting one foot in front of the other to just keep on walking! Whichever it is today, that's victory! So, don't give up. Stay positive, faith-filled, focused, and energetic.

Nowhere did Jesus ever say, "Thy skepticism has made thee whole." Your dominion starts with living from the inside-out, understanding who you are in Christ, valuing your words, and decreeing the word of God over every aspect of your life. Make up your mind to shake off the lies that hold you back. We need to glance at our problems, but stare at Jesus! When people say you can't, remember that God's word says you can!

So, never abandon hope in your life. God has perfect timing for everything. All of us need to learn to wait on Him. He will be your protector, He will be your comfort, and He will be the one that gives you all the provision you need to get through. There is always hope for the future because while we are waiting, God is working! He is up to something on your behalf and its good! His plans for you are greater than you could ever imagine!

"For since the world began, no ear has heard and no eye has seen a
God like you, who works for those who wait for him!"
Isaiah 64:4 NLT

DAY 335

1. You are walking in newness of life. That means all of life is about the possibilities of God. I pray for a shift in your season from lack and attack spiritually, mentally, emotionally, physically, relationally, and financially, to a season of abundance!

2. I pray God restores everything you lost in your life to better than what it was before!

3. I pray that God will open a door for you that no one can shut- not the devil, not the doubters, no one!

4. I pray that God will be your vindicator, that He will bring justice and promote you regardless of those trying to make you look bad!

5. I pray that God is causing all things to work together for your good today. That goodness, favor, and turnarounds are coming your way!

6. I pray that the powerful presence of God will bring the pure will of God into your life, spirit, soul, and body. That your best years still lie ahead of you, as you walk in intimacy with His heart and dare to believe that He is faithful. Let hope arise!

7. I pray for angels to be released on your behalf to minister and to battle for you in the name of Jesus. Let every struggle from your past come to an end!

8. I break every spirit of weariness over you in the name of Jesus and pray for supernatural joy and strength! You will run and not be weary! I pray that the power of the resurrection that resides in you will bring life to every situation!

9. I pray God clear any blurred vision you may have, that He opens your eyes to see spiritually what can't be comprehended naturally.

10. I pray that if you've been feeling tired, confused, or discouraged, that today is your day to lift your perspective and receive a new dream from God.

DAY 336

Just because life didn't unfold for us the way we thought it would does not mean it's over. When things don't happen on our timeline, we can get really frustrated and start living in disappointment and discouragement. Let's agree today to not allow our frustrations to push our faith, hope, and expectation over the cliff. In Jesus' mighty name, things will get better! Even when the time has passed and all seems lost, God can still redeem it!

The enemy's main tactic in our lives is deception. Fear lies to us so much about the future, so much! Notice how in every scenario, he never presents God in the situation, but He will be there!

So today, we by faith declare, "We will not live in fear and panic! God has called us, and He will faithfully lead us through! The mighty God lives in us. Therefore, we will live in the shelter of His wings and in the closeness of His love and care. His presence is in us, around us, and through us, and His voice is greater than the problems screaming at us! Our mighty God is our avenger! He will turn things around for our good! He is our redeemer, restorer, rebuilder, and rewarder! Our Redeemer lives!"

"Then they remembered that God was their rock, And the Most High God their Redeemer."
Psalm 78:35 NLT

DAY 337

Favor in the fire- we all need it. We need to be assured that even when we are going through it, God will still cause favor to work for us and, in some way, bring deliverance. Believers have favor because we are "in Christ."

So today I agree with you, that if you're walking through the fire, God is going to cause the right people to see the smoke; that He's speaking to others about you, even when it feels like He's not speaking to you; that there will always be a "fourth man" on display that others will see walking with you; that this will turn around for your good and God's glory; that you will experience opportunity for every place of opposition you face. I'm agreeing with you that before it is over you will be able to say like King David and others who have been there said, "In my distress, God enlarged me." I'm believing with you that you won't break, you'll bloom, you won't wilt, you'll blossom; that God will take you from famine to feast; that in your career, health, finances, and relationships you will rise to even greater levels of fulfillment.

"Father, I ask you to restore every lost opportunity, stolen blessing, and good thing that belongs to your children. In Jesus' name, I declare that no matter what anybody does or says, it has no power to stop the favor and blessing of God in their life today. I pray an increase over you, in favor, harvest, success, an abundance of God. In the name of Jesus, let it pour out on you! Thank you, Father, that no problem is too great, and no dream is too big. Thank you, Jesus, for your favor that lasts a lifetime!"

"I've learned that his anger lasts for a moment, but his loving favor lasts a lifetime! We may weep through the night, but at daybreak it will turn into shouts of ecstatic joy."
Psalms 30:5 TPT

DAY 338

Before you assume, learn the facts. Before you judge, understand why. Before you hurt someone, feel God's heart. Before you speak, be quick to hear and slow to speak, listen for His voice and think. Before you react, pause. Before you condemn, put yourself in their place. Before you give up today and quit, be strong, be steadfast, be strategic, one more day. Before you act, pray.

Before you focus on the disappointments, think about the blessings. If you have a family that loves you, a few good friends, food on your table, and a roof over your head, you are richer than you think. In everything you do, everywhere you go, let the goodness of God be shared with those around you.

Before you allow disappointment to overpower you about how far you have to go, remember how far you've come. God doesn't see you as a problem to solve, but as a son or daughter who He enjoys. He celebrates you and He celebrates every step no matter how small. Before you let fear dominate your vision of the future, let faith open the eyes of your heart. Before your words are released in anger and haste over yourself or someone else, let God's word be your response and confession.

Before you get so focused on what you want, remember not to miss the beauty of this day. Everything may not be perfect, there are things that need to change, but you have the grace to be happy today.

Before you give in to despair, child of God, trust the one who knows your name and keeps His promises. Each and every day, before you speak any other name, speak His name. Others may fail and disappoint, but His is the name that is above all names. He is Lord forever, and there is no one who can challenge His authority and power. He will rule forever and ever, and there is no end to His kingdom.

DAY 339

Sometimes we get caught up in life, problems, circumstances, and trouble and forget who our God is. Let's remember today and proclaim who our God is.

1. God is with me, in me, and for me today! His face smiles over me in divine favor. I have His peace in the storm, His healing in pain, His abundance in a time of need!

2. God is my way maker, barrier breaker, destiny shaper, and a good good father! He never stops believing in me and in His great destiny for my life!

3. God is the one who takes what the enemy means for harm and turns it around and uses it to His advantage and my favor!

4. God is my rock, my fortress, my deliverer, my strength, in whom I will trust; a shield for me; my glory, and the lifter up of my head! (Psalms 3:3, 18:2)

5. God is never-ending love in my life. He knows my deepest flaws, yet He still loves me outrageously! I am secure in Him!

6. God's presence will bring favor to my life and will connect me with the right people for His will to be done, open doors of opportunity, and completely astound me with His goodness.

7. God is covering me with his feathers. He will shelter me with his wings. His faithful promises are my armor and protection! No evil can attach itself to me; no plague can come near my life, my family, my possessions, or my purpose, in Jesus' Name!

8. God is my restorer. He will restore everything the enemy has stolen from me!

9. God is a healer, comforter, and provider. He takes ashes and turns it into beauty. There is no problem in my life that God's presence can't solve; no mountain it can't melt; no brokenness it can't heal!

10. God is greater than man, greater than all! He is my way today when it seems like there is no way. He will open for me and to me what no one can close! (Rev.3:8)

DAY 340

God knows everything about us, including the ugly parts, the broken parts, and the dysfunctional parts. Yet, He still believes in us. He still has a future and a hope for us.

I pray today that you are filled with great thoughts for your future, that your heart beats with deep feelings of hope and great anticipation of what God is doing and will do. I pray you won't let your vision die just because time has passed, that God's presence will keep it alive and fresh.

This could be the day, the week, the season where those things and even greater things begin to happen. You might feel stuck, but you will not be there forever. It's time to again put your hope in God and in the great future He has already put in motion for you. Things are happening behind the scenes that you can't always see. Keep dreaming, keep believing, and keep celebrating each step of faith and victory! God is faithful!

God's promises aren't a challenge for us to make them happen. They are a call to rest in Him and know that He is faithful. Keep looking unto Jesus, the author and the finisher!

Even though you have walked through seasons of barrenness, you will stand in bountiful blessings and breakthroughs! Get ready; God is for you.

"Hope deferred makes the heart sick, but a dream fulfilled is a tree of life."
Proverbs 13:12 NLT

DAY 341

Sometimes we need to stop and consider some things when we feel alone, confused about our future, or conflicted about who we are and how God sees us. Jeremiah 1:4-5 says, "Then the word of the Lord came to me, saying: Before I formed you in the womb, I knew you. Before you were born, I sanctified you; I ordained you."

God doesn't just see where you are; He sees where you can be. You were known, sanctified, ordained, and commissioned by God before you ever showed up in the nursery. You have purpose! God is saying, you and I hung out in my heart before you ever got here. I knew you before you knew yourself. You are not your mama's mistake; you are not an accident; you are not an outcast; you are not an orphan; you are not fatherless or forsaken! There will always be someone who carries a negative opinion of you; just make sure you are not that person!

Remember today, you are blessed, chosen, favored, honored, and filled with the treasures of Heaven. God sees in you what you can't see in yourself and what others can't always see as well. He knows it's there because He put it there. You are a child of God. You are amazing in ways unique to you. He continues to work with you and in you to maximize every gift He has graced you with. He has plans for you that are amazing too. God's goodness and mercy are rising up in you. His faithfulness is shining brightly and His pleasure in you will be radiant! Keep going forward in faith!

"We are like common clay jars that carry this glorious treasure within, so that the extraordinary overflow of power will be seen as God's, not ours. Though we experience every kind of pressure, we're not crushed. At times we don't know what to do, but quitting is not an option."
2 Corinthians 4:7-8 TPT

DAY 342

Our Father wants you to know how loved you are, that you belong to Him, and that He is bringing you into an even deeper revelation and understanding of your special and beautiful place in Him. God loves us with an everlasting love. It's not based on our merit or our worthiness. He loves us in spite of ourselves. We don't deserve it, and we really can't earn it, He just does.

You are chosen and set apart for such a time as this and I remind all of us today, God can take our season of pain and make it a season of purpose, our mess a message, our test a testimony. That's who He is and what He does.

I declare divine acceleration to the promises of God for your life, that every word He has given you in His Word is true. I declare the flood-gates of heaven are being opened for you and your family, that it is harvest time, that you will reap supernatural abundant blessings from every seed you have sown. Lord, let abundance be poured out in every part of each life and their family's life! I declare no weapon formed against them will prosper! God is making a way for you! Let every snare, trap, and demonic setup be overturned now.

So, keep on doing the right thing. Continue believing God. Stay in His word. Trust Him to keep His promises. Stay the course. Don't give up on your future. The forces for you are greater than the forces against you. May the Lord's presence guide your steps, open doors, overcome obstacles, and lift your cares and fears!

"Now may God, the inspiration and fountain of hope, fill you to over-flowing with uncontainable joy and perfect peace as you trust in him. And may the power of the Holy Spirit continually surround your life with his super-abundance until you radiate with hope!"
Romans 15:13 TPT

DAY 343

The enemy's strategy is guilt and condemnation. He wants us to be so beat down that we miss out on the things Jesus already paid for. Grace is not only for the forgiveness of coming up short...it's also for the guilt and condemnation of missing the mark. There is a grace for every season of your lives. Now is not the time to draw back in fear. It is a time when we must rise up in love and flourish in love. Don't confuse your mistakes with your value. The enemy will try to capitalize on shame and regret.

The Lord's perception is different from ours. While we see failures, mistakes, problems, and losses, God sees what we can be and will be. The prophet Daniel wrote, "Those who know their God will do great exploits."

Gideon was the least important person in his family's genealogy, and he didn't think much of himself either. Yet God came to him and called him a "mighty man of valor" and used Gideon to deliver the Israelites from oppression. God uses us in spite of our weaknesses. God called Gideon a "mighty warrior." God is calling us by a new name. Redeemed. Forgiven. Loved. Mighty. Overcomer. Blessed. Favored. Accepted. Healed. Called. Righteous.

"But he answered me, "My grace is always more than enough for you, and my power finds its full expression through your weakness." So I will celebrate my weaknesses, for when I'm weak I sense more deeply the mighty power of Christ living in me. So I'm not defeated by my weakness, but delighted! For when I feel my weakness and endure mistreatment—when I'm surrounded with troubles on every side and face persecution because of my love for Christ—I am made yet stronger. For my weakness becomes a portal to God's power."
2 Corinthians 12:9-10 TPT

DAY 344

Ever been disappointed? I know we all do. People and circumstances can let you down. The way we choose to deal with our disappointments and trials determines where we go next. We keep our connection to God open when we can say to Him, "With all my failures, hurts, and disappointments, I hurt, I am angry, grieved, but here I am." When we are authentic with God, He can handle our feelings and work in our hearts.

Jesus feels our pain, our grief, our sorrows, and our High Priest has a supernatural ability to identify with our weaknesses. He truly understands the things that hurt us, and Isaiah 53 says He carried our sorrows. Many people have experienced life-shattering episodes that changed everything. But God doesn't want us to be captured by hurt and disappointment and held hostage. He wants to heal every place and restore us completely.

The greatest disappointments in my life have happened when I got my eyes off of Him and on people. God holds our future and we must decide to say yes to the future He holds out to us and keep our expectation in Him. In the fires of the trial, remember that God's Word will stand, it will not return void. Remember that God works all things according to the counsel of His own will (Eph 1:11). The battle during disappointments is to keep looking into Jesus. And when we outlast the trial and come out on the other side, destiny is waiting for us and a future filled with a deep understanding of where our hope lies changes our perspective. Let's lay all our disappointments at the feet of Jesus today and say what Jehoshaphat said.

"... For we have no power against this great multitude that is coming against us; nor do we know what to do, BUT OUR EYES ARE UPON YOU."

2 Chronicles 20:12 NKJV

DAY 345

I feel the Lord's heart of compassion and desire to encourage those who are growing battle weary and on the verge of losing their hope. We have all been there in our lives at some time. Every biblical vision has a season of contradiction.

I want to release this promise over us as we go into the Christmas season and soon to be New Year.

"Return to your fortress, you prisoners of hope; even now I announce that I will restore twice as much to you."
Zechariah 9:12 NIV

Lord, let us be prisoners of hope! Captured, taken, and filled by hope that will never let us go, no matter what!

People who hold on to Your promises in the midst of everything!

People who refuse to be intimidated!

People who refuse the spirit of compromise!

People who refuse to allow someone or something small to keep us from Your best.

People who always say I will overcome every obstacle, defeat every enemy, and become everything God has created me to be!

People who know that whatever I entrust to Your hands, You will uphold, protect, guide, shape, and make better and increase!

People who know there's going to be a payback, a harvest, a twice as much that's been stolen season that's coming my way!

People who refuse to take no for an answer when You have said yes!

People who aren't just strong starters, but strong finishers and strong in the middle too!

People who have a life story that brings God glory, where people will say one day, I have never seen anything like that!

Say it today, "God favors me, loves me, and has chosen me from the foundation of the world to receive His grace and favor!"

DAY 346

The daily grind of life can take its toll. We can feel overwhelmed. Remember this about feelings; feelings are only indicators they do not have to be dictators! They can remind us that there are things that need to be addressed in our lives, but they can also deceive us into quitting or making rash decisions. When Esau traded the lasting benefits of his birthright for the immediate but temporary pleasure of food, he acted according to his feelings; he was governed by fatigue and impulse rather than by wisdom; he was tempted to satisfy his immediate desires without considering the long term consequences of his actions, and he was a slave to the flesh.

When we are tired and weary and facing the prospect of just totally backing off, we need to remember our why. When we lose our why we lose our way. We don't get burned out because of what we do. We get burned out because we forget why we do it. Our why connects with our purpose and keeps us fresh and energized.

So today, I remind you of just a few whys. Why? Because you are needed. You are needed in your church. You are needed in your community. You are needed in your family. You are needed in that place of prayer and caring. You are needed in that place of giving and loving. You are needed in this world. You are needed in so many ways. If you weren't needed, God would not have created you.

You are chosen and placed for such a time as this. Your life matters and you are making a difference. Today needs you, tomorrow needs you, and there are things that are yet to happen and people you are yet to meet that need you!

"I thank my God upon every remembrance of you, always in every prayer of mine making request for you all with joy,"
Philippians 1:3-4 NKJV

DAY 347

We all have places of pain in our lives. We all have been wounded and hurt at some point. Wherever there is the presence of ongoing pain, there is a need for healing. The first step in the healing process is learning to forgive and asking the Holy Spirit to heal our hearts. Don't confuse a hard heart with a healed heart. A heart that is healed is a heart that has removed the walls that are built by offense and can still be soft and pliable before the presence of God, but a healed and healthy heart has doors and gates. Be careful what you allow in your heart because the heart has the force to push the physical out of the spiritual. Understand the power of the heart.

Why do you think the enemy spent so much of your life trying to sow seeds in your heart? That attack was about more than just the physical act. That rejection, conversation, and trauma were designed to plant something in you your heart that would eventually push out. It is time the enemy is exposed. We must get the right seed in the soil of our hearts. Guard the soil of your heart. As we allow the Holy Spirit to rule in our heart, our heart will tell us what doesn't belong in it. Our heart is like a garden and it has a voice. Sometimes it is saying, "Don't let that in because you're going to have issues if you do."

Thank God for the open doors that promote us but thank God for the closed doors that protect us. Forgiveness is always required by God, but it does not always lead to reconciliation. Forgiveness doesn't excuse their behavior or invite it to continue. Forgiveness is a release for you that prevents their behavior from continuing to destroy your heart and future.

"So above all, guard the affections of your heart, for they affect all that you are. Pay attention to the welfare of your innermost being, for from there flows the wellspring of life."
Proverbs 4:23 TPT

DAY 348

God has a plan. You are part of that plan. You matter and make a difference. You always have something to contribute. Your life matters! You have something that someone needs to see or hear that is reflected in what you have been through. You made it through to get here and somebody else needs to know it so they can walk in the hope and assurance that they can make it through! When you've been through it and experienced delivering grace, it brings hope to others' hearts! We overcome by the word of our testimony.

Sometimes just the smile on your face is enough to give someone else the strength to go on because they know that smile comes from someone who has walked through the shadows, the darkness of the night, and come through still able to smile and reflect the goodness of God. Your praise matters. Worshipping and praising God through the storm inspires others. You matter, your story matters, your smile matters, your battles matter, your faithfulness matters, your presence matters, your persistence matters. You continuing to show up through it all matters! You're meant to make it through not just for you but to show others they can make it too! So, the next time you're tempted to feel insignificant and unvalued or to give up and give in, remember, you are not an accident, a coincidence, or a mistake. You are an awesome, amazing creation of an Almighty God. You matter! We need you. No one else can do it like you, even if it is just your smile, your voice, your affirmation, or your testimony.

"But you are God's chosen treasure—priests who are kings, a spiritual "nation" set apart as God's devoted ones. He called you out of darkness to experience his marvelous light, and now he claims you as his very own. He did this so that you would broadcast his glorious wonders throughout the world."
1 Peter 2:9 TPT

DAY 349

Don't get caught up in battles and distractions you were never meant to enter into today. Sometimes the best thing you can say is nothing because every offense does not deserve your attention and emotional energy. Do what God has put in your heart and trust Him to take care of your critics. We get off track and distracted from God's purpose in our lives when man's opinion means more to us than God's opinion.

People can be cruel with their words, opinions, and actions, or they can simply be careless with them. Be careful not to let the words and opinions of others shape your soul or steal your seeds of expectation!

We have to learn to discern between the thoughts from God and the thoughts from other sources.

God doesn't get His opinion of you from others! He has already decided that you are His, you belong, He loves you, and He wants you! Even the things others have done to you, God can turn around to use for you! In one moment, God can turn around years of pain and disappointment! He will restore to you the years that have been wasted, damaged, or lost. This is your year to get back the lost years.

So, remember today, it's not over. You are not too old and it's not too late! Don't drown in the hopelessness of not seeing a change or shift yet; you can live with hope because you serve a God of restoration! God is working even when you can't see it with your eyes and leading you into victory!

"Every seed buried in sorrow, you will call forth in its time. You are Lord, Lord of the harvest, calling our hope now to arise!"

"But as for you, you meant evil against me; but God meant it for good..."
Genesis 50:20

DAY 350

In the photo album of our life experiences, there are pictures of success and failure, hurts, heartaches, broken dreams, and ships that didn't make it to shore, along with blessings, breakthroughs, and mountain tops. Through it all, our faithful God remains our rock, our cornerstone. And because I'm "in Him" and He's "in me," because of the power of Christ living within me I can say today, "I will be thankful and love the life He has blessed me with, not just live it. I will live my identity, not just know it. I will believe the Word, and be a doer of the word, not just hear it. I will walk in discernment, not just sense it. I will live and walk in faith and love, not in fear and not just try to do because in Christ I not only can, I am!

I hear Him reassuring us today, "When the battle is over, you will not only come through it, you will come out stronger and better than you were before. By faith today, look up and see the rainbow in the clouds. Never let your problems silence what you heard from Me and don't ever let anyone convince you that there's no hope for you or that you are a lost cause. My Spirit is brooding over your life, reversing the things the enemy has plotted against you. No weapon formed against you can prosper. I'm birthing hope, love, God surprises, miracles, and open doors. Increase is on the way. You are precious to me. You are honored and I love you."

"Every single moment you are thinking of me! How precious and wonderful to consider that you cherish me constantly in your every thought! O God, your desires toward me are more than the grains of sand on every shore! When I awake each morning, you're still with me."
Psalms 139:17-18 TPT

DAY 351

If you are like me and I feel sure you are, there are things you are facing that you don't have answers for right now. When we look at what we need and compare it to what we have, it can feel overwhelming. Eventually, we encounter that place where we can feel as though we don't know how to overcome or how to proceed, but that is not the time to draw back in fear. It is a time when we must rise up in faith and know that God has a plan for our lives. Worrying does not take away tomorrow's troubles; it takes away today's peace. Our God loves to speak victory in the face of defeat, life to dry bones, and hope to dead dreams!

"May the God of hope fill you with all joy and peace in believing, so that by the power of the Holy Spirit you may abound in hope."
Romans 15:13 ESV

I choose today to be radiant with hope. I want to throw my whole life and everything I have into building a dream that comes from the heart of God, to get out there so far that without God's help, I can't get back, to not be afraid to fail. Fear of failure can cause you to do the one thing that absolutely guarantees failure, and that's not attempting anything at all. Let's counteract fear by meditating on God's promises until the picture is so clear on the inside of us that nothing can take it away from us. Let's turn our hope up. Let's look at the promise, the divine dream, the inner image, that's bigger than we are because it's built on the promises of God.

"Behold, they eye of the Lord is on those who fear him, on those who hope in his steadfast love, that he may deliver their soul from death and keep them alive in famine. Our soul waits for the Lord; he is our help and shield. For our heart is glad in him, because we trust in his holy name. Let our steadfast love, O Lord, be upon us, even as we hope in you."
Psalms 33:18-22 ESV

DAY 352

When I talk about being tired, I'm speaking about more than physical exhaustion. It's amazing what a good night's sleep can bring if you can get one. But there is tiredness that can go beyond the physical—mental and emotional weariness that can become paralyzing. Let me share with you one of my personal responses when I'm tempted to feel this way.

This takes intentionality, but try to, in some way, reach out and personally let someone else know you are thinking about them and ask God to give you something special from His heart just for them. This brings hope to their hearts as well as taking you from the "self-zone" to the "God-zone." But it's on those days of disappointment and feeling like the grind has ground me down and is getting the best of me that I am glad that I feel the need and, at times, the obligation to encourage someone else. Some of my best words have been birthed on some of my worst days.

In the days of horse and buggies, farmers would load their potatoes into a wagon and deliberately take the toughest road to market. When they got to the market, all the nice big potatoes were on the top and the small ones were on the bottom. Rough roads can make the best rise to the top. You are no different than me. We all have our own battles. Reaching out to love someone else and convey Gods heart to them in the midst of our own weariness is a beautiful step of faith that opens up possibilities for us as well as breakthroughs for them, and helps us discover things inside we never knew we had and I choose to believe my future is awesome, transformed, purified, blessed and favored. I choose to believe that He will make a way.

"The confidence of my calling enables me to overcome every difficulty without shame, for I have an intimate revelation of this God. And my faith in him convinces me that he is more than able to keep all that I've placed in his hands safe and secure until the fullness of his appearing."
2 Timothy 1:12 TPT

DAY 353

Jesus was and still is touchable. "For we have not a high priest which cannot be touched with the feeling of our infirmities..." Hebrews 4:15

I've learned and am still learning that whatever the depths of our personal pain, it is possible to be raised up. It is possible to heal. It is possible to forgive. It is possible to love and live again. Even when it's my own mess I've made, the Lord still makes a way! Therefore, no matter who or what tries to knock you down, it is important for you to know that God will always embrace you, hold you, and help you get back up again.

He is the God who restores emotionally, mentally, physically, financially, and relationally.

"Thank you, Lord, for touching, raising up, and restoring every person reading this and filling them with love, hope, peace, and strength, and turning any disappointment into fulfillment. We look to you Lord; our eyes are on you. Thank you, Jesus!"

"Arise, shine, for your light has come, and the glory of the Lord rises
upon you."
Isaiah 60:1 NIV

DAY 354

One of the greatest steps to increase in our lives is found in starting our day right. Many times, we start our day consumed with what we don't have. Around much of the world, today, people are focused on what they don't have and trying to figure out how to get it.

But for powerful things to happen in our lives, we need to get our minds on what we already have, not what we don't have!

Every day, start off by thinking about and remembering the things God has already done!!!

In Psalm 103:1-5, David said, "...forget none of His benefits—He pardons your sins, heals all your diseases, redeems your life from destruction, crowns you with lovingkindness and compassion..." Wow! That's enough to make our day great right there!

Let's stop cursing our little bit and start blessing it instead, knowing our God will bring increase to everything we give to Him!

And this kind of attitude and outlook creates faith energy. As we reflect on what God has given us already, it stirs us up to believe for more!!!

Philemon 1:6 says, "Your faith becomes effective, as you acknowledge every good thing already in you, through Christ Jesus."

So today, even if it looks like you're starting the day at a deficit, believe in the God of more than enough. Thank Him for what you do have already and then live in expectation of His goodness and provision.

DAY 355

Today, on the authority of God's word and in the power of agreement, I decree breakthrough in every area of your life in Jesus' name. Nothing will separate you from God's presence.

I decree that God's love, presence, and power will saturate every fiber of your being in Jesus' name!

I declare new hope, new vision, and new faith are coming your way in Jesus' name.

I decree that you will be radically and extravagantly blessed by God above all that you can ask or think in Jesus' name.

I decree you will walk in God's perfect will and plan for your life and have joy in the journey in Jesus' name.

I decree that perfect peace will guard your heart and mind in Christ Jesus.

I decree that your soul will be full of God's joy and peace! I break discouragement off of you in Jesus' name!

I decree that God's presence will overflow from your life in Jesus' name.

I decree that God is working all things for your good in Jesus' name.

There is greatness on the inside of you. God's maximum potential will be realized in your life in Jesus' name. I declare you will be full of hope and fresh vision in Jesus' name.

"There is no one else who has the power to save us, for there is only one name to whom God has given authority by which we must experience salvation: the name of Jesus."
Acts 4:12 TPT

DAY 356

Sometimes we get caught up in the loss and pain and forget if we stay focused on the people that left us, we'll never appreciate the ones who stayed. All of us have people in our lives who need to hear this. Those who want what's best for you are best for you. Find them and appreciate them. This is a great day to just sit back, reassess, give thanks, and realize how blessed we are. Everyone needs a "place" to believe, to belong, and to be loved. Thank you for being that "place." So many beautiful and amazing people who have made such a difference. I'm grateful for you today, grateful for the parts of my life you make so much better. Grateful for family that goes beyond skin color, nationality, socio-economic class, gender, or stereotypes, that connects us on a heart level. I can't imagine what it would be like without you, without your smile and presence, without your care and concern and faith and encouragement and love.

Thank you for staying when others left, thank you for loving when others turned away, thank you for being there even when things went wrong and it looked like there was no way out, but you didn't give up, walk out, let go, or join in with the crowd who said it was all over. My life is richer, fuller, and so much better because of you. Friend doesn't really begin to say it all. Family describes it better. God is good for bringing you in my life and I am so blessed! Just wanted you to know, I thank God upon every remembrance of you. You have touched my life, and this is my heart's desire for you.

"I thank my God upon every remembrance of you, always in every prayer of mine making request for you all with joy, for your fellowship in the gospel from the first day until now, being confident of this very thing, that He who has begun a good work in you will complete it until the day of Jesus Christ;"
Philippians 1:3-6 NKJV

DAY 357

I believe for those that are open to God's work in their lives that this new year can be a year of innovation, advancement, progress, supernatural increase, and unexplainable blessings. It can be a year of expansion, opportunities and empowerment to do great exploits. This new year can be a year for favor to explode into reality for us. But it will require an openness for transition and allowing God to interrupt our attitudes. Before achievement comes attitude! Caleb had a can-do attitude when he said, "We are well able to take the land."

The ten spies saw through trouble-shooting lenses, while Caleb saw through treasure-hunting lenses.

God's hand is so strong on your life right now. This is a strategic time and you are not alone in this journey; it is orchestrated by the Spirit of the Lord. You know it on such a deep level. This is a season of great transition. Your perspective has changed and is still changing. You are seeing yourself and your future through Father God's eyes. The pieces of the puzzle are coming together. Your willingness to step into the unknown by faith has set your free from the status quo! You are a Caleb; there is a different spirit in you. You are well able to take the land!

"Then Caleb quieted the people before Moses, and said, "Let us go up at once and take possession, for we are well able to overcome it."
Numbers 13:30 NKJV

DAY 358

Never be deceived into believing you can accomplish your destiny in life with someone else's game plan. Wearing "Saul's armor" may look impressive, but it is not yours! I'd rather have rocks provided by God than armor provided by man. Contentment with who God made you, who you are becoming, and what you possess is key to fulfilling your calling. Our greatest potential is never realized until we are willing to become a contributor to something greater than ourselves.

Success that has only us in mind leaves us empty and longing, but promotion with purpose brings fulfillment and satisfaction. This is a time and season when God is stirring the desire to do something bigger than yourself when God's direction and purpose is awakening. Too many of us are not living our dreams because we are living our fears. We are here to live a life that causes our heart to come alive. Believe with all of your heart today that you will do what you were made to do, that you will live a life of purpose. Even though there are places and areas of our lives where we feel less than or not enough, know that God will complete your incompletion! Be confident in God's power in your life today. There is nothing in the world that can come close to matching Him. No problem is too great. No dream is too big. When you become aware of God's favor, you can and will do amazing things! But remember, it's not about just waiting for the "big things." A great life isn't about big things; it's about the small things that make a big difference. Sometimes the smallest things have the biggest meaning. It takes a big person to do things that seem small and unnoticed but get ready; God is preparing you for something really small that will be connected to something really big. Never despise the day of small things. Who knows where it will lead!

"His lord said to him, 'Well done, good and faithful servant; you were faithful over a few things, I will make you ruler over many things. Enter into the joy of your lord.'"
Matthew 25:21 NKJV

DAY 359

Life is about balance. Be kind, but don't let people abuse you.
The people we allow in our inner circle will alter our future either for good or bad. There will always be people that disappoint you in life. But to have true joy and peace, you have to learn how to forgive, forget, and move on. Trust, but don't be deceived. Be content, but never stop improving yourself.

Life will challenge us every day. But God commands us to be courageous. Be confident in all you do, knowing He is with you.

Dethrone the past from becoming the dictator of your future.

Mistakes alone don't limit growth. Growth is limited by how much we fail to learn from our mistakes. Let old things pass away, behold all things are made new. (2 Cor. 5:17)

Be grateful in spite of the problems. Never speak anything over your life that you don't want to come true. Each word we speak either waters the seed or destroys it, so let's speak life.

Thanksgiving is the enemy of discontent and dissatisfaction. Everything good in your life multiplies in the incubator of gratitude. So, declare it today, "I am perfectly loved by God, filled with His presence, upheld by His promises. Thank you, Lord. It's going to be a great day."

DAY 360

We can never rise in life above our understanding of who we think we are. It's so important to discover our true identity in Christ. We believe what we think and say about ourselves more than what anybody else says. Once you know who you are, "their" opinions don't control your emotions anymore. Our lives are shaped by our most dominant thoughts because these are the thoughts that mold our beliefs. Beliefs direct our expectations and actions. Actions determine the results we get in our lives.

One of life's simplest, yet most powerful truths is this- What we consistently think about, talk about, and meditate on will eventually show up in reality. We become what we behold. If we want to live better, it starts with getting our mind right. I don't want to ever believe things about me that God doesn't believe about me. I want to see, say, and think the way He sees, says, and thinks about everything! Even on days when I don't feel blessed, successful, strong, healthy, or creative, I choose to do what God does; He calls me what I am before I become it! When you discover your true identity in Christ, stand on it, and don't allow yourself or anyone else to convince you or talk you out of it! Your bondage or breakthrough in life has a lot to do with the people and voices you listen to! Do not align yourself with what the lying spirit of fear and dread is saying. Don't fret or give into the spirit of intimidation. In Jesus' name, you will no longer allow lies and misunderstandings to lead you to believe you are defeated, incompetent, unloved, undesirable, or incapable. Nothing can stop what God is releasing into your life. The future belongs to those who belong to the one who holds the future. He is holding you up and making a way for you to come out in complete victory!

"Stop imitating the ideals and opinions of the culture around you, but be inwardly transformed by the Holy Spirit through a total reformation of how you think. This will empower you to discern God's will as you live a beautiful life, satisfying and perfect in his eyes."
Romans 12:2 TPT

DAY 361

You are never too old or too anything to get a new attitude! Never stop learning, growing, reaching, or increasing! You are not too old to begin again and to get a fresh start! Allow God to open your eyes so that you can dream, envision, see, and imagine. He wants us to go far past where we are to a new level in Him, in our personal lives, families, jobs, businesses, or relationships. No shrinking back, thinking back, going back today. I'm moving forward into God's destiny for my life! My best days start today!!!

"The eyes of your understanding being enlightened; that ye may know what is the hope of his calling, and what the riches of the glory of his inheritance in the saints, And what is the exceeding greatness of his power to us-ward who believe, according to the working of his mighty power,"
Ephesians 1:18-19 KJV

DAY 362

The right words spoken over us are like taking a spiritual shower. Let these words saturate you today, "You are loved, you are wonderfully made, you are beautiful, you have purpose, you are a masterpiece, and God has a great plan for you!

By God's grace, you'll move from pain to purpose, from hurt to health, and from wounds to wisdom! There is no one on planet earth that can separate you from the glory and the beauty of how God loves you. Nobody! God is breathing new life into your dreams and new hope into your heart! You are a chosen, set apart, child of the Almighty God! You are walking in grace today. You are walking in empowerment today. You are walking in redemption, and everything around you will be marked by new life. As you fulfill your responsibilities, it's birthing your rewards. He is shining on you, in you, and through you. Your today and your tomorrow are blessed. Be confident, be steadfast, be stirred up, be prayerful, be assured. He that began the good work in you will complete it. He will fulfill His purpose for you by His grace and for His glory!

"I pray with great faith for you, because I'm fully convinced that the One who began this glorious work in you will faithfully continue the process of maturing you and will put his finishing touches to it until the unveiling of our Lord Jesus Christ!"
Philippians 1:6 TPT

DAY 363

You never have to face another day alone. Even when it feels like you are alone in the battle, declare, "God is always with me. Because He is close to me and always available, my confidence will never be shaken, for I experience His wrap-around presence every moment. He will take my hand and lead me through to the other side, and I will be wrapped in His presence continually. He is imparting strength, guidance, energy, love, and comfort, through the good and the bad. He is always with me."

With all the chaos going on in our world right now, let's choose to trust and believe in our Emmanuel, God with us. I declare He will rescue you, carry you, and sustain you. He is getting ready to amaze you!

Some days, we have to take our eyes off of all our problems and all our unanswered questions and just place them on the One whose love never fails. It's not the time to give in or give up! God is the God of hope. He will lead you through, and He is going to cause you to radiate with hope!

"May the power of the Holy Spirit continually surround your life with his super-abundance until you radiate with hope!" (Romans 15:13) Your breakthrough is coming. Hold on, stand firm in the faith, He can work wonders when we trust Him!

"Because you are close to me and always available, my confidence will never be shaken, for I experience your wrap-around presence every moment. My heart and soul explode with joy—full of glory! Even my body will rest confident and secure."
Psalms 16:8-9 TPT

DAY 364

I'm so eternally grateful that our Father is tireless in His care for us, everlasting in His mercies, and so generous with His grace. He anticipates our weakness and meets us right there with His strength. When we feel a little (or a lot) weary, He meets as a loving Abba Father, not as a destructive critic. He meets us with the gospel, the good news, not a record of our wrongs and failings. He meets us with a smile and a loving embrace, not with scorn and contempt. He meets us with encouragement, not shame. The grace that brought us into the kingdom is the grace that can carry us through.

Let's believe today that our God is the life-giver, the one who brings all things to pass, the performer of all promises, the absolute unchangeable one. He will be all that is necessary as the need arises. He knows what we need even before we ask, and He has chosen to love us unconditionally. Thank you, precious Lord. You are our Jehovah Jireh, the one who always provides all we need in every way, even more than enough.

"He heals the brokenhearted binding up their wounds... He counts the stars and calls them all by name... How great is our Lord...His power is absolute... His understanding is beyond comprehension."
Psalms 147:3-5 NLT

DAY 365

With every new year comes new expectations, new dreams, and a new vision. As the year drags on, life tends to beat people down, dismissing those expectations, dreams, and visions of a better year. We can begin to question if we've really heard from God at all. So, how do I know if dreams, visions and desires for my life are from God?

First- A dream and vision that is from God will stand the test of His presence. In fact, it will become more real and strong when you are praying, worshipping, and meditating on the word and engaged in seeking Him. It's in those moments we really begin to "see" from a heavenly perspective for our lives.

Second- Will it enable me to not only be blessed but be a blessing? In Genesis, Joseph's family tried to destroy the dream seeds God had planted in Joseph, and if they had succeeded, they would have destroyed their own deliverance. Their deliverance was in the dreams God had given Joseph. It's always about so much more than us.

Third- God given dreams and desires will keep you on track in your life, not lead you astray. Joseph's dreams kept him on track during very difficult times when He was faced with great temptation and discouragement.

"When there is no clear prophetic vision, people quickly wander astray. But when you follow the revelation of the word, heaven's bliss fills your soul."
Proverbs 29:18 TPT

Your God-given dreams and purpose will help get you up in the morning and cause you to have hope in the darkest of nights. It will inspire you and motivate you and help keep your life on track and focused on God. I pray today you are filled with great thoughts for your future that your heart beats with deep feelings of hope and great anticipation of what God is doing and will do. Keep dreaming and believing!

Donations cans be made to:
Illuminate Ministries
312 T Schillinger Road North
#204
Mobile Alabama 36608
Or
paypal.me/illuminatemin

Scott Howard serves as the Senior Pastor at Life Church in Mobile, AL. He is the President and founder of Illuminate Ministries, designed to help people everywhere deepen their relationship with God and those around them. Scott has been married to his wife, Susan, for 45 years and they have two children and five grandchildren.